FISHING ARKANSAS

FISHING
ARKANSAS

A Year-Round Guide to Angling Adventures in the Natural State

KEITH SUTTON

The University of Arkansas Press
Fayetteville
2000

04   03   02   01   00   5   4   3   2   1

Designed by Liz Lester

⊖   The paper used in this publication meets the minimum requirements of the American National Standard for Permanence of Paper for Printed Library Materials Z39.48-1984.

Library of Congress Cataloging-in-Publication Data

Sutton, Keith B.
        Fishing Arkansas : a year-round guide to angling adventures
    in the natural state / Keith Sutton.
            p.   cm.
        Includes index.
        ISBN 1-55728-623-X (pbk. : alk. paper)
        1. Fishing—Arkansas. I. Title.
    SH471 .S88   2000
    799.1'1'09767—dc21   00-009324

To my mother, Barbara Ann Sutton,
whose love of the written word
largely shaped the path I have chosen.

Contents

Illustrations

Acknowledgments

Some of the articles composing this book were originally published in the following magazines:

"Little Red Trout" *Thicket's Hunting and Fishing Guide*, January 1993;

"Arkansas Hotspots for Ten-Pound-Plus Bass," *Arkansas Sportsman*, January 1990;

"Winter on Arkansas's Smallmouth Bass Streams" (originally published as "Make It a Smallmouth Winter"), *Arkansas Sportsman*, January 1999;

"Midway Lake for February Crappie," *Arkansas Sportsman*, February 1990;

"Greers Ferry Walleyes" (originally published as "Walleyes . . . Big Walleyes!"), *Arkansas Sportsman*, February 1994;

"City Water Bass" (originally published as "Bass in City Water"), *Field & Stream*, South Edition, September 1987;

"Caddo River Smallmouths," *Arkansas Sportsman*, January 1998;

"Crappie Lakes Nobody Fishes," *Outdoor World*, May/June 1999;

"Don't Skip the Skipjack" (originally published as "Those Other Fish: Skipjack Herring"), *In-Fisherman*, October/November 1997;

"White Lightning! White Bass!" *Arkansas Sportsman*, April 1999;

"Arkansas Walleye Hotspots" (originally published as "Arkansas' Walleye Treasures"), *Arkansas Fins & Feathers*, May 1985;

"Oxbow Crappie along the Mississippi" (originally published as "A River and Its Oxbow Crappie"), *Arkansas Sportsman*, April 1996;

"Diamond Lakes Bassin'"(originally published as "Diamond Dabbling"), *Arkansas Sportsman*, April 1993;

"Razorback Redears," *Arkansas Sportsman*, June 1993;

"Easy-Access Channel Cats," *Arkansas Sportsman*, August 1998;

"Rockin' Down the Buffalo," *Arkansas Sportsman*, May 1991;

"Oxbow Bass" (originally published as "Arkansas Oxbow Bass Fishing Is a Natural!"), *Arkansas Sportsman*, April 1994;

"The Fish That Eats Salad" (originally published as "Those Other Fish: Grass Carp"), *In-Fisherman*, December/January 1997–98;

"Summer's Hottest Hybrids," *Arkansas Sportsman*, June 1999;

"Big Cats of the Mighty Mississippi," *Arkansas Sportsman*, June 1998;

"Fishing Arkansas's Island Retreats" (originally published as "Islands in the Sun"), *Field & Stream*, South Region, June 1988;

"Warm Up on Arkansas's Summer Warmouths," *Arkansas Sportsman*, May 1993;

"Gar Wars," *In-Fisherman*, March 1998;

"Little Rock's In-Close Crappie" (originally published as "Little Rock's In-Close Crappie Lakes"), *Arkansas Sportsman*, July 1996;

"Consider the Carp," *Southern Outdoors*, August 1995;

"Battling Bowfins," *Field & Stream*, South Region, August 1991;

"Drummin' Up Summer Fun," *Arkansas Sportsman*, August 1992;

"Arkansas's Most Unusual Fish" (originally published as "The American Eel: Our Strangest Fish"), *In-Fisherman*, December/January 1996–97;

"Get the Jump on Summertime Whites" (originally published as "Slip on in to Those Summertime Whites"), *Arkansas Fins & Feathers*, July 1986;

"Arkansas Striper Bonanza," *Arkansas Sportsman*, May 1996;

"Rod-and-Reel Gar," *Southern Outdoors*, July/August 1993;

"They Call It the Streak" (originally published as "Those Other Fish: Yellow Bass"), *In-Fisherman*, July/August/September 1997;

"Bassin's Fall Lineup" (originally published as "Bassin' Our Fall Lineup"), *Arkansas Sportsman*, August 1999;

"Hotspots for Flathead Catfish" (originally published as "Top 10 Hotspots for Flathead Catfish"), *Arkansas Sportsman*, July 1998;

"Arkansas River Stripers" (originally published as "Arkansas River Rockfish"), *Arkansas Sportsman*, March 1993;

"Playground of the Ozarks" (originally published as "Angling in the Ozarks"), *Trailer Life*, March 1986;

"Capital City Saugers," *Arkansas Sportsman*, March 1995;

"Christmas Tree Crappie," *Field & Stream*, South Region, December 1990;

"Cool Cats," *Game & Fish Publications*, South Region, February 1999.

Introduction

I've been fishing my way around Arkansas, my home state, since I was six years old, and I haven't been on a fourth of our lakes and streams. You might wonder, then, what qualifies me to write a book about fishing Arkansas. I offer this evidence.

Arkansas encompasses more than 110,000 impoundments. Most are small privately owned ponds with less than five surface acres, but several hundred are public waters ranging from one acre to forty thousand acres. In addition, hundreds of natural lakes are scattered throughout the state, most of which are on public land. White River National Wildlife Refuge alone contains more than two hundred natural lakes.

Only six major river systems flow through the state—the Mississippi, White, Arkansas, St. Francis, Ouachita, and Red—but if you add to that the scores of tributaries of those large rivers, and the many tributaries of those tributaries, you discover that Arkansas streams number in the hundreds. If you could lay those streams end to end, they would stretch more than twenty thousand miles.

Knowing these things, we can make a reasonable assumption: if a person could fish on a different Arkansas lake or stream every week throughout the year, and could do this year after year, it would still take a lifetime to investigate firsthand the thousands of extraordinary fishing waters within the boundaries of this state. To my knowledge, no one has come close to achieving that end.

Other Arkansas anglers certainly have caught more and bigger fish than I, and they do so on a regular basis. Others have fished far more of the waters here than I'll ever have a chance to fish. Nevertheless, I feel fully qualified to write *Fishing Arkansas*. I feel qualified because I'm a good listener, a good observer, a good student, and an active participant.

I've fished with some of the state's finest anglers, people who know how and where to catch the fish they seek, and who do so with astounding regularity. I've listened to them and observed as they shared their secrets for landing a mess of fish. And some of it sank in.

Many of our state's fisheries biologists and researchers have been kind enough to let me pick their brains and tag along when they were on the water. The things they've taught me about Arkansas fish and fishing would fill volumes. One could ask for no better teachers.

I've read the works of those writers in this state who write well about fishing our waters—people such as Jim Spencer, Gregg Patterson, Charlie Bridwell, Gary Nelson, Don Feulsch, John Heuston, Jay Kaffka, Jerry McKinnis, Cliff Shelby, Charlie Burton, and others. I've fished with many of them—often, in some cases—and by listening to and reading what they have to say, I've learned more than I could in several lifetimes of fishing alone.

Most importantly, I have fished. I've wet a hook in *most* of the major lakes and rivers in Arkansas, and quite a few of the minor ones. I've caught every species of fish swimming in our waters that's large enough to be taken on hook and line—everything from longear sunfish to alligator gar. What I've learned is there's much more to learn, and there are many, many more waters that I must—somehow, some way—find time visit.

I say all this to prepare you for the fact that your favorite fishing hole may not be mentioned in this book. This is not due to oversight, but to a lack of space and time. No book on Arkansas fishing could be totally comprehensive in its scope. And it is doubtful any Natural State angler, myself included, will ever find time to visit the thousands of blue-ribbon fishing holes scattered across our state. Some day, perhaps, I can expand on what I've included here.

What is here is a collection of stories I have written during the past two decades about where to fish in Arkansas and how to catch the myriad species swimming in our lakes and streams. I've hardly scratched the surface of the subject matter, but if you read them thoroughly, I think you will find within these pages new knowledge about the fascinating fishes inhabiting Arkansas waters. You'll learn from some of our experts, venture to some of our most remote and productive fishing waters, and find new places to explore right in your own backyard. And if I've done a good job of this, you'll come away with a much greater appreciation for the splendid fish-filled waters that grace the most beautiful state in the nation.

Good fishing.

FISHING
ARKANSAS

JANUARY

Little Red Trout

Arkansas's Little Red River is a stream of contrasts. This popular Ozark Mountains trout stream is beautiful, running crystal clear and rice-well cold, skirted by scenic hardwood hillsides alive with wildlife. Yet on the Little Red, there is no feeling of wilderness, no sense of backcountry solitude like you find on many famous trout waters. You're rarely out of sight of boat docks and houses. You're rarely beyond earshot of other anglers.

Trout caught in the Little Red are stockers for the most part—hatchery fish raised on commercial trout chow. Yet few will ignore offerings of corn, night crawlers, or cheese, and on a good day you might catch fifty or more nine- to twelve-inch rainbows.

There are wild fish, too, though—big brown trout, sleek and magnificent, that spawn on tumbling river shoals each fall. And there are fish for fly fishers, long lean trout gone feral after years of freedom, trout that will wolfishly inhale a midge or nymph presented just so, trout that offer more challenge than your typical grocery-eating stocker.

The trout-fishing stretch of the Little Red is only twenty-nine river miles long. But the Little Red is anything but small in the hearts of trout fishermen. This stream has a big reputation and is touted as one of the finest trout streams in the South. That's partially because it produces big trout. To use the foremost example, on May 9, 1992, Howard "Rip" Collins of Heber Springs, Arkansas, landed a mammoth forty-pound, four-ounce brown trout that established a new all-tackle world record. He caught it in the Little Red on a ½₂-ounce marabou jig tied to four-pound-test line.

The Little Red finally is getting its due. For decades, the superb trout fishing here was overshadowed by the world-renowned trout fishing on another Arkansas river, the White. The White has given up not one, but two all-tackle, world-record brown trout and scores of browns topping twenty pounds. It also serves up fast-paced action

---

Anglers net an eight-pound rainbow trout on the Little Red River near Heber Springs.

for rainbow trout, fish that sometimes top fifteen pounds. Trout fishing on the White must be experienced to be believed.

The same is true for the Little Red. But in this case, an extraordinary trout fishery was outshined by a super-extraordinary trout fishery. The White became every trout angler's dream destination; the Little Red, a world-class fishery in its own right, played second fiddle to its sibling stream.

Then Howard Collins set the trout-fishing world on its ear. Collins caught the biggest brown trout ever known, and he caught it in the Little Red River. The spotlight shifted, the Little Red became the focus of attention, and, suddenly, anglers everywhere knew what a few anglers had been saying all along—that the Little Red River sits near the top of the list of the world's great trout streams.

The Little Red trout fishery was a late-comer among Arkansas trout streams. It had its beginnings in the mid-1960s following the completion of Greers Ferry Dam. Cold (40–55 degree) water tumbling through the sluice gates out of 31,500-acre Greers Ferry Lake was unsuitable for native warm-water fishes. The Greers Ferry National Fish Hatchery was constructed at riverside by the federal government as mitigation for the loss of the warm-water fishery, and soon hatchery-raised rainbow trout were being released into the Little Red. The trout thrived, and trout fans from throughout the nation came to fish for them.

Brown trout entered the picture about ten years later when introduced to the river by fly-fishing clubs. Members first planted brown trout eggs in egg boxes in the river and then stocked fingerlings with the blessing of the Arkansas Game and Fish Commission. These actions occurred in the late 1970s and early 1980s. Little stocking has occurred since 1983, but there has been no need. Brown trout do quite well on their own as evidenced by Collins's world-record catch. Browns running five to eight pounds are common today.

Cutthroat trout, first stocked in 1989, add another dimension to the Little Red trout fishery. Anglers harvest a high percentage of those released, but three- to four-pounders are fairly common. Stockings continue each year when cutthroats are available.

Rainbow trout are the "bread-and-butter" fish of local anglers. Each month, thousands are released. Nine- to twelve-inch stockers are most common in anglers' creels, but trout carryover from season to season is so good there are plenty of larger rainbows found here. With growth rates approaching an inch a month, Little Red rainbows generally tip the scales at three-fourths to four pounds each, with good numbers of five- to twelve-pounders sprinkled in. The river record weighed just over sixteen pounds.

The Little Red is full of stumps, logs, partially submerged trees, and beds of aquatic vegetation. At times, it looks more like a Louisiana bayou than a classic trout stream. The weed beds are loaded with sowbugs, freshwater shrimp, and other aquatic invertebrates eaten by trout, one reason for the stream's astounding productivity.

Fishing techniques vary with fluctuations in the river level. When water is low, most folks fly fish or anchor in a boat to bait-fish in deep holes.

Most bait fishermen opt for ultralight spinning or spin-cast outfits spooled with two-pound or four-pound line with a two-pound leader. One or two split shot are attached eighteen inches above the hook, or an egg sinker is rigged above a barrel swivel tied above the leader. The hook, a No. 10 to No. 6 gold Aberdeen, is baited with a night crawler, wax worms, corn, cheese, or salmon eggs. Then a miniature marshmallow is squeezed on the line above the hook to float the morsel off the bottom.

When still-fishing, anglers look for holes in weed beds or near timber. The bait is cast, then allowed to sink to the bottom. When a trout taps the line, the hook is set with a sharp upward thrust of the rod. Lightly set drags are important to prevent break-offs on the set, especially on the three- to five-pounders that bait fishermen catch with amazing regularity.

Most fly fishermen access the river afoot and wade, working the pools. During the brown trout spawning run, which usually starts in mid-October and runs through the first two weeks of November, the most effective fly is the egg pattern that imitates eggs laid by browns. At other times, good patterns include gray nymphs (sizes 14–18), Woolly Buggers and Woolly Worms (sizes 6–14 in olive, black, or brown), and Pheasant-tail Nymphs or Sowbugs (sizes 14–18).

Lure fishermen generally rely on small in-line spinners, small spoons and $\frac{1}{64}$ - to $\frac{1}{32}$ -ounce crappie jigs. For big browns, local guides favor either a four-inch sinking Rebel minnow or Smithwick Rogues. They drift near the bank and retrieve the lure with a ripping center-to-side motion, allowing the lure to rise and sink. This imitates a crippled baitfish and draws savage strikes from jumbo brown trout.

When water is high or on a rise due to power-generation releases at the dam, the current is too swift to anchor safely. During these periods, drift-fishing at mid-river with a salmon-egg rig is an effective tactic. Thread a ¼-ounce bullet sinker on four- to six-pound-test line and tie a barrel swivel below it. Tie an additional eighteen to twenty-four inches of leader line to the bottom of the swivel along with a No. 10, long-shanked Aberdeen hook. Bait the hook first with a one-inch plastic glow worm (available at local docks) positioned so it covers the long shank. Then add a large salmon egg, making sure the hook's point is completely hidden in the egg. Flip the bait ten feet behind the drifting boat and work it with a lift-drop action of your rod tip as you float. This is a deadly combination for trout.

Drift-fishing with corn, cheese, wax worms, and night crawlers is another tried-and-true high-water technique. A combination of lure and natural bait, one that frequently works well, is a ¹⁄₆₄-ounce marabou jig tipped with two wax worms and drifted beneath a clear bobber.

The trout fishing portion of the Little Red runs from Greers Ferry Dam at Heber Springs to the Ramsey Public Access east of Pangburn. There are several boat ramps at public access areas along the river and two walk-in accesses, one at Cow Shoals off Highway 210 east of Heber Springs and one at the Pangburn Bridge on Highway 110 at Pangburn. The latter area has a wheelchair-accessible fishing pier. Excellent bank-fishing access and camping are available at John F. Kennedy Park just below Greers Ferry Dam.

The river gets crowded at times, especially on holiday weekends, but even then it's not hard to find a good fishing hole. You may be within sight of six or eight boats, but you'll seldom have trouble catching your limit.

Is Arkansas's Little Red River the South's best stream? Some might debate that question, but few would deny it's among the best, not just in the South, but in the entire world. The best way to find out is to experience it for yourself. Plan a trip this year. If you enjoy trout fishing, that's a decision you'll never regret.

Arkansas Hotspots for Ten-Pound-Plus Bass

Catching a largemouth bass weighing 10 pounds or more is no easy task. Many dedicated bassers spend a lifetime trying without success. But despite the odds against it, catching a hawg this size in Arkansas can be done. The key is selecting the right lake, then devoting long hours to fishing it. Three of the best are Greers Ferry, Bull Shoals, and Austell.

GREERS FERRY LAKE

Greers Ferry's lunker bass potential surfaced in January 1988 when Billy Glaze of Bald Knob landed the second heaviest legal largemouth ever caught in Arkansas waters. Glaze was fishing for walleyes and hybrid stripers near the dam around midnight on January 1. The temperature was about thirty degrees, but the fishing was hot. Glaze and his brother–in–law landed two nice hybrids and three walleyes topping the 8-pound mark. Then something huge hit Glaze's CC Spoon.

"I thought I had a catfish or something when it first started fooling with my lure," Glaze recalled later. "It tapped the lure about five times before starting to pull straight down on it. I gave him a five count, then hit him as hard as I could. When I finally saw what it was, I got pretty nervous. I've caught 8-pound bass, but this thing made them look like babies."

The fish eluded the net twice, but the men finally landed it after Glaze worked the fish to the surface on the third try. Even after drying out on the drive home, the fish still weighed 16.5 pounds on a tackle-box scale. Although Glaze knew he had an exceptional fish and wanted to get it officially weighed, he decided not to wake anyone because it was now 2:30 A.M. He packed the fish on ice and went to bed.

By the next day, the bass was frozen solid. When an Arkansas Game and Fish Commission wildlife officer officially weighed the fish, it had been out of the water thirteen hours. It tipped the scales at 15 pounds, 15 ounces, just 5 ounces less than the state record caught in Mallard Lake in 1976.

The fact that Glaze caught his monster largemouth in Greers Ferry Lake comes as no surprise. This 31,500-acre Corps of Engineers impoundment sustains an excellent population of out-sized bass, and each year several fish exceeding 10 pounds are taken by visiting anglers. The lake is deep and clear, making it tough to fish, but it provides a good forage base of baitfish and has diverse structure such as deep drop-offs, long bluffs, and heavy timber.

Anglers seeking big winter bass on this Cleburne County lake would do well to follow Glaze's example. He caught his lunker offshore in twenty feet of water. Most big bass hold on deep-water structures during cold months, and finding and fishing these areas is the key to success.

BULL SHOALS LAKE

Bull Shoals Lake in the Ozarks of north-central Arkansas and southern Missouri is another lake well known for its trophy bass potential. Among the 10-pound-plus bass taken here are two former Arkansas state records. In 1960, Leroy Copeland of Ossie, Missouri, landed an 11-pound, 9-ounce record in the Big Creek Arm of Bull Shoals. Then, in 1973, another state record was snatched from the lake, this one a 13-pound, 2-ounce largemouth taken by Robert Brinkman of Bull Shoals. Missouri's current state-record largemouth, a 13-pound, 14-ounce fish taken in 1961 by Marvin Bushong of Bull Shoals, also came from Bull Shoals Lake. Although the lake is almost forty years old, it produces several hawgs over 10 pounds each year.

This Corps of Engineers reservoir covers forty-five thousand acres and 740 miles of shoreline at normal conservation pool level. One problem visiting anglers face is deciding where to fish.

In January, big bass often hold along deep main-lake bluffs where anglers work jigging spoons, tailspinners, jig-and-eel combinations, and big heavy spinnerbaits in twenty-five to thirty feet of water. The water still will be very cold, and the big bass will be relatively inactive, so present the bait slowly.

Anglers also should use bottom-contour maps to locate long deep-water points next to the old river channel or one of the big creek channels. Fish near deep water; this is where big bass live this time of year.

LAKE AUSTELL

On an acre-by-acre basis, no lake in the state can compete with the small northeast Arkansas impoundment known as Lake Austell. Located in Village Creek State Park atop Crowley's Ridge, Austell covers only eighty-five acres. Yet in one three-year period (1987–89) during which records were kept, this pint-sized impoundment produced no less than fifteen bass over 10 pounds, including six between 10 and 11 pounds, five between 11 and 12 pounds, four between 12 and 13 pounds, at least one 13-pounder, and a 15-pound, 12-ounce bass, the third heaviest ever taken in Arkansas waters. That's an impressive record for any body of water, but it's even more astounding when you consider the lake's diminutive size.

Jimmy Maners of Wynne caught the lake-record largemouth, a fish just half a pound shy of the current state record. It was around 2:00 P.M. on January 31, 1989. Maners was fishing the tail end of a long January warm spell, fighting wind in a seventy-eight-degree heat wave. Cranking a crawfish-colored Mann's +30 crankbait down to the ten-foot level in a deep hole, Maners reacted to a tap on his line and found himself tussling with the biggest bass he'd ever seen.

"I knew it was a monster as soon as I saw it," Maners said. "I figured right off it would go at least 13 or 14 pounds. I couldn't get it in my net, so I hung one foot out of the boat and grabbed it with my hand. I'd had some big bass break off in Austell before, and I didn't want this one to get away."

Good fortune smiled on Maners, and in short order, he was headed to the store to weigh his catch. "The first store I weighed it at, they said it weighed 15½ pounds," said Maners. "But when it was weighed by the game warden later that night at a different store, the scales said 15 pounds, 12 ounces. That was the official weight."

Maners's fish isn't the only fish nearing state-record size to come out of Austell. On February 25, 1987, the son of a park employee

found a dead bass floating on the lake. Turtles had eaten the fish's entrails and eyes, yet it still weighed 15 pounds. Had it been caught alive, that monster bass might have exceeded the current state-record weight.

Austell bass hold in or near deep water in January, just like bass in other lakes. But don't expect to catch a lunker without working for it.

"You can't expect to go to Austell and catch a big bass right off," Maners says. "You may fish hours or days without catching a fish. I've been fishing here every chance I've had for years, and the biggest one I caught in Austell up to now weighed 8 pounds, 2 ounces. It's tough fishing, but if you're willing to stick with it and learn the lake, then sooner or later your efforts will pay off."

Catching a bass topping 10 pounds isn't easy. It takes patience and luck. But if you want to cant the odds in your favor, try these three lakes this January. The fishing is great whether you're out at midday in seventy-degree weather or in the middle of the night in freezing cold.

James Maners of Wynne displays the 15-pound, 12-ounce Lake Austell bass he caught in January 1989.

Cold-Weather Pickerel

A buddy and I were bass fishing on an east Arkansas oxbow one January afternoon when a long, sleek fish followed my lure to the boat and milled around as if waiting to see what would happen next.

"That's a chain pickerel," my friend said. "Stick your lure in front of him and circle it around. See what happens."

I did as he suggested. The pickerel pounced on the lure and went airborne. It was something to see; the pickerel jumped several times only three feet from the boat.

Until that day, I never fished intentionally for pickerel. Few Arkansas anglers do. After that memorable battle, however, I studied chain pickerel and began fishing for them on purpose. And now, after more than a decade catching them in the weedy backwaters of Arkansas's rivers and lakes, I can say ol' chainsides has gotten a bum rap as a second-rate sport fish. This fish strikes a variety of baits with a lack of restraint unsurpassed by any largemouth. The biggest ever documented weighed nine pounds, six ounces, but even small ones are superstar fighters. Best of all, this power-packed predator fires up with the urge to feed at the same time other game fish are holed up for the winter.

Pickerel are caught year-round, but they bite so much better from November through March, when few other fish are stirring, that this seems the best time to chase them.

PICKEREL FACTS

The chain pickerel's name comes from the pattern of iridescent green "chains" marking its sides. Arkansans also call it jack, jack-pike, and snake, the latter in reference to its long, slender shape and toothy mouth. It inhabits everything from small natural lakes and tiny creeks to sprawling man-made impoundments and big river backwaters. Favorite haunts include black-water oxbows, sloughs, and streams stained dark with tannic acid from decaying vegetation. Waters in southern and eastern counties harbor the densest populations, though pickerel are common nowhere in the Natural State.

FISHING TACTICS

The key to successful pickerel fishing is seeking them as your primary quarry using appropriate tackle. Four- to six-pound line on a five- to six-foot, medium-action spinning rod is ideal—light enough so one- to two-pounders can strut their stuff, yet strong enough to tame occasional trophies.

Vegetation is the tip-off to hotspots. No matter what the season, pickerel live in weeds, and though vegetation may be sparse in January, scouting prime pickerel waters often reveals favored hideouts. Look for winter fish in five to ten feet of water along the edges of gently sloping weed beds, paying special attention to quiet, out-of-the-way locations like slow, grassy river backwaters and shallow necks connecting backwater sloughs.

Pickerel, being fish eaters, are drawn to lures mimicking baitfish. A weedless, silver spoon with a trailing pork rind is an old standard, but spinners, chugger plugs, slim-minnow lures, streamers, and even plastic worms elicit strikes. Cast along weed beds, reeling with a steady, moderate-speed retrieve; or, when using topwaters, cast to weed bed pockets, let the lure sit until the ripples die away, then twitch the lure again, continuing to the boat with a twitch-and-stop retrieve.

Live minnows allowed to swim naturally near cover sometimes take pickerel when artificial ones fail. Use a size one to four fine-wire hook, attach a split shot a foot above it, and add a small bobber. Hook the minnow through the back, then work it in and around the weed beds. Live frogs hooked through a back leg and allowed to swim across weed tops also are first-rate enticements.

Pickerel are notorious bait followers and often strike right next to the boat. At other times, they follow a bait to the boat but turn away at the last second. An alert angler usually can coax these fish into striking by presenting the bait again.

When thick weeds hinder an angler's use of more conventional fishing techniques, pickerel can be caught by "skittering." Skittering employs a ten- to twelve-foot cane pole, jig pole, or fly rod and an equal length of line. A pork frog or strip of fish belly is affixed to a stout hook, and the bait is jerked, or skittered, across openings in weed patches.

GOOD PICKEREL WATERS

Two good Arkansas pickerel producers are Lake Ouachita, just west of Hot Springs, and the lower portion of the Little Red River near Bald Knob. Both bodies of water contain beds of coontail, elodea, and other aquatic weeds. And where there are weed beds, there are sure to be pickerel.

In Lake Ouachita, look for winter fish in five to ten feet of water along edges of weed beds encircling islands. Weed beds in the backs of large, quiet coves also harbor many good fish.

When fishing the Little Red, pay attention to weed beds away from the main current. The water is clear here, and pickerel often are spotted cruising the tops of weed patches near creek mouths and in large pools.

Other Natural State waters offering good pickerel fishing include the White River and associated oxbows below Clarendon, Bayou de View, Bayou Bartholomew, the lower Ouachita River, south Arkansas's Saline River (not the Saline River of the Ouachitas), Dorcheat Bayou, and Moro Creek.

TROPHY-FISHING TIPS

The Arkansas record pickerel—a seven-pound, ten-ounce fish caught in the Little Red River in January 1979—is almost two pounds lighter than the world record, but it's possible a world-record-class fish swims in one of our backcountry lakes or streams. Good pickerel fishing in many waters is still largely untapped. Thus pickerel can attain maximum size, especially in remote oxbows, sloughs, and river swamps.

To zero in on a trophy, follow these tips. First, big pickerel are inveterate loners and will be found only in prime feeding stations, having driven away weaker competitors. Savvy anglers therefore focus on locales known to yield heavyweight chains.

Second, trophy pickerel prefer foods they're accustomed to eating. Use lures and baits that closely resemble the predominant baitfish in the body of water you're fishing.

Third, trophy-class pickerel are lazy and reluctant to leave the dark sanctuary of their favored niche. Present your bait in or very near heavy cover and keep it there for the best chance of hooking a muscle-bound brute.

Don't overlook pickerel this winter. They thrive in many Arkansas waters, and, ounce for ounce, they distinguish themselves in battle as well as any bass. Best of all, they're eager to strike this winter, providing a sure way to knock the chill off a January day.

Winter on Arkansas's Smallmouth Bass Streams

January is superb for float-fishing the scenic smallmouth bass streams coursing through Arkansas's Ozark and Ouachita Mountains. Water levels are just right for canoeing, big "bronzebacks" are actively feeding, and with fewer people on the water, you can enjoy an extra measure of relaxation.

Where should one start? Consider the following floats.

BUFFALO RIVER

Arkansas's best-known smallmouth stream is Buffalo National River. During warm months, hordes of visitors detract from the aesthetic values that attract many anglers in the first place. In winter, however, crowds are thinner, and anglers can enjoy a peaceful float through gorgeous canyons with sky-high bluffs.

The Buffalo is a model smallmouth stream, with clear, fast, oxygen-rich water and a gravel bottom and boulder beds that smallmouths love. Most smallmouths weigh a pound or less, but there are plenty, and there's always the chance of boating a three- or four-pounder.

One excellent winter lure choice is a ⅛- to ¼-ounce brown lead-head jig dressed with a No. 11 pork frog. Use your rod tip to bounce the lure across the bottom like a crayfish scurrying backward for cover. Other good lures include crayfish- and minnow-imitation crankbaits and small soft-plastic jerkbaits weighted for an underwater retrieve. Don't overlook live baits, either. Live crayfish, minnows, and night crawlers are extremely effective.

The Buffalo stretches over 150 miles of scenic mountain territory from near Boxley to its junction with the White River near Buffalo City. Good float stretches include Ponca to Highway 7 (25 miles with access points and campgrounds at Steel Creek, Kyles Landing, Erbie, and Ozark); the stretch between Arkansas Highways 7 and 123 (10 miles with accesses and campsites at Carver and Hasty); the float from

Arkansas 123 to U.S. Highway 65 (32 miles with access/camping areas at Mount Hershey and Woolum); the U.S. 65 to Buffalo Point float (27 miles with access points at Gilbert, Maumee North, Maumee South, and Arkansas Highway 14); and the final stretch from Buffalo Point to Buffalo City (30 miles with a single take-out point at Rush).

MULBERRY RIVER

The Mulberry, one of our finest Ozark smallmouth streams, gets a bit wild during high-water periods, with waters rated from medium to difficult, but still receives high marks from the fishing public. Winter smallmouth fishing is superb.

The Mulberry flows in a west-southwesterly course from Arkansas Highway 21 just north of Ozone to below Interstate 40 near Mulberry. Along the way, it passes near Catalupa, Oark, and Cass.

The first major put-in is where Arkansas Highway 103 crosses 2 miles southwest of Oark. You can take out where Forest Road 1504 crosses (11.5 miles downstream) or at the Wolf Pen Recreation Area, 2.5 miles below the 103 bridge. The second float starts at the 1504 access and ends 6 miles downstream at the Arkansas Highway 24 crossing at Turner's Bend. The Redding Campground is midway through this trip. The third major float originates at the Highway 23 bridge and continues 8.5 miles to Milton's Ford on Forest Road 1501 west of Arkansas 23. The last float, from Milton's Ford to Arkansas Highway 215 north of Mulberry, is an 18 to 20 mile trip through remote country.

Two top baits favored by local anglers are night crawlers and small jigs. Present them by casting upstream and allowing the bait to float naturally past rocks or other current breaks where smallmouths wait to ambush prey.

The best float conditions are at river levels of 2.0 to 4.0. (Readings at the scale's lower end are best for fishing.) Anything beyond 4.5 is dangerous. Visitors should watch weather forecasts closely, because heavy rain can quickly transform the Mulberry into a rampaging torrent.

Much of the Mulberry flows through the Ozark National Forest, but portions pass through private property. Take care not to trespass.

ELEVEN POINT RIVER

The Eleven Point enters northeast Arkansas from Missouri near the town of Elm Store and courses southward 40 miles to merge with the Spring River near Old Davidsonville State Park. Its name is derived from eleven principal tributaries.

The upper section in Missouri flows through national forest land and has rock bluffs typical of Ozark float streams. In Arkansas, land around the stream changes gradually from gentle hills to delta country. The lower Eleven Point's strong points are its cold, clear water; gravel bottom; abundant logs; and loads of smallmouths.

On the lower river below Dalton are steep banks of sand and gravel rising more than ten feet. These banks often are undercut and cave in, taking trees and undergrowth that clog the stream. In some places the channel is completely blocked to floaters, but the in-washed cover provides havens for outsized brownies.

Five old stone dams also require special consideration by the floater. Because of these obstructions, only experienced and careful canoeists should attempt floating the river below Dalton, and then only at low to medium stages. Above Dalton, the river is comparatively safe for novices at low to medium levels. When the river is near bank-full, it shouldn't be tackled by anyone.

Plenty of smallmouths inhabit the Eleven Point, and while an occasional four-pounder is taken, most weigh one to two pounds. Even so, the number of brownies is exceptional, and it's not unheard of to haul in a pair of smallmouths on a single crankbait.

When the water is clear, shallow-diving slim-minnow plugs on six-pound-test line are recommended. On rare occasions when rains muddy the water, spinners and crankbaits also are good producers.

This first-class smallmouth stream also offers fish a smorgasbord of aquatic foods such as crayfish, leeches, salamanders, insect nymphs, and small baitfish. Smallmouths eat these foods daily, and a fresh live bait often entices more fish than an artificial lure.

Access to the Eleven Point is available at five bridge sites. The first float from Missouri Highway 142 to the Arkansas Highway 193 bridge at Dalton covers 15.4 miles. It's 9 miles from Dalton to the Highway 90 access, and 11 miles farther to the U.S. 62 takeout area. The Game and Fish Commission has a public landing on the Black

River just below the junction with the Spring River and 4.5 miles below the end of the Eleven Point at Spring River. This last ramp is 14 miles below the U.S. 62 access.

KINGS RIVER

You'll have to look long and hard to find a better winter smallmouth stream than the Kings. Gentle and clear, the river twists through the rolling north Arkansas Ozarks, usually beneath a canopy of hardwoods. A float here is delightful and unforgettable, and cold-season smallmouth fishing is superb.

The Kings covers 90 miles from its headwaters in the Boston Mountains to the Arkansas-Missouri border. The county road access northwest of Marble is a traditional starting place. After 11 miles of deep pools, occasional rapids, and several large bluffs, floaters arrive at Marshall Ford, an access point northeast of Alabam. The second stretch from Marshall Ford to Rockhouse is a 15-mile trip through quiet backcountry. Other floats include the 7-mile stretch from Rockhouse to Trigger Gap, the 12-mile float from Trigger Gap to the U.S. Highway 62 crossing, the 12-mile run from the 62 crossing to Summers Ford (off Arkansas Highway 143), and the final 4 miles to Table Rock Lake.

Action is fast in spring and fall, but the really big smallmouths usually are taken in midwinter. Cast to still pockets, side sloughs, and pools. Skip the fast water. Good winter artificials include spinnerbaits with trailing pork rind, long diving-minnow plugs, and the jig-and-pig. In clear water, try small spinners with split fly-strip pork rind, or small crayfish-imitation crankbaits.

One of Arkansas's most precious assets is its wealth of smallmouth bass streams. We've mentioned just a few. Other excellent streams to try this winter include Big Piney Creek, the Cossatot River, Illinois Bayou, the Little Missouri, the Saline River, the Strawberry River, and the Spring.

Do me a favor, though. If you tell folks about our great smallmouth fishing, tell them to come in the spring, summer, or fall. Our winter smallmouth fishing . . . well, that's always been a secret 'tween us Arkies. I vote we keep it that way.

FEBRUARY

Midway Lake
for February Crappie

Midway Lake in Lee County ranks high among Arkansas's best February crappie fishing lakes. Crappie fishing is downright tough on many lakes this month. Finicky slabs frequenting deep prespawn haunts are hard to find and harder to catch. But on Midway, a broad, shallow oxbow, the water warms early, and February anglers load their coolers with one-, two-, and even three-pound crappie.

Midway's name is derived from its location. On some maps, this one-thousand-acre natural lake is called Council Lake. That name never stuck. Because the lake is midway between Arkansas and Mississippi, straddling the state line between West Memphis and Helena, local folks dubbed it Midway Lake, and that's the only name now commonly used.

Location also plays an important role in Midway's astounding productivity. The lake is an oxbow of the Mississippi River, lying entirely within the Mississippi River levee in a territory well known for producing giant crappie. A fertile soil base and river overflows keep lake waters rich in nutrients and food animals. Buckbrush, cypress trees, fallen timber, and other woody cover are abundant, and fish find ideal spawning grounds in the lake's shallow brushy flats. All this combines to produce the large population of big crappie that draws anglers here from throughout the tri-state region of Arkansas, Tennessee, and Mississippi.

Midway is shaped like a horseshoe with one fat arm and one skinny arm. The northeastern arm gouges a four- or five-mile channel through the Delta flatlands, but this section is narrow with few first-rate crappie fishing areas. The southeast arm stretches about the same distance but is broader with a greater variety of crappie habitat and structure. Most crappie anglers concentrate their efforts here.

On the east shore of this section are two large points, known as

---

Midway Lake, a Mississippi River oxbow, serves up plenty of big February crappie.

the Big Killdee and Little Killdee. Each is blanketed with buckbrush (button willow), a first-rate crappie cover. The lower east side, especially the southeast corner, also provides excellent fishing with a lot of buckbrush, cypress trees, and fallen timber attractive to crappie.

The west shore abuts the Mississippi River levee. This bank is skirted by bushes, logs, and treetops and has long stretches of riprap. It seldom produces the same quantities of big crappie found elsewhere in the lake, but it, too, is sometimes a productive fishing area.

The west shore of Midway Lake also is the site of Fowler's Boat Dock. E. O. Fowler, the proprietor, has been serving Midway anglers many years, and there's no person more familiar with the ins and outs of fishing this natural paradise.

"In a normal year, February is a choice month for catching crappie on Midway," Fowler said when interviewed. "The crappie are going real good. We usually have some warm days in February, and folks troll for crappie and catch some real slabs and a lot of them. Yo-yo fishing is excellent, too.

"Usually, if it's a normal year, the water is lower in February. Midway is a shallow lake, and if the water isn't too high, it warms earlier than deeper lakes in the surrounding area. So crappie turn on here in February, though it's mid–March a lot of times before they start hitting good on other lakes."

In February, most big stringers of fish are caught by trolling.

"Trolling out in the middle, that's usually the best way to catch crappie in February," Fowler said. "Most anglers that time of year use minnows, though some prefer jigs. Either one or a combination of both is good. They carry six to ten poles spread on the end of the boat, and if there are two parties in the boat, they'll have some poles around the sides and toward the back."

Midway crappiers have devised some ingenious rigs called trolling boards to facilitate their efforts. These are custom made by each angler to fit the style of boat they use. A board is cut to conform to the shape and size of the boat's front seat or deck. Then several rod holders are attached so the trolling poles are pointing different directions in a half circle at the front of the boat. The trolling boards are clamped to the seat or deck using C-clamps and can be easily removed to provide additional seat space.

When trolling, the boat looks like a big spider moving through the water with legs pointing in all directions. The angler starts using a variety of baits rigged at different depths. When using six poles, four might be rigged with a variety of jigs in different colors and sizes, and the other two with minnows. Two baits might be set at two feet deep, two at four feet, and two at six feet. This permits the angler to test different baits and depths until he finds crappie. Once it's established that crappie favor a certain depth or bait, then all the poles are rigged to conform to that preference.

"In February, crappie are usually caught three to four feet deep, sometimes even shallower, from two to three feet," Fowler said. "Because the lake is shallow, you're actually fishing fairly deep at four feet. On average, the lake is just six to eight feet deep, though there are a few potholes that drop down twelve to fifteen feet."

Most folks troll from north to south on the lake's broad south-east arm, starting at mid-lake just out from Fowler's launching ramp and moving up and down the lake in a zigzag pattern until fish are found. Some use electric motors to power their troll. Others drift-fish, allowing the wind to carry them along. When they reach the end of productive trolling grounds, they move back and start again.

When a crappie hotspot is found and several fish have been caught, fishing efforts are concentrated in that specific area until the action tapers off. Then the anglers move to another locale and the search for fish begins anew.

When the Mississippi River gets high, water spills into the lake, and crappie may move into shallow cover, even in February.

"If the river stays in here for a period of time, a few weeks or so," Fowler said, "there's excellent fishing around the brush. Fishermen get back in the bushes and do real good on yo-yos or poles."

Fishing with yo-yos is very popular on Arkansas crappie lakes. Yo-yos are automatic fishing devices hung singly on tree limbs, brush, or other handy places. Line is pulled off a spool, and a catch is set to hold the line at the preferred depth. A minnow is baited on a hook at the end of the line, and when a fish hits, the catch is released and a spring causes the line to be rewound on the spool. This sets the hook, and then the yo-yoer comes around periodically to remove his catch and reset the lines.

Although the river flows into Midway periodically, this doesn't typically occur during February. "On the average, it's usually March or April before the river gets into the lake," Fowler said.

Nevertheless, because river overflows have a dramatic influence on crappie fishing conditions, anglers need to be aware of changing water conditions. The best way to do this is to monitor the Mississippi River gauge at Memphis. Local newspapers usually print the river stage daily.

"When the river is at any stage below 21 feet on the Memphis gauge, it doesn't affect this lake at all," Fowler said. "On normal years, the river will come into the lake at 21.5 to 22 feet. However, when we have a lot of beaver dams, the river may rise an additional six inches to a foot before it comes into the lake."

When the river does enter the lake, anglers should closely watch the gauge to determine if water levels are rising or falling and at what speed. Some anglers prefer fishing during a rise; others prefer a fall. Most agree that the speed of the fluctuation should be relatively slow. Fishing during a slow fall or slow rise is generally very good, but during a fast rise or fall, crappie action usually is poor.

Perhaps the best thing about Midway is the size and quantity of the crappie you catch. "In February, you see a lot of two-pound crappie," Mr. Fowler noted, "and I've weighed lots of three-pounders in February, too. The average crappie runs near a pound here, and there are plenty to be caught. We have a lot of limits caught during February."

So when those bluebird days come round this February, and the crappie fishing itch has gotten you antsy, give Midway Lake a try. They may not be hitting every day, but if you're persistent, sooner or later you'll get into some of the best fishing for jumbo slabs you've ever experienced.

Greers Ferry Walleyes

In the world of walleye fishing, Greers Ferry Lake is hallowed water. This 31,500-acre Corps of Engineers impoundment in north-central Arkansas is the home of the world-record walleye, a twenty-two-pound, eleven-ounce fish caught here by Al Nelson on March 14, 1982. Local fisheries biologists give reliable reports of walleyes nearing, perhaps exceeding, this benchmark, that have been captured and released during walleye studies in Greers Ferry.

Greers Ferry has produced more twenty-pound-plus walleyes than any body of water. Nelson's gargantuan fish topped a twenty-one-pound, nine-ounce state record caught by Ed Claiborn in March 1979. The record prior to that was Mrs. Neva Walters's twenty-pound, six-ounce Greers Ferry walleye caught in November 1979. Another extraordinary fish was a twenty-pound, nine-ounce walleye caught by Thomas Evans on February 10, 1989.

To put this in perspective, consider the fact that twenty-pound-plus walleyes have been verified from only five states—Missouri, Kentucky, Tennessee, Virginia, and Arkansas. And none of the other states can boast the number of giants taken from Greers Ferry year after year.

Greers Ferry Dam on the Little Red River at Heber Springs was dedicated in 1963 by President John F. Kennedy. The project's intent was flood control and recreation; the ultimate creation was a 31,500-acre walleye-fishing paradise. It's here where another world-record walleye, a huge female fish topping twenty-three pounds, probably will be caught; and if it is caught here, it will surprise no one, especially not Tom Bly.

"I fully believe this lake has the potential to produce a new world record," says Bly. "A few years ago, I saw a walleye larger than Nelson's world record, and there are other giants out there, too."

The state-record-sized walleye Bly saw was released and may be swimming in Greers Ferry even now. Bly, you see, is a fisheries biologist with the Arkansas Game and Fish Commission, and that huge fish was captured and stripped of its eggs during the commission's

annual walleye project, a project that provides the fertilized walleye eggs that state fish hatcheries need to raise stocking-size fingerlings. Bly lives at Heber Springs and is involved with all aspects of walleye management on Greers Ferry.

"If you're after a big walleye," he says, "the best time to fish is from December through February. The biggest fish are females, and their eggs are fully formed toward the end of that period, giving them extra weight. They're feeding heavily prior to spawning, so you're more likely to catch one. During the spawn, they may quit feeding altogether."

Most walleye anglers fish Greers Ferry from mid-February through early April during the spawning season. When the water temperature approaches fifty degrees, walleyes ascend the four upper forks of the Little Red River—the South Fork, Devil's Fork, Middle Fork, and Archey's Fork. Males arrive at spawning sites first and later are joined by females. Both sexes at this time occupy long, deep pools below swift riffles. Ripe adults move into shallow gravel-bottomed shoals to spawn at night.

"The upper forks of the Little Red receive intense fishing pressure during this time," Bly says. "Action for one- to four-pound walleyes, the small males, is fast-paced. They strike out of aggressiveness brought on by the spawning urge. And there are hundreds of them, so you catch more. Action on big females is always slower, because they're fewer in number."

Bly says many anglers believe the large upper forks are the only place walleyes are likely to be caught, when, in fact, other locations are equally productive during this season.

"Some of the best fishing areas are feeder creeks where there's a good inflow of water into the lake," he says. "Good ones include Peter Creek, Drip Creek, Hill Creek, and Lynn Creek. There aren't as many walleyes in the creeks, but there's a good possibility an angler could hook a sizable fish."

Bly notes that some Greers Ferry walleyes spawn at mid-lake

On the Devil's Fork of the Little Red River above Greers Ferry Lake, walleyes on spring spawning runs provide fast-paced action for savvy anglers.

sites on gravel points. He theorizes some of these are northern-strain walleyes stocked years ago.

"Most Greers Ferry walleyes are river fish," he says. "They evolved in these river systems and continue to migrate up the tributaries to spawn, just as they have for ages. Studies done by Texas A&M University indicate these may be a special strain of walleyes different in genetic and behavior patterns than those found in northern waters.

"When we learned we had a special strain of walleyes in the lake, we discontinued all stocking of non-native walleyes immediately," he continues. "But prior to that, during two or three years when we didn't have enough native fish for supplemental stockings, we introduced some northern-strain walleyes into Greers Ferry. I think these fish have a greater tendency to spawn in mid-lake areas—on gravel points and such—than the native walleyes do. Those are the places where they spawn in northern lakes. And anglers who know how to fish these locations usually can find plenty of walleyes."

Greers Ferry anglers also should know this is not just a spring or spawning-season walleye fishery.

"There's a small group of knowledgeable fishermen here who catch walleyes during all seasons," Bly reports. "They know the lake, and they know where walleyes are likely to be found during each season. They take home fish consistently."

Many fishing tactics, lures, and baits are used to catch Greers Ferry walleyes. Jesse Finch of Heber Springs caught a 16.4-pound walleye in late February 1991 while trolling a deep-diving Rebel minnow-style crankbait, a very popular fishing technique here. Bottom fishing with small live bluegills or creek chub minnows is a common and productive strategy, and, according to Bly, many walleye anglers troll or vertical fish with jigs or jig-minnow combos. Some anglers fish from boats, but, at spawning time, just as many settle onto their favorite section of river bank, fire up a lantern, and watch their baits work lazily below the spawning shoals. Some wade-fish in the shoals.

Is there another world-record walleye swimming in Greers Ferry? If so, will it ever be caught? The answer to both questions is maybe. The odds certainly are good that a new record will surface someday on this beautiful Ozarks lake, but it's anybody's guess about when.

Perhaps it will happen this year. Perhaps you'll be the one who does it. Visit Greers Ferry this February and sample the best fishing for giant walleyes America can offer.

City Water Bass

If you know the impact late winter–early spring weather and water conditions have on bass fishing patterns, and are willing to invest a little extra time to locate your quarry, February can produce outstanding bass fishing on Arkansas's many first-class public fishing waters.

Some will head for one of the Natural State's huge U.S. Army Corps of Engineers impoundments—lakes like Ouachita, Bull Shoals, or Beaver. Others opt for the smaller confines of our Game and Fish Commission lakes, state park lakes, or old river oxbows. When water conditions permit, river fishing on waters like the Arkansas River also is popular with February bass fishermen.

If you haven't tried them, you also should consider fishing some of the state's many city-owned water-supply lakes. Dozens of these man-made impoundments are scattered from border to border near the cities of Benton, Booneville, Camden, Charleston, Clarksville, Dierks, Eureka Springs, Fayetteville, Ft. Smith, Mena, Nashville, Newark, Newport, Ola, Paris, Pottsville, Prairie Grove, Siloam Springs, Van Buren, Waldron, and many others. All harbor populations of largemouth and/or spotted bass, and February bass fishing on these neglected waters is, at times, nothing less than superb.

Three of the best, and largest, of Arkansas's city-water bass lakes are Maumelle, Winona, and Brewer, all in central Arkansas less than an hour's drive from Little Rock. Here's the lowdown on February bass fishing in these waters.

LAKE MAUMELLE

Maumelle is the largest of Arkansas's many city-water fishing lakes. Owned by Little Rock Waterworks, this lake covers 8,900 acres eight miles west of Little Rock. Primary access is along State Highway 10 between Little Rock and Thornburg.

Maumelle harbors good numbers of largemouth and spotted bass. Fish may be scattered in February, but if it's a normal February —cold during the first portion and slowly warming toward the end—the bass will locate primarily along the north side of the lake. Maumelle runs west to east, thus water along the north shore warms before the remainder of the lake.

Early in February, bass fishing here usually is slow, but many anglers are able to entice largemouths by vertically jigging grubs and spoons around deep points, humps, and creek or river channel drop-offs. Nearly all the timber on the lake bed was cut when the lake was impounded in 1957, so anglers can't rely much on visible cover like dead snags and brush when trying to pinpoint fish. A sonar fish-finder unit is an invaluable, and often times necessary, aid for locating underwater structures that concentrate schools of fish.

As the water temperature rises toward the fifty- to fifty-five-degree mark late in the month, largemouths begin hitting crankbaits, spinners, and jig–pork frog combinations around rocky points, stumps, and shoreline rubble. Some of the best fishing grounds during this time include the North Shore Cove, situated near the mid-point of the north shore, and the shoreline reaches from this cove back toward the lake's west end. Days following periods of warm rain can really send bass on a feeding spree, so whenever possible, try to plan your fishing excursions to coincide with those times.

Spotted bass are another popular target for Maumelle's black bass fans. In fact, Maumelle is considered by many to be one of the best spotted bass lakes in Arkansas.

Again, the best fishing in February is likely to be along Maumelle's northern shore, and again, these bass are typically found around underwater structures like stream channels, rock humps, points, and piles of gravelly rubble. Rocky shoreline ledges that extend down into fairly deep water seem especially attractive to big spots.

Islands west of the North Shore Cove are productive sites for spotted bass fishing, as are the waters around Workman's Island and the western end of Big Island and the cove just north of Workman's Island. You can't beat live crawfish for bait, but the jig-and-pig and other deep-working crawfish imitations are reliable as well.

One big handicap for Maumelle bassers is the extremely clear water. To make the best of this situation, use only ten- to twelve-pound-test line at the most, and remember that the best fishing will usually be during low-light periods—early and late in the day and during periods of cloudiness and rain. Make long casts when possible and keep a low profile on the water. This helps avoid spooking already finicky fish.

LAKE WINONA

Just south and west of Lake Maumelle is another city-water hotspot. Lake Winona, a Little Rock water-supply lake like Maumelle, is in the Ouachita National Forest, seven miles west of State Highway 9 at Paron.

Completed in 1938, Winona is among the oldest of the state's man-made public fishing reservoirs. Like Maumelle, it is extremely clear much of the year, and though small—1,240 acres—the average depth is thirty-five feet, with some holes dropping to one hundred feet. These two characteristics—depth and transparency—make light line important, not only to avoid spooking wary clear-water bass, but also to get lures down to depths where fish are likely to be feeding.

During early February, Winona's largemouth bass frequent deep water, often holding along the channel of the Alum Fork of the Saline River, which was dammed to create the lake. Secondary creek channels branching off the main river channel also hold bass concentrations. A sonar fish-finder helps pinpoint this underwater structure. Watch the sonar for blips that indicate bass suspended around stump beds, points, cuts, and other prominent features along the channel drops.

Shad, crayfish, and sunfish are the primary bass forage in Winona, and lures imitating these animals are good choices. A silver spoon allowed to flutter down through the water on slack line provides a convincing imitation of a dying shad and often will be nailed by hungry bass. Deep-diving crawfish-colored crankbaits, one-ounce jig-grub combinations, live crawfish, and live minnows also are popular with local anglers.

As the water warms, largemouth bass migrate to shallow flats and coves adjacent to deep-water reaches. During the latter half of February, if several warm fronts have passed through, largemouths usually can be found by casting spinnerbaits, vibrating plugs, or crankbaits around shoreline stumps and buckbrush.

The prespawn locational pattern for spotted bass focuses on the secondary creek arms of Lake Winona, arms which traverse the lake bottom in nearly every large cove. As the water temperature reaches the low fifties, the fish move to the junctions of smaller creeks and the old river channel, and then begin slowly moving up the creeks toward more shallow water.

Late in the month, as the water temperature rises, many spotted bass move close to shore near steep ledges. High banks with broken rock in combination with clay are good places to begin prospecting. The fish also may school on rocky points from five to fifteen feet deep, depending on water clarity and sunlight. If it's a fairly dry month and the water remains clear, the fish drop into deeper water, and anglers catch them by working small jig-grub or jig–pork frog combinations bounced stair-step fashion down the points. When the water is highly colored after heavy rains, spots lie in shallow water, four to five feet deep, against steep banks. A good presentation in this case is slowly crawling a small crawfish-imitation crankbait or live crawfish parallel to the bank face.

BREWER LAKE

Another topnotch February bassing spot is Brewer Lake, on State Highway 92 four miles north of Interstate 40 at Plumerville. Opened for fishing in 1983, 1,100-acre Brewer was built as a municipal water supply for Conway, fifteen miles to the east. Fishing pressure often is heavy.

Among the notable features of Brewer Lake are numerous fish attractors scattered across its bottom. Prior to Brewer's filling, timber cleared from the lake bed was placed in a series of fifteen-by-fifty-foot brush piles. These brush piles now lie ten to twenty-five feet below the surface and are prime hideouts for the lake's largemouth bass year-round. None rise above the surface, so a sonar unit is necessary to locate them.

In February, bass may be between the brush piles and the shoreline, holding above the brush or down in it, or ranging between the inundated creek channels and brush piles. When a brush pile is found, throw a jig-grub combo, counting it down to just above the brush tops, then retrieving it with a slight jigging motion. Crankbaits also produce well when fished over the brush, alongside it, between the brush and the shoreline, and between the brush and the creek channels. A very effective technique is bumping the brush piles—allowing the lure to stop and begin to float up, then resuming the retrieve. Many strikes occur just as the crankbait starts to dive again.

Another February bass hotspot is the area in front of the dam; the area has two types of structures—riprap and a steep bluff—that almost always hold fish. Some of the largest bass from the lake are taken by anglers working crankbaits along the riprap. The steep bluff, which drops down to seventy feet deep in the old Cypress Creek channel, is a good spot for fishing spoons, grubs, or, as the water warms, plastic worms. Hopping lures down the ledges or working them around small points can be very productive.

Other areas to prospect for February bass include several inundated farm ponds, the brushy edges of which often hold bass; a big hump, actually an old cemetery, northeast across the lake from the south boat ramp, on top of which bass often feed; and the submerged roadbed of an old highway that runs in and out of the lake near the west shoreline. Ditches alongside the old road are filled with brush and often hold good fish.

City-water lakes often are overlooked by Arkansas bass fans. But if you catch it right, fishing for largemouth and spotted bass can be fast-paced and exciting. When planning your February fishing itinerary, don't forget to include Maumelle, Winona, Brewer, and other municipal water-supply lakes among the waters you consider.

Caddo River Smallmouths

For five minutes, Richard Lancaster fishes a half-submerged treetop, dancing a jig-and-pig through this likely bass refuge. Nothing happens. The fisherman twitches the bait by moving his rod tip, then reels in a bit more line. The jig darts, flutters, settles, darts again. No takers.

A sharp pull and the bait scurries quickly over the bottom, mimicking a crawfish seeking safety. Still nothing. Another cast, another promising spot.

This time, to Lancaster's delight, a fish strikes. He sets the hook, and his adversary begins an acrobatic performance packed with pizzazz. Six times the fish jumps.

Lancaster plays the fish gently but commandingly—two qualities that do not blend easily. But he combines them, achieving something stronger than either alone.

After another sustained run, he gains control and leads the gleaming fish to the canoe. He gets a thumb lock on the fish's lower jaw and scoops it from the river. It's a beautiful fish, but at four pounds or so, it doesn't look like a trophy. In fact, if it were a largemouth bass, it wouldn't draw much attention from the angler.

This fish is no largemouth, however. In fact, to hear Richard Lancaster tell it, the difference between this fish and a largemouth is like the difference between a thoroughbred race horse and a mule. It's a "brownie," precisely what Lancaster has been fishing for—a bronze-colored, scrappy smallmouth bass. And a four-pound brownie is something to glow about.

"This river gives up some of the biggest smallmouths I've ever seen," says Lancaster. "It's a beautiful float trip, too, with some of the best scenery in the Ouachita Mountains. That's why I keep coming back. Smallmouth fishing like this is hard to find."

Richard Lancaster of Lonoke introduced me to the Caddo River on that trip more than ten years ago. It was the first time I floated this extraordinary river, but it wasn't my last. I've returned time after time through the years to experience the blue-ribbon smallmouth fishing there, and I can say without reservation it's among the finest smallmouth rivers in Arkansas. Catching several dozen one-half- to four-pound smallmouths during a good day of fishing is not unusual.

The Caddo begins life as a trickle of water in southwestern Montgomery County, but the upper section from the headwaters to Norman is only floatable following extended periods of rainfall. After clearing Black Springs, then Norman, the upper stream continues more than twenty-seven miles, skirting the towns of Caddo Gap, Glenwood, and Amity before entering the headwaters of DeGray Lake.

Though anglers floating the Caddo are seldom far from civilization, the river is peaceful and custom-made for smallmouth bass. Its waters are clear, cool, and fast-flowing, and there's a good mix of long deep pools and rapids. Big rocks, shale ledges, and deep runs under steep banks and downed timber offer shade, food, and protection from the current. That's where you find smallmouths.

Many local smallmouth anglers prefer live baits, particularly live crayfish and minnows, but any artificial one imitating the smallmouth's natural prey usually proves productive. Plastic worms and salamanders, crayfish- and minnow-imitation crankbaits, and the pork-frog–jig combination all are worth trying.

Caddo River brownies usually rest behind rocks or other current breaks and wait to ambush food passing in the current. You'll catch more bass if you present your bait the same way. Cast upstream and let the bait drift with the current on slack line. Guide the lure past as many large rocks as you can, hopping it along with short flips of your rod tip. Make the retrieve slow.

If you want to catch a big bass, pick a day in December, January, or February. Winter canoe traffic is light, so boat-wary smallmouths aren't as likely to have lockjaw. You may have the river all to yourself, another big plus.

If fish size is unimportant, you can visit the Caddo any time and enjoy a productive trip. Autumn is an especially fruitful fishing season, with colorful hardwoods blanketing the surrounding hillsides. During spring, you may catch spawning white bass and walleyes in the lower reaches, in addition to smallmouths. Summer fishing excursions also can provide memories of first-class angling.

No matter when you fish, try to be on the river before the sun comes up. Smallmouth activity peaks near dawn. In contrast, the worst periods for river smallmouths usually come on the heels of hard cold fronts, regardless of the season. For a day or two after a front comes through, bass fishing usually takes a nosedive.

The uppermost Caddo River fishing float starts at a small bridge in Norman and ends eight miles downstream at an old low-water bridge just west of Caddo Gap. To reach the low-water bridge, turn west from Highway 8 at the Caddo Gap Post Office and go one-quarter mile.

The second fishing float covers six miles from Caddo Gap to Glenwood. The takeout is at the U.S. Highway 70 bridge. This is all Class I water, with no problems for novices except two tight S turns and a few canoe-grabbing trees.

The float downstream from Glenwood is a slower version of the upper sections. Pools are longer, and the rapids lose some of their intensity. It's perfectly suited for novice canoeists wanting to catch some nice smallmouths. You can float eight miles to the Arkansas Highway 182 bridge north of Amity or thirteen miles to the Arkansas Highway 84 bridge northeast of Amity.

The Caddo also can be floated below DeGray Lake to its confluence with the Ouachita River. This short stretch is one of the most convenient in the state, crossed by Interstate 30, U.S. Highway 67, and Arkansas Highway 7. The smallmouth fishing, however, is poor compared to the river's upper reaches.

The Caddo River provides a beautiful, peaceful setting for a smallmouth junket. Visit it this season and match wits and brawn with the smallmouth bass, one of the cagiest, smartest, and most classic fighters in Arkansas waters.

MARCH

Crappie Lakes Nobody Fishes

She lies in the back of beyond, an emerald-green jewel hidden behind a lattice of saw briars, crossvine, and rattan in the heart of an Arkansas swamp. Few people know of her existence, and only a handful of those know her with the intimacy that she and I have shared.

When last I visited her, an alligator crossed her breadth and swam alongside the leaky wooden johnboat from which I fished, eyeballing me like a cat eyeballs a plump baby bird about to tumble from its nest, before vanishing 'neath the lady's glaucous veil of duckweed. A pair of bald eagles fished with me that day, carrying bluegills to a nest high atop an ancient cypress where a single downy chick waited to be fed. Wood ducks squealed as they raced by overhead. Rain crows clucked, and peepers peeped. The staccato drumbeat of pileated woodpeckers chiseling for grubs echoed through the wilderness.

To visit the lady, I motored many miles down the back of the great river to a point far from the nearest town. Tying my johnboat to thick oak steps placed here years ago by some now forgotten individual, I clambered to the top of the steep river bank and followed a barely discernible path through a hundred yards of jungle to the lady's edge. A screen of tupelos, cypress, and buckbrush narrowed my field of vision, but I soon spotted the old wooden boat awash near shore. No one knows who owns it anymore, but ownership is not an issue in this lonely corner of the world. The boat is there for whoever comes along.

I tipped the hand-hewn cypress craft to empty it of water, then placed inside it the cane pole and coffee can full of jigs I brought along. Water edging the oxbow was shallow, and I had no difficulty pushing my way to the outer boundary of the cypress trees using a sweetgum pole cut from a nearby thicket. As I tied a squirrel-hair jig to my line, I saw a spritz of tiny shad erupt beside a button willow bush, a sure sign that largemouth bass were hunting there. But I wasn't after bass.

Arkansas encompasses many small lakes in remote places where crappie fishermen can enjoy a peaceful outing.

Dipping the jig into the convoluted folds at the base of a hollow cypress, I found my quarry. Its subtle strike almost fooled me, but I saw the line go slack and set the hook with a sharp upward snap of my wrist. A brief battle ensued. The fish darted this way, then that, in the darkened recess of the tree, and I thought for a moment its frenzied efforts might beget its escape. This time, however, it was not to be. As the fish weakened, the springy cane pole slingshotted it from its hidey-hole, and I quickly swung it over the transom.

The big crappie glistened like a silver ingot. Its weight approached two pounds, much larger than the crappie I usually catch in man-made waters pressured every day by hoards of anglers. I laid it in water that had seeped into the bottom of the boat and continued fishing.

Over the next hour and the next and the next, I caught crappie after crappie after crappie. A few were larger than the first, including one barn door that measured three lengths of a dollar bill. Most weighed a pound to a pound and a half by my estimation, and I rarely fished more than five minutes without catching one.

The lady—this gorgeous little oxbow lake in the back of beyond —had once again blessed me with her bounty. That evening, before I turned away and headed up the path that would lead me back to my boat on the river, I offered her a silent word of thanks.

Only rarely do I visit this isolated pool, and when I do, I go alone. A friend who introduced me to the lady nearly fifteen years ago made me promise I would never reveal her whereabouts to another soul. I intend to keep that promise because this is not a place where I want to see other people. The charm that draws me there is the charm of solitude and natural splendor. People do not belong there.

My friend goes there to fish for bass. I have not told him about the hundreds of huge crappie I've caught there, and I don't intend to; he's happy enough fishing for bass. The giant gar and bowfins living in the lake feed on the crappie and keep them from stunting. The lack of fishing pressure lets them grow large. I know of only a few other lakes where crappie grow so big and are so abundant, and those, too, are isolated waters that rarely have human visitors.

If I gave you a few clues, and you had the desire, you could find my little hideaway and fish it yourself. The land on which it lays is public ground. Fishing is allowed year-round, except for a brief period in winter when the area serves as a sanctuary for waterfowl. I don't intend to provide you any additional clues, however, so you'll be better off finding your own hideaway where you can fish for crappie away from the crowds. All it takes is a little homework.

Begin your search on large tracts of public land such as national wildlife refuges, wildlife management areas, and national forests. The key word here is large. Remote lakes by their very definition must be surrounded by large tracts of land where access by vehicle is difficult or impossible. Identify such spots, then write or call the agency in charge and determine how to obtain a map. Topographic maps are best, as they provide more detailed information that will help you determine the best means to reach the body of water you choose to fish. Call local fisheries biologists and ask if this is a lake where good numbers of crappie are likely to be found.

White River National Wildlife Refuge encompasses more than two hundred oxbow lakes. Only a few dozen have easy access; the rest rarely are visited by fishermen, and all harbor untold numbers of slab crappie. With a topo map and GPS unit, anyone can pinpoint these remote lakes. Walk in with a belly boat and a minimum of tackle, and you can catch crappie on some waters that haven't seen another angler in decades.

Two large national forests in Arkansas—the Ozark and Ouachita —cover millions of acres holding scores of seldom-fished crappie lakes. Some have roads to their edges, but because the banks are steep and no launch ramps are available, the few people who fish them usually do so from small open areas on shore. By sliding in a lightweight inflatable boat or canoe, I've fished remote hotspots loaded with jumbo crappie. Consult personnel on national forests to find similar locales.

Proper timing may be required to reach some out-of-the-way crappie lakes. One oxbow I like to fish, for example, is surrounded by swampy, snake-infested ground in the backwoods of Henry Gray–Hurricane Lake Wildlife Management Area near Bald Knob. Walking in is not an option, but in spring, when local rivers flood, it's possible to motor up a bayou to within a hundred yards of the lake. A few local anglers who know about the lake's rich bounty of giant crappie devised a set of wheels that can be placed under a small johnboat, allowing two men to pull it through the woods between the bayou and lake. It's back-breaking work, but the rewards make the effort worthwhile.

Some unfished crappie lakes lie in plain view with easy access. One I've often fished lies on public land right beside Interstate 40. Thousands of people drive by it every day, yet I've never seen another person fishing there. With a belly boat and an ultralight spinning outfit, it's easy to fish around the lake's beaver lodges and flooded tupelo trees where I sometimes catch two-pound-plus crappie. Lakes such as this don't offer the quietude many anglers seek, but they provide a good option when there's not enough time for a backcountry junket.

Crappie lakes devoid of people offer treasures not found in other places. To be on the water on a beautiful day, resting in the shade of giant cypress trees; to be in a place untouched by human hands, a place where crappie grow as big as dinner plates and rush to take the offerings you lay before them; to come home fully spent, empty-handed or bearing food for the table; to sit by the fire and relive the time you were there and long for the time when you can be there again—this is crappie fishing at its best.

Don't Skip the Skipjack

As far as I can tell, there are only two good reasons to fish for skipjack herring. Neither has anything to do with the fish's culinary qualities, for skipjacks are about as edible as bicycle tires. Size is no attraction, either. The world record—a three-pound, twelve-ounce skipjack caught in Tennessee's Watts Bar Lake—was colossal. Arkansas's record weighed only two and a half pounds. Skipjacks are not exceptionally beautiful, nor challenging to catch.

Why fish for skipjacks, then? First of all, skipjacks are extraordinary bait for giant catfish. Their flesh contains dense concentrations of scented oils, and these oils are highly enticing to flatheads, blues, and channels. It matters little how you present the bait—live, dead, whole, cut, filleted. Hungry cats gobble up skippies like a toddler eating chocolates. Heavyweight striped bass gorge on skipjacks, too, and live herring bait is hard to beat when you're after a trophy-class striper.

Perhaps the best reason to fish for skipjacks, though, is simply because it's pure, unadulterated fun. Hook one of these silvery, streamlined fish, and the reason for its name becomes immediately apparent. It skips across the surface of the water like a flat stone, leaping again and again and again. Tussle with one on ultralight tackle, and you'll be amazed that so small and slender a fish exhibits such sporty qualities.

The skipjack herring is closely related to shad and alewives. Anglers know it by many nicknames, including nailrod (my favorite), river herring, golden shad, river shad, skippy, and blue herring. When seen skipping across the water, pursuing the small fishes that comprise most of its diet, its symmetry and color catch the eye. The iridescent blue-green back and silvery sides flash in the sun.

Skipjacks inhabit open waters of large freshwater rivers and occasionally wander into brackish and salt waters along the Gulf Coast. They range from the upper Mississippi River Valley to the Gulf, and from Florida to Texas. In Arkansas, they occur in the Mississippi, lower White, Arkansas, lower Ouachita, and Red Rivers.

The species is highly migratory, moving about continuously in

large schools. Until recently, it was believed to be anadromous, migrating up rivers from the sea to spawn in fresh water. It's now known to be entirely a freshwater form, but fishermen report distinct upstream runs in spring.

Most skipjacks are an incidental catch for anglers pursuing white bass, saugers, and other panfish. But many who catch them this way discover that fishing for skippies, specifically, can be just as much fun as chasing more popular game fish.

A long, sensitive ultralight spinning combo amplifies the enjoyment of skirmishing with these pint-sized pugilists. The average skipjack weighs a pound or less, so two- to six-pound-test line is ample. Light line also permits long casts with the small lures that work best—jigs, spinners, streamers, and tiny topwater plugs. Small, live minnows also nab them.

Jigs ($\frac{1}{64}$ to $\frac{1}{32}$ ounce) are perhaps the most commonly used skipjack lures. Small white bucktails are favored by skipjackers on the Mississippi River, where these little scrappers are abundant. But style is of little importance it seems, for skipjacks just as readily strike tube jigs, curly-tail jigs, marabou jigs, and other designs. Two or more jigs often are fished tandem on the same line, and multiple catches on a single cast are common.

The tailwaters below Arkansas's big-river dams serve up some of the best skipjack fishing, especially in spring when lock-and-dam structures hinder the skipjack's upstream migrations. Enormous concentrations assemble in these reaches, and at times the water's surface flashes like a mirrored globe twirling above a disco dance floor as schools of skippies caper in the swirls. A fortunate fishermen may land dozens, perhaps a hundred or more, in a single afternoon spent casting around lock walls, power-generation channels, and wing dikes.

River junctions also are skipjack hotspots. The boiling eddies created when two big delta rivers converge seem especially attractive to these fish, perhaps because this type of water also attracts enormous concentrations of small food fish. Large schools of skipjacks often churn the surface of the swirling water as they pursue young-of-the-year shad in late summer and early fall. Here, the largest skipjacks

---

Skipjack herring aren't good to eat, but they make excellent catfish bait.

Skipjack herring are fun to catch on light tackle.

often are found in association with white bass, small stripers, or other game fish, an additional bonus for the lucky angler.

I remember a week spent on a houseboat moored just upstream from the confluence of the White and Mississippi Rivers in southeast Arkansas. We spent most of our time fishing for the monster catfish that call this world home. But each morning at dawn, we motored to the juncture of the two vast rivers and fished for skipjacks.

If there's a more beautiful sight than a thousand skipjacks flashing like fireflies in the glow of a Mississippi River sunrise, I've never seen it. It started slowly at first, a skippy here, another there, gamboling on the water's surface. Every now and then a little spritz of elfin shad would spurt from the water with a skipjack close behind. Then as the sun rose and that rich tangerine light saturated the river bottoms, the skippies rose, and the water's surface became textured by their dance. Leaping, flashing, leaping, flashing—thousands upon thousands of them were gorging on the rivers' great bounty of shad.

Sometimes it lasted an hour or more; sometimes only a few all-too-brief minutes. But each day we were there, and each day we cast to boiling schools of skipjacks as they did their dance. When we had enough to bait our trotlines that day, we'd stow the rods and take in the extravaganza. And when it was over, we always wished it wasn't.

Some anglers never outgrow the stage where catching big, powerful sport fish is all that matters. For them, fishing has no meaning unless they catch a limit of bass, trout, stripers, or other "meaningful" fish—the bigger the better.

For others, though, fishing is an end unto itself. It clears the mind and soothes the soul. It matters not what kind of fish are caught, or how many, or how big. These folks are out to have fun, to relax, to take in the outdoors. And, for them, the simpler pleasures are enough to satisfy.

It's for this latter group that skipjacks were tailor-made. They're not good to eat. They don't get very big. They have no status. But fishing for skipjacks is among the best of all ways to enjoy a March day outdoors.

White Lightning! White Bass!

For a few short weeks each spring, savvy Arkansas anglers can participate in some of the fastest fishing of the year. This is the season when white bass carry out their spawning activities, and fishermen who know where to find them and how to catch them enjoy fun-filled hours where a fish caught every cast is not unusual.

Generally speaking, small streams provide better white bass fishing than large ones because the water is easier to cover and you can find the fish more readily. Given a choice, fish the feeder streams that flow into the Natural State's large impoundments. Feeder streams flowing into other, larger streams will have white bass runs, but they won't be as big as the runs occurring on streams that connect directly with large lakes.

Timing the spawning run is critical to success. If you go fishing at the wrong time, you won't catch any whites no matter how many use the stream for spawning. Fortunately, it's easy to time the run by tracking the water temperature in the stream you plan to fish. When the water temperature hits fifty degrees, schools of white bass gather near the mouths of feeder streams. These prespawn fish are eager feeders, and one usually can catch them with minnow-imitation lures—jigs, spoons, spinners, crankbaits—worked in ten to twenty feet of water. A sonar fish-finder can simplify the process of finding a school of whites, but you can do OK without one; where you catch one white bass at this stage in the game, you'll catch a bunch of them.

More and more whites gather at tributary mouths as the water warms. When it hits the magical temperature of fifty-eight degrees, the upstream surge begins. In the southernmost reaches of Arkansas, that phenomenon may occur in early to mid-March. In the northern tier of counties, it may be well into April. The spawning run can last as long as a month, but, typically, it starts and ends within the span of two weeks. A cold snap during the run can bring things to a

When white bass move upriver on their spring spawning runs, Arkansas anglers gather to catch them.

shuddering halt, but the only thing that will completely mess up the fishing is a torrential rain that puts the tributary streams into flood stage.

Where should you fish? That's the most difficult question to answer. Arkansas has good white bass fishing in all quadrants. But as I said before, the best white bass spawning streams feed major impoundments. That's where you should fish if you want to be in the center of action.

LAKE HAMILTON

This 7,200-acre Entergy lake on the Ouachita River at Hot Springs offers excellent fishing for these scrappy sport fish. In March, white bass congregate in the basins of Little Mazarn, Big Mazarn, Glazypeau, Kelly, and Hot Springs Creeks, awaiting the water temperature that will send them swarming up the streams to spawn in mid-April. Anglers swarm with them. Banks are lined with fishermen, and limit catches are common. Most white bass anglers must pursue their quarry from boats, however, because most shoreline property on Hamilton is privately owned. Tandem-rigged jigs, small spoons, crankbaits, and live minnows are among the most popular white bass enticements.

LAKE NORFORK

Though best known for its top-notch largemouth, crappie, and striper fishing, this 22,000-acre Corps of Engineers impoundment in Baxter and Fulton Counties serves up excellent white bass fishing as well. Small horsehead spinners like the Roadrunner are popular with local anglers fishing Brushy Creek, Big Creek, Diamond Creek, Tracy Cove, Bennett's Creek, and other tributary areas. During the April spawning run, it's not unusual to catch fifty to a hundred in a half day of fishing, including many in the two- to three-pound range.

BEAVER LAKE

Many anglers consider Beaver Lake near Rogers in northwest Arkansas the number-one white bass hotspot in the state. There are good reasons for this. This 28,220-acre Corps of Engineers impoundment has many large creek and river tributaries where white bass congregate to spawn, and a forage base of shad keeps them healthy and abundant year-round.

The lake is fed by one fork of the White River; that fork goes back south and east as far as Crosses, Delaney, and St. Paul. The West Fork of the White ranges southwest as far away as Winslow, West Fork, and Greenland, while the Middle Fork travels northwesterly about halfway between and paralleling Arkansas Highway 16 and U.S. Highway 71. These three forks add up to many miles of prime water where you can always find springtime action.

War Eagle Creek, the fourth largest tributary, flows in from the east side of the lake. In this stream, whites can travel only as far as the dam at War Eagle Mill, where they congregate in huge numbers to create an excellent fishing site. You'll find spawning whites well into April in all these waters.

TABLE ROCK LAKE

The White River below Beaver Lake has a northerly flow and becomes the headwaters of Table Rock Lake. During spawning runs, fish in this lake follow the urge to migrate upstream and run up the river (south) to the base of Beaver Dam. This short-stopping effect crowds white bass by the millions around the shoal areas from the tiny town of Beaver all the way to the dam.

In this area, you'll rarely go wrong using live minnows, lead-head jigs, or a combination of the two. For minnows, use a heavy sinker tied to the end of the line to drag the bait to the bottom. The minnow is lip-hooked on a small, single hook attached to a dropper line tied a few inches above the weight.

Lead-head jigs must be also have enough weight to carry them to or near the bottom. For shallow water, lighter jigs—$\frac{1}{16}$ to $\frac{1}{8}$ ounce—work well; in deeper or more turbulent water, some anglers go as heavy as an ounce.

When using a jig-minnow combo, consider adding a No. 8 treble hook as a trailer. To do this, tie a short length of line to the bend in the jig's hook and tie the treble hook on the other end.

Hook a live minnow through the lip with the jig hook, then hook one barb of the treble hook in the minnow's tail. This rig sounds complicated, but it helps nail soft-hitting winter white bass on the slightest nibble.

LAKE OUACHITA

Lake Ouachita, a 40,000-acre Corps of Engineers lake west of Hot Springs, is a sleeper lake in terms of white bass fishing. Stripers and black bass draw the attention of most Lake Ouachita anglers. But in March and April, white bass get a flash of attention from local anglers enjoying the fast-paced action that spawning fish provide in major tributaries. This huge lake produces some enormous linesides. Every day during the spawn, many honest three-pounders cross the fillet table.

Most fishing is done during the height of the spawning run in March or April in primary tributaries. The headwaters of the lake—the Ouachita River, especially—give up enormous numbers of whites. Small in-flowing creeks sometimes hold a few spawners, but better fishing is available in large tributaries like the South Fork of the Ouachita at Mount Ida and the North Fork below Mount Tabor.

Prespawn fishing also can be good. Just prior to their spawning runs, whites begin schooling at the mouths of creeks and streams, and many are caught by anglers trolling across points adjacent to these tributary mouths. Small deep-diving crankbaits imitating shad garner lots of fish, but other shad imitations that work deep perform well, too.

GREERS FERRY LAKE

All feeder streams of Greers Ferry are attractive to white bass when they make their spawning migrations. Peter Creek, which enters the lake from the northeast a few miles up-lake from the dam, is one of the most popular white bass hotspots and produces many fish in the three- to four-pound range. The four forks of the Little Red River above the lake—Devil's, Archey's, Middle, and South Forks—also offer opportunities for catching lots of jumbo whites during the spawn.

Whites and hybrid stripers move up the tributaries at the same time, and the same tactics usually result in mixed stringers. Ultralight tackle is OK for whites, but if you use it, you take a chance of losing any sizable hybrid that might come along. Good lure choices for both species include ¼-ounce jigheads with three-inch grubs, ¼-ounce Rat-L-Traps, or two-inch crankbaits in shad colors.

BULL SHOALS LAKE

Bull Shoals Lake (45,440 acres in north Arkansas) produced the two largest white bass ever recorded in Arkansas. Both were caught on April 15, 1984, at the tail end of the spring spawn. One weighed five pounds, two ounces. It was caught by William Garvey of Indianapolis, Indiana. The other fish—our current state record— weighed five pounds, four ounces. It was caught by Garvey's fishing partner, William Wilson, also of Indianapolis.

Bull Shoals white bass tend to be hefty and in excellent shape. Two-pounders are a dime a dozen, and the big egg-laden females often push the four-and-a-half-pound mark. When they ascend feeder creeks to spawn, it's not unusual to find them in only one to two feet of water.

In March, the male white bass, mostly one- to one-and-a-half-pound fish, show up on the shoals and bars in the mouths of tributaries, usually in ten to fifteen feet of water. Jigs, grubs, Rat-L-Traps, and tailspinners such as the Little George will take them. In late March or early April, as the water warms, male whites ascend the spawning streams and soon are joined by the females. After spawning, both sexes return to the main lake. It's during their upstream and downstream runs that most whites are caught, often by bank fishermen working the streams with spoons, small crankbaits, or live baitfish. Good areas to try include Big Music Creek, Sugarloaf Creek, West Sugarloaf Creek, and Carolton Hollow Creek, all on the south (Arkansas) side of the lake.

LAKE MAUMELLE

Lake Maumelle is an 8,900-acre water-supply lake owned by Little Rock Waterworks. Just a few miles west of Little Rock off

Arkansas Highway 10, the lake is extremely popular with white bass anglers. When the whites are ready to start their spawning runs in mid- to late March, the question starts making the rounds in fishing circles throughout town: "Are the whites running on Maumelle yet?"

Most spawning activity is concentrated at the west end of the lake where the Big Maumelle River flows in. Anglers gather on the lower ten miles of river, some fishing from boats, others from the banks. Night fishing seems to be most productive, especially when casting small spoons, spinners, and live minnows. Fishermen often have a hard time finding a good spot to fish because people are crowded shoulder to shoulder on the more easily accessible stretches of river. Most will agree, however, that the possibility of catching several two- to three-pound whites per night makes any extra effort worthwhile.

LAKE GREESON

Lake Greeson is a 7,260-acre Corps of Engineers impoundment just north of Murfreesboro. White bass here run upstream into the Little Missouri River to spawn. During the run, anglers line both sides of the river for one-half to three-fourths of a mile above the Highway 70 bridge. Some fish from boats as far upriver as they can go. Good action also is found in the long lake fingers reaching up into the many feeder creeks.

DEGRAY LAKE

DeGray Lake covers 13,400 acres northwest of Arkadelphia. It features a white bass spawning run on the upper end where the Caddo River enters. White bass also are taken where major creek tributaries such as Brushy Creek enter the lake. Fishing from a boat is the most common method used to go after spawning whites. Look for them around gravel bars in fairly shallow water. Before and after the actual spawning, you can find whites in the bays at the mouths of the creeks. Trolling or casting small jigs is a good way to catch them.

LAKE DARDANELLE

Constructed in the 1960s by the U.S. Army Corps of Engineers, Lake Dardanelle is one of the state's premier white bass lakes. This honeyhole on the Arkansas River lies right beside Interstate 40, spreading westward from Dardanelle Lock and Dam at Russellville to cover approximately 35,000 acres in Pope, Yell, Logan, Johnson, and Franklin Counties. The Interstate 40 connection lends accessibility to the entire length of the lake's north side. On the south side, the same convenience is provided by State Highway 22.

Dardanelle contains varied structures attractive to white bass—coves, tributaries, rock piles, shallows, flats, jetties, and islands. On warmer days in the latter part of March, whites start moving up into creeks and small rivers that feed the lake. Spawning time is near, and as the water warms, they move into these tributaries to look for spawning sites.

Two excellent white bass fishing areas are the Spadra Creek and Little Spadra Creek arms just south of Interstate 40 at Clarksville. In those areas you'll find five- to ten-foot depths that jump up to two- and three-foot flats where white bass stage prior to and after the spawn. This area produces lots of whites ranging from one to three pounds and more. The Shoal Creek area near New Blaine on Arkansas Highway 22 provides similar conditions.

Another good area to try is where Illinois Bayou runs in and crosses Interstate 40 on the east end of the lake at Russellville. The dark, shale bottom around the interstate bridge conducts heat better, the water warms earlier, and that's a place where many anglers catch early white bass.

These are just a few of the many productive white bass spots you may want to try. Lake Dardanelle is 50 miles long and has 315 miles of shoreline, so if one place doesn't pan out, try another. Sooner or later your efforts will pay off.

Arkansas Walleye Hotspots

For more than fourteen years, the big female walleye survived the dangers of Bull Shoals Lake. Now, the warming March waters brought her again to Little Music Creek to fulfill her natural urge to spawn. The water temperature was only forty-four degrees, but a warm spring rain had begun to fall, so the spawn was sure to soon begin.

The sleek golden walleye was sticking close to a long, sloping point near the mouth of the river. She and several smaller females were schooled near a cluster of boulders in forty feet of water. They took every opportunity to pick off passing shad and other small fish.

Most walleyes in the school with her were females. Many males already had moved upstream to seek out the spawning grounds. Yet, a few males lingered behind, awaiting warmer temperatures.

On the second day, the walleye sow began growing restless. She somehow sensed the time was at hand for her to complete the migration that meant spawning was but a few days off. The other females sensed it also. An uneasiness swept through the school. Already the last few males had left the females to make the upstream journey.

On the third day, the walleye began swimming slowly up the mouth of the stream. Her stomach was swollen and distended, and she felt uncomfortable as the skin on her belly was stretched tight. The school traveled only at night, moving to shoal areas to feed in late evening and returning to deep water before daylight. The opaque milky appearance of their eyes was due to a unique structure, very efficient at gathering available light. The retreat to deeper and darker water during the daylight hours was in response to the dazzling effect of direct daylight.

The female walleye always was a special fish, being both exceptionally large and intelligent. None of the females around her was as big or as old. With her belly full of roe, she was now over twenty-three pounds. Her many years of life had honed a fine edge on her survival instincts.

It was the cautious nature of the giant female walleye that saved her life on her twilight sojourn up the stream. Several males began bumping and rubbing her while she swam over the spawning beds.

Even though this activity occupied most of their time, none of the ready-to-spawn fish were adverse to snapping up a careless baitfish that came too near. The female heard the whining sound of the outboard when it entered the river, but it had disappeared several minutes earlier. That familiar noise was replaced by the low hum of a trolling motor that drew ever closer. The sound held no fear for the big female or the other walleyes.

Suddenly, the female heard a light splash near the upper end of the deep pool. She turned quickly, hoping the disturbance would send dinner scurrying her way. An unusual vibrating noise was coming toward her. The gentle rattling was unlike any sound she had ever heard, but certainly it meant food. She stiffened with anticipation as the sound drew near. When the long silver creature that emitted the tantalizing sound bumped over the gravelly bottom at the edge of the pool, the female darted toward it with her mouth open wide. But, rather than inhaling it, she stopped short of striking and just watched as the morsel bounced by. The female's instincts told her something wasn't quite right. She wanted to strike but something inside warned her away.

The big walleye had barely settled back down when she heard the splash again. This time the excitement was too much to stand. The creature would not escape a second time. It drew closer to the female on the rocky river bottom where she waited in ambush. She heard it skating across the gravel, and, suddenly, it danced into sight before her. When the walleye extended her jaws to suck in the creature, a wave of water pushed her aside as a large male raced in to claim the female's dinner.

Then, from the surface, the female could see a light hanging over the edge of a huge, dark object. A distant memory from her past flashed through her mind and panic sent her instinctively back to the safety of darkness, deep below the intruders.

By week's end, she dropped her roe at random over the bottom of Little Music Creek. The males flanking her fertilized the eggs, and soon after, the ancient ritual completed, the big female and her companions returned under cover of darkness to the black depths of Bull Shoals Lake.

Could a walleye this size really be swimming in Bull Shoals

Lake? Some experts think so. We know for sure that many big, wary walleyes swim in this Ozark Mountains impoundment, and it's possible one might near or exceed the weight of the current world record, a twenty-two-pound, eleven-ounce walleye from Greers Ferry Lake. Considering the growth potential of our unique race of southern walleyes, and the lack of fishing pressure through most of the year on Arkansas waters, we could see a new world record from any one of the many bodies of water here that hold good populations of these sporty game fish.

BULL SHOALS LAKE

This federal reservoir on the White River boasts a good population of lunker walleyes. Presently, most angling in this Ozark impoundment takes place during the three- to four-week spawning period. This probably accounts for better than 50 percent of the walleye catch, with much of the remainder being accidental main-lake catches. Although walleyes in the lake are not as easy to locate as some other fish, they are plentiful and underfished. Attention on Bull Shoals is generally focused on the fantastic lunker largemouth bass population while the lunker walleye fishing has garnered almost no publicity.

Bull Shoals covers 45,440 acres with 740 miles of shoreline. Walleye fishing is best during the late winter–early spring season in the abundant coves and hollows entering the lake throughout its length. Likely spots include East and West Sugarloaf Creeks, Big Creek, Brushy, Charley, Trimble, Big Music, and Little Music Creeks. The lake has yielded several lunkers in recent years, including at least one seventeen-and-one-half-pound fish.

While big and small walleyes are caught at all hours of the day, night fishing is the most productive strategy. Walleyes are basically nocturnal creatures, most active during low light and dark hours. Fishing at these times increases your chance for success. This is true no matter what the season when you fish. Most larger fish taken from Bull Shoals are captured well after dark, particularly during the summer and fall, but also during the spring spawning run.

Another important aspect of walleye fishing is proper presentation of your lure or bait. Walleyes are bottom-dwelling fish. It is important to put your offering at the right level and keep it there throughout the length of your retrieve or troll. And since spawning walleyes aren't very hungry and are unlikely to chase a lure, it's important to place a lure very close to a fish and move it past at a speed that is slow enough to let it make a lazy swipe at it.

Most fish caught during the spawning runs are taken on artificial lures. The favorite is a slender, three-hook floating-diving bait known locally as the "long-billed Rebel." Live minnows also are effective, as are spoons, Hellbenders, Bombers, minnows, and June-bug spinners trailing night crawlers. Jigs tipped with pork rind or plastic tails also are productive baits.

Casting along the main channels from the mouth of the river upstream is best, since walleye movement is going to occur in these places. Some locals set camp under lantern light on the river banks and spend the night during the runs fishing with set poles rigged with live minnows or long-billed Rebels. The baits are positioned to remain stationary in the current like a minnow trying to swim upstream. Of all the methods, trolling accounts for the most walleyes, but because more territory can be covered, and because anglers use this technique for several other species, that stands to reason.

NORFORK LAKE

Norfork Lake, another north-central Arkansas reservoir, also has an excellent lunker walleye population. Located on the North Fork of the White River, this twenty-two-thousand-acre impoundment was completed in 1944. The same baits and tactics employed on Bull Shoals are equally effective here.

Brushy Creek and Big Creek near the dam are two of the best spots to look for early season walleyes on Norfork. In the central portion of the lake, anglers should pay attention to the area around Fall Creek near Float Creek, Pigeon Creek, and Buzzard Roost. The Bennett's River arm of the lake produces good fishing around Bennett's Bayou, Little Creek, Jenkins Branch, and Walker Branch.

Much of the natural spawn in Norfork takes place in the upper end in the North Fork River, and three creeks in this area—Lick, Cain, and Barren—also are hotspots.

In the early 1960s, the Arkansas Game and Fish Commission built a nursery pond adjacent to Norfork, hoping to beef up the walleye population. Walleye fry were released into the pond, held until six inches long, and then released directly into the lake each year. Norfork profited greatly from this operation and several million walleye have been stocked in Norfork over the years. Today, the Game and Fish Commission continues to carefully monitor and manage the walleye population on this and other Natural State lakes.

LAKE OUACHITA

Walleyes have been swimming in Arkansas's Lake Ouachita, albeit in small numbers, since the Ouachita River was impounded by Blakely Mountain Dam in the early 1950s. As with Bull Shoals, publicity for Lake Ouachita generally has centered on other species. An aggressive walleye-stocking program begun by the Game and Fish Commission in the early 1970s has since produced a top-notch "jack-pike" fishery. That, however, still seems to be a state secret.

In February and March, walleyes move up the upper Ouachita River as far as Mount Ida to spawn. The population is fairly small, and the catch rate doesn't seem so great when compared with Norfork or Bull Shoals, but those who go out after them from late winter to late spring usually can count on catching limits.

Walleyes swim in many other waters throughout Arkansas. It's possible that, with the greater attention being paid this sport fish, some of these other places may start showing up as hotspots, even if the fish taken aren't of world- or state-record caliber. Currently there are populations of walleyes in lakes Beaver, DeGray, Catherine, Hamilton, Blue Mountain, Hinkle, Greeson, Dierks, and Gillham. Lake Nimrod has been stocked with walleyes, and Lake Greeson is periodically stocked.

Good streams include the Arkansas and upper White Rivers, the Eleven Point, the Fourche la Fave, the Strawberry River, Petit Jean River, Caddo River, the Saline River, and the Little Missouri River.

In 1962, a record fifteen-and-one-half-pound walleye was caught in the South Fork of the Spring River about two miles south of Hardy. Other streams with moderate walleye populations are the War Eagle and Kings Rivers. Even the Black River produced a record fish in 1963, although walleyes normally don't thrive in the more turbid streams of eastern and southern Arkansas.

Looking for walleyes in big and small waters alike may seem like a difficult task, but if you understand some basic aspects of walleye behavior and can adapt your efforts accordingly, you can find the hotspots.

The only mysterious thing about Arkansas walleye fishing is that so few anglers fish for these magnificent game fish. For walleye anglers who want to fish on uncrowded waters sporting good walleye populations, the Natural State's untapped bonanzas are certainly worthy of consideration. The fish are there. It's the fishermen who aren't.

APRIL

Oxbow Crappie
along the Mississippi

They are orphaned waters, deserted offspring left behind by an unwitting parent. Seen from the air, they prompt visions of crystal rainbows braided into the delta heartland, sea-green pools strewn up and down Ol' Muddy like scattered emeralds from a broken necklace. On second glance, you grasp something more overwhelming. You envision young serpents embraced in the writhing coils of a powerful meandering snake; godforsaken waters in country as rugged and worn as a blacksmith's apron.

These are the Arkansas oxbow lakes spawned from the Mississippi River—Island 40 Chute, Dacus, Horseshoe, Midway, Whitehall, Mellwood, Chicot, Grand, and others. Chances are, you haven't heard about some of them, but there's a good reason for that.

Consistent action for one- to two-pound crappie is a mainstay on these waters, and folks who know about it would just as soon keep it under wraps.

I have a special love for the Mississippi River oxbows. When I was young, my mother would wake me at three in the morning so I could rendezvous with old Uncle Guy for a junket to the oxbows. We would arrive at Midway or Whitehall or Mellwood at an ungodly hour and be fishing for crappie before daybreak. I remember nebulous curtains of mist hanging over the water like fog on a Scottish moor, and the croaking *kuk-kuk-kuk-kuk* of coots bobbing through the buckbrush. I recall the traditional vittles—"Vyeenee" sausages, soda crackers, and short Cokes—and the itchy butt I got from sitting too many hours on a too-hard boat seat. I recollect painted morning skies shrouding galleries of ancient cypress trees, and Uncle Guy's coffee-can spittoon perched precariously beside him on the edge of his banged-up johnboat.

It's the fishing, though, I remember most. We looked, I'm sure,

A happy angler displays a 1-pound, 12-ounce oxbow crappie. In oxbows along the Mississippi River, this is considered an average-sized fish.

like a colossal spider blowing across the lake's surface, half a dozen cane poles jutting from both sides of the boat as Uncle Guy sculled us slowly across the lake.

Uncle Guy knew all the honeyholes, and before long a pole would flex and bob, and we'd pull a calico slab over the transom and throw it in the fish basket. There were times when two, three, even four poles would bend at once, and Guy would fuss at me in a gravel-voiced whisper, urging me to hurry—"Get 'em in, boy! Get 'em in!"—lest a big papermouth elude us. There were always plenty of dandy crappie to take home at day's end, and these jaunts with Uncle Guy grew into a lifelong passion for oxbow crappie fishing.

I always get a special feeling when fishing on an oxbow lake, a feeling that's missing when I fish man-made impoundments. Unless you've experienced it, it's hard to explain.

Fishing a Corps of Engineers reservoir, a wildlife agency lake, or a city-water reservoir can be spectacular. But those lakes are built by men. And despite the fact that many man-made lakes share some of the same qualities oxbows have, the natural feeling prevailing on the oxbows just isn't there.

Fishing the oxbows is a back-to-nature experience. When you're jigging for crappie in the shade of ancient cypress trees, your mind wanders back to a time when our country was still wild and uncharted. The bottomlands surrounding the oxbows teem with wildlife, and, on most, the setting is beautifully pristine. Best of all, you'll find plenty of rip-roaring crappie action. If you know what you're doing, a day's fishing can produce fifty or more keeper-size crappie, with several heavyweights anchoring your stringer.

Originating from the same parent stream, these oxbows along the Mississippi River are sibling lakes, figuratively speaking, and as such have many common characteristics. Each is basically U-shaped. All have abundant woody cover, primarily buckbrush and cypress, providing homesites for crappie.

The average depth of each lake is six to eight feet; the shoreline is shallow and extensive. Standard crappie baits such as jigs and minnows almost always produce. Fast-paced crappie action is the rule, not the exception, on most visits.

ISLAND 40 CHUTE

On the northern end of this "Land of the Barn-Door Crappie" is Island 40 Chute, a popular lake due to its proximity to Memphis, Tennessee. The lake is full of old willow tops, stumps, and brush and thus offers excellent crappie habitat.

Like its sister lakes inside the levee, "The Chute" is subject to flooding during wet years. As the Mississippi River spills over into the lake (around fifteen feet on the Memphis river gauge), crappie anglers must watch water-level fluctuations closely to determine the best fishing times. Crappie may be caught during a slow to moderate rise (say, maybe three inches per day), but fishing is more difficult than during steady conditions. Forget fishing if the river is rising six inches or more daily.

APRIL

Crappie fishing on a slowly falling river is good, but if it's falling hard, forget it. Crappie prefer the water level steady or falling slowly.

Some of the best crappie angling comes when the river has almost dropped out of the lake following a period of high water. As the backwaters slowly return to the lake, the river run-out area on the east end becomes a great crappie hotspot. At other times, fishing the outer stumps across the lake from Dailey's Camp, a local angling concession, is very productive. Drifting and trolling three to six feet deep with minnows is best during summer and winter.

A county road running east from Interstate 55 and Arkansas Highway 77 just north of Marion, Arkansas, leads to the community of Gammon and Dailey's Camp.

DACUS LAKE

Three miles south of Island 40 Chute is Dacus Lake, another crappie hotspot popular with Memphis-area anglers. Many nice stringers of crappie come from this lake, and many will have several fish in the one-and-one-half- to two-pound range.

Dacus floods when the Mississippi River is between twenty-one and twenty-two feet on the Memphis gauge, and slow falls or steady conditions are best during high-water periods. When the river subsides, usually in April or May, the water stabilizes and crappie fishing really picks up. Use jigs or minnows around buckbrush, fallen trees, and brush piles. Hotspots include the pockets of buckbrush along the northeast bank and the creek flowing into the lake near the southeast end.

Dacus is within sight of the Interstate 40 Mississippi River bridge at Memphis. Access is via the Mound City Road exit off Interstate 40 westbound.

HORSESHOE LAKE

This twenty-five-hundred-acre oxbow is a Mid-South favorite. Crappie numbers are excellent, though most fish run small.

Horseshoe lies outside the Mississippi River levee, so fishing is more reliable and predictable. Look for fish around piers and boathouses, along the old river channel, and around the bases of Horseshoe's many cypress trees. If you can locate some of the brush piles sunk by local anglers, you'll have a hand up on the competition.

To reach Horseshoe Lake from West Memphis, drive west on Interstate 40 to Exit 271 at Lehi. Follow Arkansas Highway 147 south fifteen miles to the lake.

WHITEHALL LAKE

Whitehall Lake, or Old Walnut Bend, is reached off the Mississippi River levee road from county roads branching off Arkansas Highway 131 near Raggio. This four-mile-long oxbow offers some of Arkansas's most consistent fishing for giant crappie.

Good stringers of Whitehall crappie often come from fallen treetops near a gallery of big willows on the lake's east side. Buckbrush, which is abundant in the lake, also harbors big slabs.

While most Whitehall anglers use minnows for bait, jigs or jig-minnow combinations also are hot. It's a good idea to carry a dozen different colors in $\frac{1}{16}$- and $\frac{1}{32}$-ounce sizes. On a good spring day, it's not unusual to fill an ice chest with a limit of crappie a pound and up.

OLD TOWN LAKE

Old Town Lake, southwest of West Helena, is considered by many to be the best lake for jumbo crappie in east Arkansas. This old Mississippi oxbow is separated from Old Muddy by a levee and drains into Big Creek in the White River drainage. Fishing conditions are not highly influenced by any river, however, and water levels are generally stable, a definite advantage for visiting crappie anglers. The lake is at the town of Lakeview on Arkansas Highway 44 in Phillips County.

Old Town offers excellent fall fishing, but fishing during the spawn is extraordinary. As the water warms in April, crappie fishing gets hot. The lake is extremely shallow, less than six feet throughout, and most fish are taken on minnows and jigs around the bases of big cypress trees and in brush and treetops.

MELLWOOD LAKE

Continuing south on Highway 44, it's a short drive to another crappie carnival. Mellwood Lake, near the town of the same name, in Phillips County is actually a spur jutting off the main body of the Mississippi River. This hook-shaped body of water has a well-deserved reputation as an excellent barn-door crappie hotspot.

During March and April, it's common for a pair of anglers to catch as many as 150 crappie daily. The average weight per fish is around a pound, but most limit stringers are anchored with many fish that tip the scale at two to three pounds.

Because Mellwood is always mated to its parent stream, the Mississippi, fishing success is in large part dependent on water level conditions that may fluctuate greatly from day to day. High water floods hundreds of acres of vegetation and makes pinpointing crappie concentrations a bit difficult. The best fishing is during low-water periods when willow sticks and tops are exposed.

LAKE CHICOT

At fifty-three hundred acres, this southeast Arkansas lake is the country's largest oxbow. It also is one of the Natural State's top crappie lakes. Visiting anglers find an extraordinary population of one-pound-plus slabs.

The lake was divided into upper and lower portions by a dam constructed in 1948, and the lower end is where most crappie are caught. The lower lake has always had a good population of big crappie, but before a lake renovation project was completed in 1986, few people fished here because the water was so muddy. Since the renovation, the water has cleared tremendously, and more folks are visiting, catching lots of crappie up to two pounds or more. Chicot is outside the river levee, so it's uninfluenced by the Mississippi's rises and falls.

Lake Chicot is at Lake Village in extreme southeast Arkansas and can be reached from several points on U.S. Highways 65 and 82.

There are dozens of oxbow lakes along the Mississippi River in Arkansas, and most provide great year-round crappie action. Consider visiting one or more next time you're looking for a back-to-nature setting in which to enjoy some first-rate angling opportunities.

Beware, though. Once you've had a taste of oxbow fishing, man-made waters won't hold the same satisfaction they once did. Angling for oxbow slabs gets into your blood. It's like heaven on earth.

You can keep all those man-made waters. I've found my treasure in the little jewels Mother Nature hid behind the big river's banks.

Diamond Lakes Bassin'

It all started with the water.

In 1541, Hernando de Soto became the first European to discover the steaming thermal springs in what is now Hot Springs, Arkansas. For over 450 years, people have come to this area to enjoy the pleasures offered by the forty-seven natural hot springs.

Today, water is still one of the Spa City's main drawing cards. But most visitors come here not for a bath in one of the city's hot therapeutic springs, but to enjoy the family vacation paradise created by the area's four "diamond" lakes—Catherine, Hamilton, Ouachita, and DeGray. Covering a combined total of almost 63,000 acres, these four sparkling impoundments on the outskirts of town are a magnet for fishermen and water sports enthusiasts. All offer top-rated spring fishing for largemouths and/or spotted bass.

LAKE CATHERINE

Lake Catherine is the oldest of the four "Diamond Lakes." It came into being in 1924 when Arkansas Power and Light Company (AP&L) constructed Remmel Dam on the Ouachita River just east of Hot Springs. The 1,940-acre, eleven-mile-long lake was named after the daughter of Harvey Couch, the founder of AP&L and the man who originated the concept of building hydroelectric dams on the Ouachita River. Black bass are the main drawing card for many visiting anglers.

"People around here complain about Catherine being a hard lake to fish," said Brett Hobbs, fisheries biologist for the Arkansas Game and Fish Commission. "The lake has a good largemouth bass population, with fish up to ten pounds. But they're tough to catch. Spotted bass, or Kentuckies, also are present, but they're not as numerous as largemouths. When you catch one, though, it'll probably be a good one."

Hobbs, who lives in Hot Springs, is responsible for managing the public fishing waters in Fisheries District 8, an area that encompasses lakes Catherine, Hamilton, Ouachita, and DeGray. He also is an ardent bass angler and often fishes for Diamond Lakes black bass

"Some of the best bass fishing areas on Lake Catherine include the state park bay, Couch's Pocket, and Spencer's Bay," said Hobbs. "If I was going there to fish in the spring, I'd fish one of those three areas."

The state park bay is a small backwater area adjacent to Lake Catherine State Park near the east end of the lake off State Highway 171. Spencer's Bay, or Spencer's Pocket, is a broad finger of water on the lake's north side that runs parallel to U.S. Highway 270 at the eastern edge of Hot Springs. Couch's Bay is another long, distinct, north-shore arm just a short distance up and across the lake from the state park. According to Hobbs, anglers should look for bass holding near woody cover in these and other areas.

"There are a lot of stumps in Spencer's Bay," he said. "And Couch's Bay has a lot of trees fallen from the bank. The lake has a lot of current going through it, and much of the cover where you find bass is stuff the current has deposited in various areas. Some outside bends in the river channel will be good places if you have a sonar unit to locate brush and timber along the drop-off. Work ledges on the edges of creek banks along the main channel, too."

Good lures? "The jig-and-pig is always a good springtime bait on Catherine," said Hobbs. "If you can find timber and work a jig-and-pig near that, that's a good possibility for a big bass. If you're fishing shallow flats, maybe fall back on a Carolina-rigged worm or a spinnerbait. Crawfish crankbaits worked parallel to some of the drop-offs will be good, too."

LAKE HAMILTON

In 1932, Carpenter Dam was built on the Ouachita River above Lake Catherine. The dam was named to honor Flave Carpenter, a pioneer peace officer who first discovered the Remmel and Carpenter dam sites while searching for outlaws along the river and recommended the sites to Harvey Couch. Couch named the resulting seventy-two-hundred-acre, eighteen-and-one-half-mile long impoundment Lake Hamilton in honor of his attorney, C. Hamilton Moses, who assumed the presidency of AP&L after Couch's death in 1941. The lake borders almost the entire southern edge of Hot Springs.

"In spring, largemouth bass fishermen on Lake Hamilton do good fishing Carolina-rigged plastic worms and lizards, and spinner-baits," said Brett Hobbs. "Fishing is good in several major creek basins—the White Oak Creek basin, Williams Creek, Little Mazarn Creek, and Fourche Loop Creek.

"To find largemouths in Lake Hamilton, look for shallow water next to deep water. You need to find shallow flats going into embayments off main creek channels. Then look for brush piles. Since Lake Hamilton is an old lake, and it's somewhat restricted on natural cover, local anglers have put many brush piles into the lake. Use sonar to look for the brush piles, then when one is found, bump the brush with your lure. If a bass is there, he'll take it."

Docks are another place to investigate when seeking Hamilton's spring largemouths. Several thousand homes line the lake's shore, and there's a fishing dock with nearby brush piles behind almost all of them.

"When fishing docks, look for signs of crappie fishermen, such as chairs and rod holders and crappie lights," Hobbs noted. "You can work those docks in particular and generally find brush by them. That saves time when you're trying to find bass."

Spotted bass comprise a significant portion of the black bass catch on Lake Hamilton, but, according to Hobbs, catching these scrappy fighters requires different fishing tactics.

"The best way to catch Kentucky bass in the springtime is by fishing live crawfish off the points," he said. "The hardest thing about this is finding the bait. You can buy live crawfish at a few area bait shops, but not everyone carries them, so you'll have to look around. Fish them with just a hook and a split shot, letting them sink down and tight-lining them on or near the bottom."

DEGRAY LAKE

DeGray Lake, a 13,800-acre Corps of Engineers impoundment on the Caddo River, is twenty-one miles south of Hot Springs via

State Highway 7. Completed in 1972, this deep reservoir is a real challenge for bass anglers; but, according to Brett Hobbs, three- to six-pound largemouths are common, and seven- to eight-pounders are not unusual. Spotted bass comprise only a small portion of the lake's black bass population.

"DeGray is a good springtime bass lake," Hobbs said. "Usually, I go straight to the big bay just north of the Caddo Bend point."

Caddo Bend is a long peninsula on the north shore west of DeGray State Park, where the Caddo Drive recreation area and campground is. The bay lies between the Caddo Drive and Arlie Moore campgrounds.

"A lot of baitfish flock into that bay in spring," said Hobbs. "It's especially hot if you get some high water. The baitfish will be in the edge of the trees, and bass will be right on top of them. Try fishing spinnerbaits, a Smithwick Rogue, or a jerkbait like a Sluggo. Anything that imitates a shad is good for bass. The De Roche area, east of the DeGray State Park Lodge, is also good during high water."

If the lake's not high, Hobbs recommends fishing around beds of elodea around islands and underwater humps. "There are some humps near the mouth of Brushy Creek, as well as south of the DeGray Lodge in the main part of the lake," he noted. "Some actually come out on top of the water. The weed beds are around those humps. Work them with spinnerbaits, Smithwick Rogues, or Carolina-rigged centipedes."

LAKE OUACHITA

Forty-thousand-acre Lake Ouachita is the largest lake lying entirely within Arkansas. Owned by the Corps of Engineers, this deep, crystal-clear reservoir was impounded by construction of Blakely Mountain Dam on the Ouachita River in 1953.

Ouachita provides excellent fishing for largemouth and spotted bass. According to Hobbs, "Ouachita yields some real good bass every spring. There's always the possibility of catching a seven- or eight-pounder, and occasionally we see largemouths up to ten pounds."

Hobbs recommended Glen Warren as the best source of information about spring bassing on Lake Ouachita. Warren guides fishermen on lakes Ouachita, Hamilton, and DeGray. From January through June, he's on the lakes every weekend at least.

"In spring, I hardly ever fish the timber on Ouachita," said Warren. "This time of year, the largemouth bass are normally in the moss—in beds of hydrilla, water milfoil, or elodea. You can usually find the weeds with a depth finder in fifteen or twenty feet of water."

The Shad Rap is Warren's favorite spring bass lure. "Once you've found a weed bed," he said, "move out away from it, then cast the lure out, crank it down deep, and bring it in with a stop-and-go retrieve. Work the bait right along the top of the moss. The fish will come up for it."

Warren noted that the Shad Rap works best when bass are around the deeper, outside edges of weed beds. If that doesn't work, try fishing a Rattling Rogue in shallower water on the inside edge of the weeds. "We fish the medium-runner that gets down about five feet and work it using a real fast stop-and-go retrieve."

A short green plastic worm is another of Warren's favorite artificials. "Rig it with a small leadhead, then swim the worm around the weed beds and get ready for strike," he said.

Spotted bass usually are in fairly deep water in spring, said Warren. "You'll catch a lot of them on small plastic worms, crawdad crankbaits, and jig-and-pigs; but they'll be deeper than largemouths, in timbered pockets, moss, or on the deeper rocky ledges. I've seen them as deep as forty feet that time of year. Probably the best lure for spring Kentuckies is the jig-and-pig."

Follow the advice of these veteran Diamond Lakes anglers and you, too, can enjoy fast-paced bassing action. April is a top time to do it, so get out there and try while the fishing is good.

Razorback Redears

Shellcracker, government-improved or GI bream, yellow bream, chinquapin, cherry gill, stump-knocker, tupelo bream, strawberry bream—the redear sunfish has as many nicknames as a boy named William. But whatever you call it, the redear sunfish is one of the finest fighters for its size in freshwater.

The largest of the true sunfishes, the redear is a favorite of Arkansas bream anglers. These spunky panfish are found statewide, and, during spring and summer, Natural State fishermen swarm to blue-ribbon redear waters to get in on the year's best action.

Of course, whether or not a redear is actually a panfish depends on your ideas about panfish. A fish that fights like a smallmouth and frequently exceeds a pound and a half doesn't exactly fit the classic definition of panfish—or the classic pan. If you're discussing eating qualities, however, the redear is a panfish extraordinaire. When rolled in cornmeal and fried golden brown, the thick fillets from these chunky little sunfish form the entree for one of the best meals you'll ever sit down to eat.

Redears resemble their close cousins, the bluegills, and many anglers don't make any distinction between the two. They're both "bream," and they're both good to eat and fun to catch. There are, however, important differences, both in how they look and how they behave.

Redears aren't as colorful as bluegills, but they're handsome fish nevertheless. The back is usually olive-green, fading to silvery-green sides checkered with brown or green mottling. A yellow wash colors the belly on adult fish. The mouth is very small, and the pectoral fins are long and pointed.

The name "redear" is a practical designation based on the color of the "ear" flaps at the rear edge of the gill covers. Bluegills have dark bluish or black ear flaps, as do redears. But on adult redears, the margin of the ear flaps is usually orange or red. Males are more brightly colored than females and sport a bright, cherry-red border.

Redear sunfish are considered special prizes by Natural State bream fishermen.

Females and young usually have a pale orange border. No other sunfish found in Arkansas are so marked.

Another distinctive redear characteristic is the set of hard, tooth-like grinders or "shellcrackers" (hence the nickname) in the throat. These allow redears to crunch the shells of the snails, tiny clams, and other aquatic invertebrates that form most of their diet. They spit out the shells and chug-a-lug the rest like a Cajun at a crawfish boil.

Feeding habits of redears and bluegills also differ, a fact that may account for the absence of redears on many bream anglers' stringers. Bluegills feed anywhere from the water's surface to the lake bottom, but redears feed almost exclusively on the bottom, a habit requiring special fishing tactics.

Size is the redear's most unique attraction. Two pounds is exceptionally large for most sunfish, but some lakes produce one- to two-pound redears with astounding regularity. In Arkansas, redears usually average eight to ten inches in length and about a half pound in weight. The state record, caught by Glenda Tatom in Lake Bois d'Arc in May 1985, weighed two pounds, fourteen ounces.

Redears have a definite preference for warm, clear waters with no noticeable current. They tend to congregate around logs, standing timber, stumps, roots, and green aquatic vegetation. They prefer deeper water than most other sunfish, sometimes moving to depths of twenty to thirty feet in summer.

During most of the year, redears remain scattered, making it difficult to find schools. But during the spring-summer spawning season, they congregate in colonies to spawn. Bedding areas of one-quarter to one-half acre are found in some lakes, but the average "bed" has about the same dimensions as a school bus. They like to nest in lily pads, usually in two to eight feet of water, but you can find them almost anywhere you might find bluegills—around cypress trees, brush, stumps, and logs, or even on open sand and gravel bottoms. Redears usually return to the same bedding areas year after year, so a site that produced fish during this year's spawn should continue producing fish in succeeding years.

Spawning begins when the water temperature nears sixty-six degrees. Late April through early June is prime spawning time in Arkansas, but spawning may continue into August.

Most bream anglers love to catch redears, but many don't know the proper way to do it and often go home without a single redear for dinner. There are two important things you must remember to score consistently on these burly bream.

First, redears are bottom feeders, and if you're presenting your bait anywhere except very near or on the bottom, you'll miss most fish. Most anglers expect to catch redears using the same techniques used for bluegills. But in most cases, this just won't work. Bottom-fishing tactics are the only ones that regularly catch shellcrackers.

Second, redears are very finicky. They're less likely to be caught on artificial lures than other panfish, and even when fishing with live bait, you have to determine the specific bait they want and the best way to present it.

Let me give an example. A friend and I were fishing for redears on a small east Arkansas lake. We were using almost identical ultra-light spinning outfits while bottom-fishing with worms, perhaps the premier redear bait. And we were fishing the same beds of spawning fish. Problem was my buddy was catching lots of redears, and I wasn't catching any.

"I can't figure it out," I told him. "You're catching 'em one after another, and I can't get a nibble. And we're doing everything the same."

"Not everything," he said. "You've got a split shot on the line and I don't."

I didn't really think the addition of a single split shot could make any difference. But when I removed it from the line, I started catching redears.

Lesson? If you think you're doing everything right but you're not catching fish, try varying your method of presentation ever so slightly. Even a small variation like a split shot may keep these persnickety devils from biting. Redears are fussy beyond compare, and you have to vary your presentation until you figure out exactly what they want.

Perhaps the most important key to redear fishing success is picking a body of water where redears are abundant. In Arkansas, this isn't hard to do. Almost all our lakes and many streams have healthy populations of redear sunfish.

Some of the state's best redear lakes are in eastern and southern portions of the state. Perhaps the best of the best is Bear Creek Lake, a 625-acre impoundment in St. Francis National Forest near Marianna. This popular fishing lake produces numerous redears in the one-and-one-half-pound class each year, and two-pound-plus shellcrackers always are possible.

Most timber that once stood in Bear Creek has rotted and fallen. Veteran redear anglers usually work the shallow waters of the lake's many long fingerlike coves in spring and summer. After the spawn, redears stay along the edges of underwater creek channels in deep, fairly open water.

Lake Chicot, Arkansas largest oxbow at fifty-three hundred acres, is another super redear hotspot. Fishing action starts earlier in the year here than on most Arkansas redear lakes, thanks to Chicot's extreme southern location. Chicot is just a few miles north of Louisiana at the town of Lake Village in extreme southeast Arkansas.

Big redears are abundant here. Most anglers fish around cypress knees, brushy tops, and buckbrush. Several public fishing piers also are heavily used, with brush sunk around them as fish attractors. When the lake's jumbo redears are bedded up in late spring and early summer, loaded-down stringers are the rule rather than the exception.

If you want to enjoy a real get-away-from-it-all redear excursion, head out for one of the two hundred or so oxbow and overflow lakes on White River National Wildlife Refuge. The largest one only covers a few hundred acres, but nearly all these little gems have the capacity to produce limit stringers of three-quarter-pound redears every day during peak fishing months.

If you're willing to do a little searching in the refuge, you can find prime redear fishing lakes that you can have all to yourself, even during the peak of the spawning season. Many lakes are accessed by well-traveled roads and are heavily fished, but there are some that have gone unfished for years. Pack a topo map and a belly boat, and you can enjoy redear fishing in the most primitive surroundings Arkansas can offer. Flip a worm out on the bottom beside a cypress tree and get set for action. Redears too big to reach a hand around are the hallmark of these picturesque waters.

Bois d'Arc Lake also is a shellcracker honeyhole as evidenced by the state record redear caught there in 1985. Located in south Arkansas near Hope, this six-hundred-acre Game and Fish Commission lake is full of dead snags and buckbrush that harbor big redears. Bank-fishing from the levees on the north, south, and west sides is very popular, but boating will allow you to fish some coves and timber haunted by one-and-one-half- to two-and-one-half-pound shellcrackers.

Lakes in other parts of the state also are worth checking out. Lake Millwood with its vast shallow waters and abundance of freshwater shrimp, a redear favorite, is a shellcracker heaven. Lake Conway in central Arkansas produces two-pound redears from its log jams and lily pads. Merrisach, Cox Creek, White Oak, Hinkle, Catherine, Horseshoe, Felsenthal—the list goes on and on. If you live in Arkansas, you're probably just a short distance from good shellcracker waters.

Any angler who gets acquainted with redear sunfish will be abundantly repaid in good old-fashioned fishing fun. Redears are persnickety and hard to catch at times, but the possibility of catching a sunfish topping one and a half or two pounds makes it all worthwhile. Don't let spring pass by without giving them a try on one of the many excellent lakes in Arkansas.

Easy-Access Channel Cats

Catfish are among the largest Arkansas game fish. Flatheads grow to 140 pounds here, blues over 116, and channel cats over 50. If trophy-class whiskerfish are your quarry, the Natural State is a great place to be.

Of course, not all catfish anglers are interested in pursuing giant fish. Many Arkansans are just as happy when they can sit under a shade tree on a small lake and catch a few small channel cats for dinner. For them, catfishing is a way to relax or to enjoy a few hours fishing with the kids. If a big cat is caught now and then, so much the better. But catching big fish is secondary to just being there, enjoying the outdoors and tussling with a decent fish now and then.

Channel cats are tailor-made for this kind of fishing. They're stocked in hundreds of small lakes and ponds throughout Arkansas, so they're easily accessible to every angler. They're abundant, easy to catch, and excellent to eat. More importantly, you don't need a megabucks bass boat, expensive rods and reels, and a suitcase-sized tackle box full of pretty lures to catch them. A cane pole or cut-rate fishing combo works just fine, and the only hardware required is a few hooks and sinkers, a stringer, and maybe a lawn chair to sit in. Make a short drive to that little lake down the road, and you can be catfishing in no time at all.

Try some of this "backyard" fishing. Take your children along or some kids from the neighborhood. It's fun. It's relaxing. It's enjoyable. And the fish you may catch provide superb eating.

Here are some places to try.

LITTLE ROCK AREA LAKES

If you live in Little Rock or North Little Rock, there are at least six small lakes within a few minutes drive of you that offer good bank-fishing for cats. The Game and Fish Commission stocks

---

The many small city lakes scattered around Arkansas offer excellent bank-fishing opportunities for anglers after channel catfish.

catchable-size channel cats in all these waters, and at times the fishing is extraordinary.

MacArthur Park Lake lies in the corner formed by Interstates 30 and 630. Take the Ninth Street exit off Interstate 30 for access. **River Mountain Park Lake** is just off Highway 10 west of Interstate 430. Access is from Southridge Drive.

Three of these lakes are in southwest Little Rock. **Hindman Park Lake** is off West Sixty-fifth Street near the south end of University Avenue. Watch for the signs. **Holt Street Lake**, in the Southwest Kiwanis Park, is accessible from the Colonel Glenn Road exit on Interstate 430. Drive east on Colonel Glenn about one and a half miles to Holt Street, turn left and you'll wind up at the park. **Ottenheimer Park Lake** is in Cloverdale. Turn onto Azalea Drive just north of the intersection of Chicot and Baseline Roads and watch for the signs.

The **Burns Park Golf Course lakes** are in North Little Rock. Take the Burns Park exit off Interstate 40 just east of Interstate 430.

OTHER CITY LAKES

Little Rock isn't the only Arkansas city with public catfishing lakes. There are dozens of these small man-made impoundments scattered from border to border. Among the best are Lake Atalanta in Rogers (sixty acres), Bald Knob Lake (two hundred acres), and Siloam Springs City Lake (thirty-five acres). Small city-owned lakes also are found in or near the cities of Benton, Booneville, Camden, Charleston, Clarksville, Dierks, Eureka Springs, Fayetteville, Fort Smith, Mena, Nashville, Newark, Newport, Ola, Paris, Pottsville, Prairie Grove, Van Buren, Waldron, and many others.

Some of these lakes were built primarily to provide a reliable water source, but in each case, recreation possibilities figured highly in city planners' development strategies. Most of the lakes have excellent bank-fishing areas and park facilities like picnic tables. Channel catfish are stocked regularly, and though often overlooked by the bulk of Arkansas's fishing populace, late summer catfishing on these neglected waters is, at times, nothing less than superb.

STATE PARK LAKES

At least seven of our state parks provide outstanding catfishing on small lakes within park boundaries. As an added bonus, the parks with fishing lakes also have picnic areas, campsites, and other outdoor recreational facilities, making them ideal destinations for a weekend or week-long family getaway.

Lakes Dunn and Austell, sixty-eight and sixty-four acres, respectively, are encompassed by seven-thousand-acre Village Creek State Park near Wynne. Both are best known for producing lunker largemouths, but catfishing in these waters isn't shabby either. Channel cats are abundant, running to over five pounds. Excellent bank-fishing is available, especially along the dams.

Sixty-four-acre **Lake Bailey** is a favorite with folks camping in Petit Jean State Park in southwest Conway County. The lake lies adjacent to the camping area, with excellent bank-fishing access around its entire perimeter. Regular stockings of channel cats maintain good fishing.

In Woolly Hollow State Park near Greenbrier, **Lake Bennett** draws notice from cat fans. It covers only thirty-three acres, but channel cats are common, and bank-fishing is excellent.

Other state park catfishing hotspots include thirty-one-acre **Lake Walcott** in Crowley's Ridge State Park (Greene County), the eight-acre lake in Devil's Den State Park (Washington County), a three-acre lake in Logoly State Park (Columbia County), and an eleven-acre lake in Old Davidsonville State Park (Randolph County).

GAME AND FISH COMMISSION LAKES

At only ten acres, **Lake Bentonville** is about the size of a large farm pond. It's tailor-made for bank-fishing, with easy access to the shoreline around the entire lake.

Small channel cats are abundant, and there's a good chance for catching a big cat, too. The Centerton State Fish Hatchery is just four miles away, and when brood catfish grow too large to fit in the hatchery's twenty-five-gallon spawning barrels, they're often stocked here.

Lake Bentonville is in central Benton County, just south of

Arkansas Highway 102 within the city limits of Bentonville. The entrance is clearly marked by signs on Arkansas Highway 102, one-half mile west of the intersection of U.S. Highway 71 and Arkansas Highway 102.

Crystal Lake, one mile east of Decatur, is another Benton County Game and Fish lake that exemplifies the old saying "good things often come in small packages." This clear, spring-fed impoundment covers only sixty acres, but its sterling catfishing opportunities make this diminutive treasure a favorite with many northwest Arkansas anglers. The lake supports a healthy population of channel catfish.

Crystal is chock-full of fish-holding structures and cover. The lake bottom is a hodgepodge of inundated points, peninsulas, and valleys, and there are extensive stump fields in many tiny inlets. One especially good fishing area is the stump field on an underwater peninsula just out from the Decatur airport hangar on the west bank.

Signs mark the two turnoffs to the lake—one on Arkansas Highway 59 one mile north of Decatur and one on Arkansas Highway 102 one mile east of Decatur. A parking area and picnic area accessible from Highway 59 are near the dam on the lake's northeast end. The Highway 102 access on the southeast end leads to parking and bank-fishing areas and a fishing pier.

Lake Hindsville is a pool of serenity beside a hurry-scurry sea. At thirty thousand acres, nearby Beaver Lake provides most everything a visitor could want—great fishing, skiing, tourist attractions, and much more. But Beaver doesn't offer the same type of relaxed, get-away-from-it-all atmosphere prevailing on Hindsville. Twenty-acre Hindsville provides a welcome respite from the crowds in this heavily populated region.

Hindsville is one of the oldest and smallest lakes built by the Game and Fish Commission. But the lake's age and size haven't diminished its popularity with local anglers. The rippling waters of this elfin treasure embrace lots of fighting channel cats, plus a few blues, and Hindsville remains a favorite with shade-tree fishermen.

Hindsville is in northwest Madison County, three miles west of its city namesake. Signs on Arkansas Highway 68 northwest of Hindsville direct traffic onto the gravel access road circling the lake.

Truman Baker Lake, three miles south of Waldron in Scott

County, was built by the Arkansas Highway and Transportation Department during excavation for the U.S. Highway 71 bypass around Waldron. Fill dirt remaining from the construction project was used to impound the fifteen-acre lake in a low-lying spot adjacent to a highway rest area.

Truman Baker is an ideal spot to take the kids fishing for channel catfish. No drive-in access is available, but visitors can park at the rest area and carry their gear a short distance to bank-fishing areas around the lake. The adjacent rest area has rest rooms, water fountains, covered picnic tables, and parking.

Other small Game and Fish lakes offering excellent bank-fishing for channel cats include fifty-acre Gurdon Lake (Clark County), one-hundred-acre Horsehead Lake (Johnson County), and twelve-acre Gator Pond in Dagmar Wildlife Management Area just west of Brinkley.

Before April ends, give these lakes a try. Catfishing is excellent this month, and it's a sure bet that savvy anglers will catch a few cats to eat when visiting these often overlooked waters.

MAY

Rockin' Down the Buffalo

Rock bass don't get much respect. A half-pounder is a whopper in most waters, and fishermen usually consider them little more than a freebie—it's fine if you catch one, fine if you don't.

Despite their small size, though, rock bass have a lot going for them. Ounce for ounce, they're among our most sporty panfish. They're aggressive, widespread, plentiful, easy to catch, and excellent eating when properly prepared. Rock bass give an angler the sense of having faced a challenge and won, and fishermen who overlook these spunky little fighters miss out on a lot of panfishing fun.

The name "rock bass" is commonly applied to three very closely related species of Arkansas panfish: the Ozark bass, a native of the White River drainage in north Arkansas; the shadow bass, found in several widely scattered streams throughout the state; and the northern rock bass, an introduced species found only in the Illinois River drainage in northwest Arkansas. We'll use the name "rock bass" interchangeably when discussing this group. Though they are scientifically distinguishable, all three look very much alike. They have big mouths, long chunky bodies, bulging blood-red eyes, and splotchy olive-and-gold markings. The color and size of the eyes have led to the appropriate common nicknames, "redeye" and "goggle-eye."

Although the range of these fish seems to indicate unusual adaptability, they're actually quite specialized. Rock bass sometimes are found in impoundments but prefer cool, clear streams with, as the name implies, plenty of rocks.

Creeks and rivers strewn with boulders, gravel, or rock rubble provide ideal habitat. Rock bass are, in fact, partial to streams suited to smallmouth bass and share many with them.

One of Arkansas's best rock bass streams is the Buffalo National River, which runs through 150 miles of the Ozark Mountains. Shadow bass and northern rock bass aren't found here, but Ozark bass, known locally as goggle-eyes, are plentiful.

To sample the pleasures of the Buffalo's excellent Ozark bass

Ozark bass, a type of rock bass, are among the most common panfish in the Buffalo River.

fishing, I accompanied Marcus Kilburn of Little Rock for a fishing junket on this, one of America's most beautiful streams. Kilburn has been an ardent rock bass angler for most of his life and has been fishing for Ozark bass on the Buffalo for more than a decade.

It was immediately obvious that Kilburn is exceptionally adept at catching these scrappy panfish. "See those rocks in that pocket?" he asked as we walked the stream bank opposite a deep pool. "That's an ideal spot to catch a goggle-eye."

With that, Kilburn proceeded to prove his theory. He cast a ⅛-ounce black jig to the precise spot he'd pointed out, then let the lure fall. Something struck the bait ferociously before it had moved more than a few inches.

The fish at the other end of his line fought valiantly, moving to and fro in a deep, broad-sided run. At first, the bow in Kilburn's rod convinced me he had hooked a smallmouth. But when the fish declined to jump and display the smallmouth's typical acrobatics, I knew otherwise. After a short but impressive battle, Kilburn landed an eight-ounce Ozark bass.

After putting the fish on a stringer, Kilburn cast to the same spot. "There's never just one," he said with a grin, as the lure settled into the pool. And sure enough, he caught a second Ozark bass just seconds later. Three more followed on the next dozen or so casts, all taken from that single pocket.

I was a bit skeptical when Kilburn first touted his talents at catching rock bass. After just fifteen minutes of fishing, though, he'd caught more than I'd seen in my entire life. I was convinced. Now, I said, "Tell me how it's done." He started by discussing the phenomenal rock bass fishery in the Buffalo River.

"I've fished for goggle-eyes in a lot of Arkansas streams," Kilburn said. "Illinois Bayou has a lot of them, and Sylamore Creek above its junction with the White River (near Mountain View) also is very good. I've fished other good streams, too, but day in and day out, the Buffalo has the best quality rock bass fishing."

Though Ozark bass inhabit nearly all of the Buffalo, some places provide better fishing than others. Kilburn centers his efforts around deep pockets with good cover.

"You won't find rock bass on long shoals like smallmouths," he told me. "To pinpoint fish, I look for big rocks and other obvious cover—what we call hides—in deep pools. They may be around woody cover, but I generally catch more around rocks, just like their names suggests. Rock ledges, drop-offs, overhangs—all are good places to fish. Submerged rocks seem especially good. People can't see them, so they don't fish them much. But if you find a submerged rock, fish around it. Those areas have lots of rock bass."

Eddies are another type of hotspot Kilburn looks for. He noted, "An eddy is anywhere you have fast water, and off to one side is a body of still water. It might be just past a shoal where the water starts to peter out. It might be a wide shoal, and there are eddies on either side of the shoal. Fishing cover at the edges, where fast and slow water meet, is an excellent way to find rock bass.

"Rock bass usually are suspended. You can never tell exactly how deep they'll be, but they're generally deeper in winter than they are in summer. But you never fish on top for rock bass. You always fish three to fifteen feet deep, depending on what hole of water you're fishing."

Ultralight tackle seems most appropriate for fish that seldom weigh a pound, but Kilburn prefers heavier tackle.

"I don't use ultralight tackle," he said. " I like a stiffer rod, medium to medium-heavy, because often you're jigging, and usually you're fishing deeper. You need extra backbone in your rod to set the hook. A rock bass's mouth is tough, and you must set the hook pretty hard. Ultralight will work, but I'd rather have a stout rod tip so when I feel a fish, I can set the hook in a hurry."

Six-pound-test line is another Kilburn standard. "You use the same basic equipment you would for smallmouths," he said, "but you need to keep a pretty small line, because rock bass often don't have a very noticeable hit. It'll just feel like a weight, a pull, or a tug.

"The heavier your line, the harder it is to feel a strike," he continued. "Plus, you don't need heavy line for rock bass. They'll fight hard initially, but they don't make the big powerful runs a smallmouth will. I wouldn't go over six-pound-test ever."

When it comes to willingness to attack a lure, few game fish can compare with rock bass. Whether you label them gullible, aggressive, or just plain eager, goggle-eyes are suckers for properly presented artificials. Small plugs, spinners, jigs, flies—all these and more can be used to entice these bantam brawlers.

"My favorite lure is a ¹⁄₁₆- to ¹⁄₈-ounce jig," said Kilburn. "My favorite color is gray or smoke, but you have to fish and find what they want. If the water's real clear, I try to use a lure that's real clear or light colored—white or yellow or something like that. If the water's dark or dingy, then I'll go to a darker lure—black or motor oil or maybe green. I carry a variety of colors, and styles, too—gitzits, twirly tails, flip tails. That's what it takes. One time they may want a gitzit, next time they want a twirly tail. You never know.

"Size is also important. I wouldn't go any smaller than a ¹⁄₁₆ ounce or any larger than a ¹⁄₈ ounce. The eighth is easier to cast, plus it falls a little quicker and seems to fall more like rock bass want to hit it. You can use a smaller jig, but rock bass prefer larger lures."

Live crayfish are another weapon in Kilburn's arsenal of rock bass catchers. "Crawdads are the best live bait, period," he pointed out. "Don't use big ones. Use small ones, not longer than two inches. You usually can't buy crawdads, and if you do buy them, they're typically not the right color. In mountain streams, crawdads have chameleon characteristics. They change colors to adapt to whatever the bottom is. So you're better off catching crawdads in the stream you're fishing or in a feeder creek."

Kilburn collects crawdads the old-fashioned way—picking up rocks and looking under them. "Keep them in a bucket with fresh water," he said. "Use just enough water so they stay wet, and put some rocks in."

Though many rock bass anglers fish with only the crawdad's tail, Kilburn uses the whole critter. "A whole crawdad works better than just a tail," he said. "I run a hook up through the tail and leave the barb exposed. I use a sinker just heavy enough to get to the bottom. I don't use a bobber. I fish with a tight line, because you're a lot better off reacting to feel rather than sight. I wrap a loop of line around my finger so I can feel it better. Then, when they bite, I can set the hook at the same time."

Wade-fishing and canoe fishing are both popular on the Buffalo. Regardless, of which method you use, however, when you catch one rock bass, stop and fish for more.

"If you catch one," Kilburn said, "stop and fish that area thoroughly, because there's a good chance several goggle-eyes will be there. I've heard of twenty fish being caught off one rock. With smallmouths, you may catch fifty fish in fifty different places. But with goggle-eyes, you may fish the exact looking place in the same hole of water and not catch another one, because all goggle-eyes in that hole of water are in one or two hides.

"Fish each hide thoroughly. You might catch one and throw out six or eight more times and think, well, there aren't anymore there. Then that ninth throw you might let it sink a little deeper or work it a little faster, and they'll grab it. They might be three feet over from where you thought they were, or five feet over. It can get down to that. If you miss it by six feet you're not gonna catch another one. When they're grouped like that, you have to put it right in front of them."

Water conditions also influence fishing success. "I'd rather fish the river when it's just a little high," Kilburn said. "Not anything that would be considered unfloatable, but a foot to a foot-and-a-half above normal.

"When the water is low, it's not good because you've got to get too close to them to catch them. They may scatter because they can see you. When it's real high, you can't get your bait down there where they are because of the current.

"Rock bass also seem to bite better if the water's a little dingy. A little bit of color is preferable, because the fish can't see as well; and because there's food floating around, I think it increases feeding activity."

If Kilburn's techniques for catching rock bass seem simple, that's because they are. All anglers, young and old alike, can apply his methods and enjoy a fast-paced outing for goggle-eyes.

To give it a try, head for the Buffalo this May.

Oxbow Bass

It was a perfect bass hideout. Gnarly buckbrush lined the edge of an inundated ditch coursing across the bottom of the oxbow. Adjacent to the buckbrush was a long log as big around as Santa Claus, the upper end of which was suspended atop two cypress knees protruding from the water beneath their parent tree. The bottom end projected down into the brushy edge of the little ditch, creating a shady hiding place ideal for a big bass.

A bass was home, alright. But when my fishing buddy Jim Spencer knocked on its door with a big spinnerbait, he wasn't prepared for the fish's response.

Jim's cast was exemplary. The lure fell beside the log, sinking into the shadowy recess below. He hadn't turned his reel handle a full revolution when the fish struck. The bass inhaled the spinnerbait, shot for cover, and did a loop-de-loop around the butt of the log. It mattered not that a 190-pound man held the end of the line opposite the bass. The fish, a 6- or 7-pounder, broke the water's surface, flipped its tail, and was gone.

Jim reeled in his slack line and laid his rod across the boat seats. Then he pulled out a bandanna and wiped beads of sweat from his forehead.

"I hate to whine," he said. "But that son of a gun didn't play fair."

It's true; the term "fair play" seldom enters the oxbow bassin' equation. Bass in these backcountry waters are brawlers. They fight dirty and make their relatives in bigger, man-made lakes look like a bunch of wimps.

Maybe it's the extraordinary fertility of oxbow lakes that gives bass the upper hand. In these natural waters, every fish seems to have an extra measure of strength and stamina.

Maybe it's the marriage of confined living space, generally shallow water, and dense cover that makes oxbow bass so good at line-busting and throwing hooks. These fish know every inch of their

---

Peace and beauty are qualities that draw bass fishermen to Arkansas's remote oxbow lakes.

home territory—every root wad, treetop, snag, and brush pile—and they use that familiarity to discomfit their human antagonists.

Maybe it's the beauty of oxbows that causes these problems. When you're fishing beneath five-hundred-year-old cypress trees, watching bright yellow warblers flit through the foliage overhead, the serenity can lull you into a state of total relaxation. Reflexes get sluggish, and, consequently, lots of bass get the best of you.

It doesn't matter, really. Oxbow lakes serve up great bass fishing, and if oxbow bass get the jump on us more often than usual, it's a small price to pay for the privilege of being there.

In fairness, I must tell you that Jim Spencer catches more oxbow bass than he misses, or at least as many. I chose the opening story to illustrate a point. But I might just as easily have chosen another where Jim set the hook and fought the bass into submission. On the day that big bass got the best of him, he caught another over six pounds and several more in the two- to five-pound range. He might have caught more, but we spent most of the day bream fishing.

Few people are as intimately acquainted with Arkansas's oxbow lakes as Jim Spencer. Jim lives in Little Rock but was raised in the flatlands of southeast Arkansas with gumbo mud caked between his toes. He cut his teeth on this brand of oxbow-lake fishing. In fact, he caught his first fish at age eighteen months out of an eastern Arkansas oxbow lake.

The serenity of the oxbows is a major attraction for Jim and anglers like him.

"Big impoundments are too crowded," he says. "Waters that are big enough to show up on highway maps have a way of attracting a lot of attention, and not just from fishermen. Sailboaters, swimmers, divers, and water skiers also flock to these places, and on pretty weekends, it can look like a floating circus out there.

"I suppose there must be a little hermit in me, because I can never make myself feel truly comfortable when I'm a part of that scene. It's enjoyable—all fishing is—but every once in a while, I get a bellyful. That's when I pack my stuff and head for the river-bottom oxbows, because I know I'll find peace and quiet there."

Arkansas anglers can find scores of bass-filled oxbows in eastern Arkansas. "I'm not about to reveal the locations of my favorite oxbows," Jim says, "but there are plenty of lakes you can find and fish on your own if you do a little homework. Topo maps, which you can get at the Arkansas Geological Commission in Little Rock, are great sources of information for people who aren't familiar with the river-bottom systems in the state. Buy maps showing the river systems along the lower White, the Mississippi, the lower Saline, the lower Ouachita, the lower Cache, the Black, and the St. Francis. The best oxbows show up as dots or squiggles of blue alongside the big rivers. Some are close to roads or the river channel, some are a half mile or more from anywhere. Some have names, but many don't.

"Some east Arkansas oxbows are fairly well known and are at least partially developed. A few examples are Mellwood Lake near Elaine, East Lake near Clarendon, and Lake Chicot near Lake Village. All three are oxbow lakes, and all three are excellent for bass fishing. But they're also much more crowded than the smaller river lakes I usually fish, because they have easy access and have been widely publicized.

"There are also some fairly crowded river lakes in other parts of the state, like on White River National Wildlife Refuge. There are scores of lakes in the refuge flanked by all-weather roads and equipped with developed boat ramps. Escronges Lake south of Ethel is a good example. One morning a few years ago, I counted 115 vehicles parked at the boat ramp/camping area beside that little two-hundred-acre lake.

"The thing is, that's an extreme situation. Most river lakes don't get that kind of pressure. On the same day I counted all those vehicles at Escronges, a buddy and I waded mud and dragged a little flat-bottom boat behind us into a small lake less than a mile from Escronges. And we didn't see another fisherman all day long. It's these smaller lakes that serious oxbow bass fishermen look for."

When you choose a lake to fish, you'll need some sort of boat. Jim says many of the small, out-of-the-way lakes have boats in them, and, in most cases, an informal system of free use prevails, provided that a boat borrower is willing to give up the craft if its owner happens to show up and wants to go fishing. Many of these little lakes don't have boats in them, however, and you'll have to carry your own.

"It goes without saying that the lighter the boat is, the better it's suited for this type of fishing," says Jim. "I prefer lightweight ten- or twelve-foot johnboats, but canoes work well, too. I've even fished out of rubber rafts and belly boats on occasion, but I don't recommend it as a regular thing."

The proper time of year to plan an oxbow bassing trip is another important consideration. According to Jim, the best time to fish any oxbow lake is during or immediately after the period when the annual flood waters are receding.

"This can occur any time between March and July in east Arkansas," Jim notes. "But as a general rule, the annual floods leave in April or May. You may have to watch the river stages in the newspapers over a period of time before you determine the river gauge numbers when fishing is best. But when you figure out that magic number, you don't want to forget. When the main river is ready to drop completely out of the lake, the bass fishing can be little short of unbelievable.

"One day a friend and I were fishing the run-out on a little White River oxbow, and we caught about forty bass, one after another, as quick as we could shake one off and cast a spinnerbait back out. They hit in pecking order. The first five or six we caught were in the lunker class, up to five or six pounds apiece. Then the size began slowly tapering off. We caught some medium-size bass, three- to four-pounders, then some a little smaller than that. The last few we caught were in the half to three-quarter pound range."

The tackle best applied to oxbow bassing varies considerably from the standards of big-lake anglers. Jim prefers bait-casting rigs with slightly shorter rods than are currently popular.

"About five and a half feet is generally the best rod length for oxbow fishing because of the cramped quarters of the boat and the tight, brushy fishing conditions you usually encounter," he says. "You don't need the big tackle boxes that are standard equipment in your bass boat, either. What you need is a small tackle box with a dozen ¼- to ½-ounce spinnerbaits, an assortment of six- to eight-inch plastic worms, a couple of chartreuse- or crawfish-colored crankbaits, and two or three of your favorite surface lures. If you can drive to the bank or close to it, you may want to haul a trolling motor, too. But if you're looking at a longer haul into the lake, it's not worth the trouble. Take a short sculling paddle instead."

Fishing techniques in oxbow systems aren't terribly complicated. When I fish with Jim, we generally work the shoreline cover carefully, probing every nook in the brush and every likely log or cypress tree, changing lures and presentations until we find one the bass find appealing that day.

"One thing to remember when fishing oxbows is that even though the bottom is relatively flat and uniform in depth, the outside bend of the lake is almost always a little deeper than the inside bend," says Jim. "This can be important in summer and fall when oxbows are lower and water is warm. Summertime water temperatures in oxbows can sometimes reach into the nineties, and when this happens, bass concentrate on the deeper side of the lake during midday. They lay in the shadows of logs and cypress trees where the water temperature is more to their liking.

"The best oxbow fishermen change their tactics to fit this situation. They work the shallows with spinnerbaits and other noisy lures early and late when bass are actively feeding. They fish deeper water with worms and slow-moving, bottom-bouncing lures during midday."

Oxbow fishing certainly is not for everyone. It's a muddy, dirty business. There are mosquitoes, sweat bees, and snakes to contend with. You must work harder than if you launched your bass boat in Bull Shoals or Ouachita. But if you like catching fish, you might find the trouble is worthwhile.

"If you have a decent knowledge of bass fishing, there will be days when you catch fifty or more bass while fishing an oxbow lake," Jim says. "When weather and water conditions are right, fishing is spectacular.

"The thing is, catching fish is secondary to just being there. You can go all day and not see another boat, or even hear a plane. The scenery takes you back to a time when the South was still wild and uncharted. It's refreshing and peaceful. And when the bass are hitting, there's only one way to describe it. It's heaven on earth."

Amen.

Bullheads: The Neglected Catfish

The bullhead gets a bit of begrudging admiration now and then, but its name isn't dropped by anglers looking for status. In fact, the bullhead—a fish that will pounce upon any offering of edibles with wild abandon, a fish that strikes hard without any pretense of caution, a fish with catholic tastes, a fish that fights tenaciously and tastes superb—is entirely ignored in many areas where it is extremely common.

Why is a fish with such laudable sporting characteristics neglected by Arkansas anglers? Well, the bullhead is ugly as a roadkill troll, a fact that does nothing to help its reputation. It is slimy, it stabs careless anglers with its rapier-like fins, it grubs on the bottom like a rooting hog when looking for dinner, and it will live—quite happily—in the fish world's equivalent of a slum. A three-pounder is a behemoth.

Many folks love bullheads, nevertheless.

WHICH CAT IS THAT?

Bullheads have colorful nicknames. "Horned pout" seems universal and was derived from the fish's sharp pectoral fins, or "horns," and from the European word "pout," which means big-headed fish. The nicknames "greaser" and "slick" also are widely used and refer to the thick layer of slime that coats all bullheads. Other colloquial names used in Arkansas include polliwog, polly, paperskin, mudcat, stinger, snapper, butterball, bullcat, and bullpout.

Three species inhabit Arkansas waters. The largest is the black bullhead, a common resident of ponds, reservoirs, oxbow lakes, streams, and swamps throughout the state. The state record, caught in Point Remove Creek in 1986, weighed four pounds, twelve ounces.

The brown bullhead is native to Arkansas but is very uncommon here. In *Fishes of Arkansas,* Henry Robison and Thomas Buchanan note that the species "has been stocked in several impoundments by

A mess of bullheads provides the makings for a fine dinner.

the Arkansas Game and Fish Commission, and all recent records from the state reflect these stockings. A stable, reproducing population of brown bullheads currently exists in Sugarloaf Lake in Sebastian County, and we have collected individuals as large as 4 pounds there." The brown bullhead prefers moderately clear, heavily vegetated streams and lakes and is one of the most-sought members of the bullhead clan because it averages quite large. None has been submitted for the Arkansas record book; the five-pound, eight-ounce world record came from Georgia's Veal Pond in 1975.

The yellow bullhead is the most widely distributed catfish in Arkansas, after the channel cat. It occurs statewide but prefers clear, gravel- and rocky-bottomed, permanent streams. It avoids strong current, however, and thrives in many Arkansas reservoirs. A four-and-one-half-pounder caught in Mormon Lake, Arizona, in 1989 is the largest ever taken on rod and reel. No Arkansas state record has been established.

FISHING STRATEGIES

There is nothing difficult about catching bullheads. Anyone who has fished for channel cats can catch bullheads with essentially the same methods.

Bait choices are legion. Bullheads are the fish world's equivalent of barnyard hogs. There's hardly anything they won't eat. Live crayfish, minnows, night crawlers, shad, catalpa worms, salamanders, leeches, maggots, tadpoles, or toads will do just fine. Dead stuff like chicken liver, mussels, shrimp, and fish guts are on the menu as well. Weird things, too, like dog food, corn, soap, sour grain, hot dogs, marshmallows, bread, cheese, and even bubblegum are acceptable. Indeed, bullheads will engulf anything remotely resembling food, so you'll probably catch one sooner or later no matter what your bait choice.

These nocturnal feeders aren't temperamental, but most bullhead anglers soon learn that no bait is more effective than a wad of worms on a hook thrown out on the bottom. Bloody chicken liver rates a close second, but stinkbait concoctions and mussel meat also are first-rate enticements.

Almost any type of tackle works, but it's best to go light to savor your rock-'em-sock-'em battles with these little cats. Four- to eight-pound line is appropriate. Hooks for bullheads range in size from No. 4 to 1/0.

Bullheads may bite throughout the day but usually feed most actively at night. Weed-bed edges, river bends, channel drops, underwater humps, inundated ponds, boat docks, and long points all are worth investigating. Don't sit in one place without moving, unless you're catching fish. When fishing is slow, a move of just a few yards can boost your catch considerably.

The simpler your fishing methods, the more you will enjoy bullhead fishing. Your fishing strategy can be as unencumbered as using a cane pole and small hook to dunk a worm or piece of liver in late evening. Fish on the bottom, using a split shot or a small slip sinker to carry your bait down. Or use a bobber to float the bait just slightly above the bottom. You needn't fish deep or far from shore.

Bullheads are notorious hook swallowers, so take plenty with you. You sometimes can remove the hooks with a disgorger or long-nosed pliers. But it's quicker to cut the line and wait to retrieve the hooks when you clean the fish.

Whether you unhook your fish or simply snip the line, it's wise to avoid the bullhead's sharp pectoral and dorsal spines. Contrary to popular folk beliefs, it's these spines, not the whiskers, that bullheads use to "sting" unwary anglers.

CLEAN WATER EQUALS GOOD EATING

As with other fish, the bullhead's flavor varies according to the quality of water from which it came. Fish from muddy or polluted waters may have a strong objectionable taste, but if you catch bullheads in clean water and put them on ice soon after being caught, they'll provide the entree for some delicious meals.

Regardless of where you catch them, always skin the fish and remove the dark red flesh along the lateral line. This rids the dressed fish of most unsavory flesh.

RELAXING SPORT

One of the nicest things about bullhead fishing is that it calls for a maximum of sitting and socializing and a minimum of the frenetic foolishness that "fancier" fish demand. Kids of all ages enjoy the thrills, the laughs, the delectable meals, and, most of all, the companionship a bullhead junket provides. There may be prettier fish, more challenging catches, and better table fare, but the bullhead remains a blue-ribbon choice for relaxing, good-times fishing.

MAY

The Fish That Eats Salad

To catch a grass carp, toss a salad. Throw in some cherry tomatoes, some lettuce, celery, pea pods, a bit of watercress, some duckweed, coontail, pondweed, and muskgrass. OK, so it's not your regular salad, and chances are, you never figured on using vegetables for bait. Don't worry; grass carp will like it, just the same.

These giant Asian minnows, also known as white amurs, are vegetarians, you see. They shy away from "normal" baits like kids eyeing a plate of liver and onions. Cast some veggies their way, though, and they'll rush in like a kitty to a can opener.

And why, you may ask, would you want to hook a grass carp in the first place? Because, my friend, these underrated ruffians often weigh 40 pounds and more. Specimens topping 110 pounds are known, and grass carp of any size immediately go airborne when hooked. Battling one on rod and reel is like tussling with a tail-hooked tarpon. In fact, long, sleek grass carp resemble tarpon, with big silvery scales and an upturned mouth. They're not at all like common carp with their barbeled, vacuum-cleaner snouts.

Grass carp are good eating, too. A platter of deep-fried strips won't last long at a fish fry. And chances are, there are lakes and ponds near your home with plentiful grass carp that could use a little thinning.

Grass carp were introduced into the United States in 1963 when the Bureau of Sport Fisheries brought seventy fish from Malaysia to the Fish Farming Experiment Station at Stuttgart, Arkansas. Amurs are native to larger eastern Asian rivers with Pacific drainages, including their namesake, the Amur River on the Chinese-Siberian border. Introductions expanded their range to India, Europe, New Zealand, and, according to some researchers, at least forty U.S. states.

The experimental imports did what they were supposed to do—eat excessive aquatic vegetation—and by the early 1970s, the Arkansas Game and Fish Commission began using grass carp to control weeds in public waters. The amur's mouth is toothless, but in the throat are large, comblike teeth that grind the salad it eats. One carp can eat two to three times its weight daily and may gain five to ten pounds a year.

By the early 1970s, amurs were being caught by commercial fishermen in the Mississippi, Arkansas, and lower White Rivers of the state, and by 1978, more than one hundred Arkansas lakes had been stocked with them. In 1976, twenty-five tons were reported taken by commercial fishermen. By 1984, sixty-eight tons were caught annually.

Today, white amurs thrive in scores of lakes and rivers statewide. Arkansas produced two world records, including a sixty-five-pound, fourteen-ounce amur caught in 1995 in Horseshoe Lake. That fish is still our state record. Specimens from our waters commonly weigh fifteen to twenty pounds.

Early grass carp introductions were controversial from the get-go. Some claimed they were needed to control vegetation, providing a natural alternative to costly chemical and mechanical controls. Grass carp opponents saw nothing "natural" about importing an Oriental fish and releasing it to become a fifty-pound intruder gobbling up bass habitat.

The controversy continues. Some states allow stocking sterile fish produced in hatcheries; a few outlaw grass carp completely. Amurs offer a trouble-free, ongoing method of weed control when stocked at the conservative rates recommended by fisheries biologists. But when weeds are in check, biologists recommend reducing by at least 50 percent the number of grass carp in a pond or lake. That's where fishermen come in.

Ken Perry, a fisheries program coordinator for the Missouri Department of Conservation, outlined a simple method for catching grass carp in an agency newsletter. First, he scatters two or three cups of fermented corn in shallow areas of the lake he's fishing. "Fifty pounds of cracked corn cost next to nothing at a feed store," he says. "Fill a quart milk jug with cracked corn and add water a few days before fishing." The soured corn attracts carp to the fishing area.

Next, Perry employs his secret weapon—cherry tomatoes. Canned corn, earthworms, and other baits work, too, but these also attract catfish and bream. With tomatoes, Perry says, you can target grass carp specifically.

Perry's fishing rig consists of a long, limber rod-and-reel combo spooled with light monofilament line to which is tied a single, heavy-wire No. 1 hook without a sinker. The reel is placed in free spool so that line plays out freely when a fish takes the bait. If there's no bite in thirty minutes, Perry changes spots.

"Many lakes that need grass carp taken out are privately owned," Perry says. "Often the owners will be delighted to get rid of the fish, but be sure to get permission first."

In waters where most weeds have been eliminated, amurs are especially easy to catch. They often feed at the surface and quickly rise to hooked bits of aquatic vegetation, vegetables, even French fries floating in the water. Warm months offer the best fishing; feeding activity slackens when water temperature falls below fifty-seven degrees.

In *Fishing for Buffalo,* Rob Buffler says that floating doughballs also take hungry grass carp. His recipe calls for mixing equal parts peanut butter, Rice Crispies, and crushed cornflakes. "Place a grape-sized glob of this mixture and a green party marshmallow on a two-inch square of white, sheer pantyhose," says Buffler. "Stretch it tightly over the doughball and tie up the ends with green thread to make a ball. Roll the ball in green food coloring." Thread a baitholder hook through the panty-hose material and cast the ball into waters where grass carp feed. With luck, a giant amur will rise and take the bait.

Grass carp may never become standard fare in the waters of America, but they're widely available and offer great fun for anglers who like tackling "those other fish." If you're not embarrassed by the thought of fishing with a tomato or French fries for bait, give amurs a try. Somewhere out there, a one-hundred-pounder is lurking.

JUNE

Summer's Hottest Hybrids

It started slowly—a ripple here, a ripple there, on the mirror-like surface of DeGray Lake. The sun was breaking the horizon, and from our position near one of the lake's many islands, we watched as the spectacle unfolded.

Off to our right, a spritz of shad broke the surface, exploding like silvery shrapnel in every direction. There was a swirl beneath the school, then another swirl a bit farther off. More shad erupted to our left, and another school behind us. More swirls, more shad, and more and more and more.

The water now started to boil, churning like a witches' cauldron as thousands of tiny fish fled predators yet unseen beneath the water. Half an acre of water seemed to take on a life of its own.

My companion, Dave Gould, launched a clear topwater plug from his end of the boat. As soon as it touched down, he gave it a twitch with his rod tip, and *blam!* A fish was on.

I launched my own attack, casting a shallow-diving, shad-imitation crankbait toward the frothy water. It, too, was attacked as soon as it made contact. And from the bend in my seven-foot rod, I knew my opponent was sizable.

Dave landed his fish first, seven pounds of striped muscle. He quickly released it, then cast again. Once more, there was a powerful, almost instantaneous strike, and he was battling another bruiser.

My fish was a twin to Dave's seven-pounder. I released it, then cast again to the maelstrom of water. This time, I saw the fish before it hit. A fin sliced the water, running on a collision course with my lure. I twitched the bait ever so slightly, then held on tightly as the fish smashed the lure and tried to yank the rod from my hand.

I was startled at the unbridled energy exhibited by my quarry. The fish ran in broad arcs fifty feet from the boat, darting this way then that, peeling line against the drag. But soon it tired, and I brought its five-pound bulk over the transom. So much fight for so

A dandy hybrid striped bass comes to the net in Beaver Lake.

small a fish, I thought. I've never caught a largemouth of similar size that could compare to this miniature torpedo.

Over the next quarter hour, we caught and released eight or ten fish apiece, all of them between five and ten pounds. It was my introduction to Arkansas's hybrid striper fishing, and I was left breathless in the wake of the frenzied battle on DeGray Lake.

THE HISTORY OF ARKANSAS'S HYBRID FISHERIES

If ever an Arkansas fishing "marriage" was made in heaven, it was the one that joined striped bass and white bass to create hybrid stripers, with Game and Fish Commission fish hatchery personnel doing the officiating. And like most good marriages, the Arkansas hybrid fishery keeps getting better with age.

Events leading to these nuptials began in the 1960s when North Carolina fisheries biologists crossed a female striped bass and a male white bass to create a third fishing sensation—the hybrid striper, also known as the "wiper," "sunshine bass," or "Bodie bass." Hybrids don't reproduce like prolific white bass or grow to gigantic sizes like stripers, but they exhibit good characteristics inherited from both parents. Like the white bass, hybrids grow fast. A year-old fish may weigh over two pounds, and after four years, hybrids weigh as much as ten pounds. Twelve- to fifteen-pounders frequently fall to Natural State anglers.

According to Jay Kaffka in a spring 1978 article in *Arkansas Game and Fish Magazine,* Arkansas got into the hybrid striper act by accident. By the early 1970s, stripers had been successfully introduced in Lake Maumelle just west of Little Rock, and this lake supplied broodstock stripers. Biologists set nets in the lake's upper end to secure eggs and milt from large adult stripers to carry out an artificial spawning program. In 1975, however, biologists found an abundance of ripe female stripers but few male stripers. Rather than allow the eggs to die for lack of milt, biologists quickly secured male white bass that had been trapped in abundance and crossed the eggs. A few weeks later, several thousand two-inch hybrid fingerlings were released into DeGray Lake, the first Arkansas lake stocked with this hatchery-produced game fish.

Greers Ferry Lake at Heber Springs became the second Arkansas lake to receive hybrids in 1976. That year, the Greers Ferry Lake nursery pond was stocked with 1.1 million hybrid fry obtained from Georgia. Half a million of those fry grew into fingerlings that were released in Greers Ferry.

Additional waters stocked in the years since then include lakes Catherine, DeQueen, Chicot, Millwood, Storm Creek, Beaver, Hamilton, Hinkle, Charles, Maumelle, Shepherd Springs, Nimrod, Harris Brake, Horseshoe, Norfork, Ft. Smith, and Neark and the Little River.

When hybrid stockings first started, no one was sure if the new fish would thrive in our waters. It was soon obvious, however, that the hybrid striper was a rising star on the Arkansas fishing scene. The first state record was established on July 9, 1976, by a one-pound, two-ounce hybrid from DeGray. The record fell an astounding twenty-four times during the next twelve years. Eighteen records came from DeGray Lake, three from Greers Ferry, two from the Little River, and one from Lake Hamilton.

The first twenty-pound-plus hybrid came from Greers Ferry in 1988—a twenty-pound, eleven-ounce record caught by Bill Brown of Shirley. DeGray gave up a twenty-one-pound record in 1989, and Bull Shoals entered the spotlight in 1996 with a twenty-two-pound, one-ounce record. Then, on April 24, 1997, Jerald Shaum of Shirley landed the whopper of all whoppers—a twenty-seven-pound, five-ounce Greers Ferry hybrid that was soon certified and now stands as the all-tackle National Freshwater Fishing Hall of Fame and International Game Fish Association world record.

BIOLOGY

The hybrid striper is ideal for stocking in Arkansas's large, man-made impoundments. It doesn't adversely affect native predators because it occupies a separate area, the open water of a lake. Although many anglers believe hybrids feed substantially on black bass and other game fish, Arkansas studies show that shad make up 85 to 95 percent of the hybrid's diet, and game fish such as bream and bass comprise only a small portion of their meals. In this respect, hybrids are important, because shad aren't adequately consumed by native fish in large, deep reservoirs. Hybrids keep their numbers in check, so large shad don't become overpopulated and detrimental to sport fisheries.

Because hybrids don't reproduce in Arkansas waters, the Arkansas Game and Fish Commission maintains populations by periodically stocking the lakes where hybrids are found. Although the number of hybrid-stocked lakes is small, these muscular fish offer exciting fishing opportunities. Let's look at five of the best lakes to try this season.

GREERS FERRY LAKE

Greers Ferry was the focus of nationwide attention when Jerald Shaum caught his world-record hybrid in 1997. A large percentage of the hybrids stocked each year in Arkansas are released in this 31,500-acre Corps of Engineers impoundment, and since the stocking program began, Greers has always been considered one of Arkansas's two best hybrid lakes, the other one being DeGray Lake.

Greers Ferry anglers use many tactics for hybrids. One of the best in summer is night fishing with eight- to ten-inch live gizzard shad. Typical tackle is a six-and-a-half- to seven-foot medium-action rod paired with a bait-casting reel spooled with twenty- to thirty-pound-test monofilament. A one-ounce egg sinker is threaded on the main line above a barrel swivel. Below this is a three- to five-foot leader to which is tied a 5/0 Kahle hook. The shad are hooked through the upper lip and nose, then the rig is dropped to the depth of the thermocline, usually about eighteen feet. This is usually done with the boat anchored near inundated offshore timber.

The egg-sinker rig allows the shad to swim naturally, and when hybrids cruise into the area, the bait becomes agitated, and its action is telegraphed to the rod tip. The angler then sets the hook and the battle begins. Five- to eight-pound hybrids frequently fall to anglers using this tactic, but all fishermen here are keenly aware that another world-record-class fish is always a possibility.

DEGRAY LAKE

Anglers on DeGray Lake near Arkadelphia have two things on their minds in summer—hybrid stripers and white bass. Both species run together, feeding on schools of shad, with the best action in the hours around dawn and dusk. Look for schools thrashing the water's surface near the dam and around the islands between the state park lodge and Iron Mountain.

Most in-the-know anglers prepare for this type of fishing by rigging some rods with topwater lures and others with spoons or crankbaits. Good choices include topwaters like the Smithwick Devil's Horse, the Boy Howdy, Cordell's Crazy Shad prop bait, small buzzbaits, Heddon's Zara Spook, and Storm's Chug Bug popper, and subsurface lures like Norman's Little N crankbait, Rapala's Shad Rap, Bagley's Killer B, and Luhr-Jensen's Crocodile spoon.

When you see fish breaking, move close. Put your trolling motor down so you can follow the school, then stay so you're about a cast away. Just before the fish start breaking, you may want to start throwing a spoon or other subsurface lure. Then once they're coming up, start throwing topwater baits. When they go down again, try a spoon again. A big school of hybrids tends to break up into several smaller schools if you stay with them. But stay with one school until you don't catch any more fish in that area.

Set your drag properly to avoid big-fish break-offs; fifteen- to twenty-pound hybrids always are possible in DeGray.

BEAVER LAKE

Beaver Lake supports healthy populations of hybrid striped bass. In summer, this twenty-eight-thousand-acre Ozark Mountains impoundment serves up fast-paced action for these hard-hitting sport fish.

Among the best fishing areas are creek mouths, including the mouths of War Eagle Creek, the White River, Ford's Creek, Cedar Creek, and Rambo Creek. Live shad is the bait favored by local anglers, most of whom pinpoint schools of hybrids using a sonar unit, then suspend a shad above the fish using a balloon tied around the line with a simple overhand knot. The balloon signals a strike and will break or slide up or down the line when a big fish hits. Hybrids also run schools of shad on the surface this season and can be taken by sight-casting shad-imitation lures to schools of fish churning the water. Average fish run eight to twelve pounds, but true heavyweights also are possible. The unofficial lake record weighed twenty pounds, eight ounces.

DEQUEEN LAKE

DeQueen Lake north of Texarkana covers only 1,680 acres, so hybrids are never far away when you start fishing. Hybrid stockings are infrequent, but fishing pressure is light, and the hybrid population is healthy. Some local anglers take forty to fifty hybrid stripers daily when fishing DeQueen.

One productive method for catching DeQueen hybrids is the umbrella rig. This rig, which resembles the framework of an umbrella, has two heavy wire crosspieces attached to a three- to five-ounce weight. Each crosspiece has steel leaders on each end, in the middle and in the center. Attached to each leader is a ⅜-ounce Road Runner (a horsehead spinner) tipped with a plastic shad trailer. Nine lures can be fished simultaneously when using this rig. It resembles a school of shad, thus attracting hungry hybrids. Catching two or more hybrids simultaneously is not unusual when trolling an umbrella rig near main-lake points that run into feeder creeks, flats, or underwater humps.

STORM CREEK LAKE

The only east Arkansas hybrid lake is Storm Creek, a 420-acre U.S. Forest Service impoundment just north of West Helena in St. Francis National Forest. Hybrids were first stocked here in 1982 to help control shad. Today, seven- to eleven-pounders are common. Hybrids have been in the lake long enough that someone could catch a twenty-pounder.

Local anglers usually fish near dawn and dusk when hybrids are most active. Most fish the main body of the lake or around points, trolling with a Rapala Shad Rap or other deep-diving lure. The line is allowed to run out sixty or seventy feet behind the boat to get the lure running twelve to fourteen feet deep where summer hybrids usually are found.

A sonar fish-finder helps pinpoint underwater structures where hybrids are holding. Look for a drop-off or other prominent structure. There are few such areas in Storm Creek, and wherever you can find a change in contour, that's where you should fish.

At one time, biologists were touting the hybrid striper as the fish of the future for America's anglers. Here in Arkansas, the future is now.

JUNE

Big Cats of the Mighty Mississippi

I felt like Huck Finn. I was barefooted. A straw hat sat atop my head. A big paddle wheeler, the *Delta Queen,* was passing by on its way up the Mississippi River. And a catfish was nibbling on my line.

It was summer 1995. A friend and I were fishing from a sandbar on a lonely stretch of east Arkansas's Mississippi River. A crescent moon painted a ribbon of silver light across Ol' Muddy's broad, dark surface. We watched for an hour as the big cruise boat crept upstream, lit up like a courthouse square on Christmas Eve. From somewhere within its depths came the brassy sound of Dixieland jazz. A barred owl hooted in the woods behind us, creating an eerie combination of natural and man-made ragtime.

"There he is!"

We were both laid back comfortably on the warm, moist sand. But suddenly my partner stood, grabbed his pole from its forked-stick prop, and yanked back on it hard. His rod tip immediately made a nosedive, signaling the presence of something sizable at the other end of his line. "Got him!" he said.

His rod arched. His drag sung. *Zzzzzzzzzzz. Zzzzzzzzzzzzz!*

"Maybe he's got you," I noted.

The fish fought valiantly, but so did my friend. After a five-minute battle, he beached the fat channel cat, which croaked incessantly at the injustice of it all. Ten pounds it weighed, maybe more. It was just one of two dozen 3- to 15-pounders we'd take home that night.

We caught mostly channel cats that evening but also a couple of nice blues and flatheads. All three species are abundant in the Mississippi's fertile waters, and all reach substantial sizes. In fact, the Mississippi River probably produces more giant catfish year in and year out than any body of water in the United States. And the stretch of river running along the border of Arkansas produces some of the biggest of those catfish.

Take blue cats, for instance. Three of the largest documented in recent years were caught in the Arkansas portion of the Mississippi River.

This 28-pound Mississippi River blue cat is considered small by catfishermen who frequently fish in this huge body of water. Hundred-pounders always are possible.

On May 29, 1995, John D. Harmon of Dermott caught a 116-pound, 8-ounce blue cat on a trotline in the Mississippi River south of Yellow Bend near Dermott. The gargantuan fish was fifty-five inches long, with a girth of forty-two inches. It established a new unrestricted-tackle state record for the species and is one of the ten largest blue cats documented since the 1800s. The current rod-and-reel world record taken from Tennessee's Cumberland River in 1998 weighed 112 pounds.

Raymond Gray of Osceola caught a record blue catfish on September 27, 1995, while fishing the Mississippi River near Osceola. Using a rod and reel with skipjack herring for bait, he subdued a 96-pound giant that smashed the old state record of 86 pounds, 15 ounces established in 1983.

John Stortz of St. Charles caught another over-hundred blue— a 102-pounder—on a trotline in March 1999. His came from the Arkansas section of the river near Rosedale, Mississippi.

Blues over 100 pounds always are a possibility in this massive river, and as more and more catfishermen ply these waters with rod and reel, the probability that a new world record will be caught here increases substantially. In the minds of many, there's no doubt that a 150-pound blue lurks somewhere in the Mississippi. The question is, will it ever be caught?

The Mississippi is a mother lode of giant flatheads, too. Fifteen- to 30-pounders are common as costume jewelry at a flea market. Forty- to 70-pounders probably are caught somewhere along the river every day during summer. And once again, the possibility of someone catching a world-record-class fish is a distinct possibility.

Channel catfish are extraordinarily abundant in the Mississippi as well, and catching fifty or more during a night's fishing is not unusual for savvy anglers. Most range from 1 to 5 pounds, but specimens exceeding 10 pounds usually will anchor the stringers of serious fishermen.

The Mississippi River in Arkansas stretches across a lengthy piece of ground, running the length of the eastern boundary, from near

With the Benzal Railroad bridge looming in the background, an Arkansas catfishermen displays a 38-pound blue cat caught downstream in the Mississippi River.

Blytheville on the north to near Eudora on the south. Deciding where to fish can be a daunting task.

Catfish in the Mississippi are like catfish everywhere. They usually hold near distinctive bottom structures or cover, favoring areas offering easy access between deep and shallow water—river channel drop-offs, humps, holes, outside stream bends, log jams, toppled trees, etc. High densities of catfish occur wherever this structure is found, and for all practical purposes, if you can find good habitat, it doesn't matter where you fish.

Were I to choose the areas I consider best for catfishing, I would recommend the junctures of the Mississippi and large tributaries like the St. Francis, White, and Arkansas Rivers. River "crossroads" like these often hold heavy concentrations of catfish, and the knowledgeable catter in the right place at the right time can enjoy fast-paced fishing unlike anything he or she's ever experienced.

Catfishing is excellent year-round, although most of the annual catch is taken during summer. When possible, fish at night. Daylight hours are productive at times, especially on overcast or rainy days, but as a general rule, the best catfishing is at night.

Trotlines are the favored fishing method on the main river channel. Rod-and-reel bait fishermen ply the river along its entire length in Arkansas. Within the fraternity of visiting and local anglers, you'll also find many who fish using jugs and limb lines.

During summer's heat, blue catfish in the river often move to deep pools and channel edges, following schools of baitfish. The baitfish—shad, skipjack herring, and others—are continually seeking comfort zones where plankton, young-of-the-year baitfish, and other foods are available. They may move several times and several miles during each twenty-four-hour period, or they may remain relatively stationary. Wherever they go, however, blue cats will follow, with most holding in loose schools beneath the baitfish where they feed on the dead, dying, and unfortunate.

Find the baitfish and you'll find the catfish; that's the key to capitalizing on this pattern. One way is using sonar to probe deep-water habitat for big fish holding beneath baitfish schools. Most will be on or near prominent bottom structures like channel breaks, humps, and holes. When anglers see "blips" indicating the possibility of a big cat beneath schooling baitfish at a specific depth, they anchor their craft, count off the right amount of line, and place a piece of cutbait or a live baitfish right in front of a fish. Some use a "stacked minnow" rig in this situation. Several large minnows are hooked through both lips on single hook. These are then presented at the proper depth beneath a float or balloon. Blue cats find the struggling "school" of crippled baitfish irresistible.

Outside bends of the river are among the most productive hotspots for big flatheads, especially where trees have toppled into the water and the river has gouged deeply into the bank forming undercuts. Potholes or slight depressions in the river bottom also tend to concentrate flatheads, as do the upstream sides of underwater humps, and shallow flats and drops near tributary mouths. Use live fish baits exclusively—shad, skipjack herring, bluegills, small carp, and suckers, or bullheads. Flatheads aren't scavengers like their brethren and are only enticed with live baits.

Look for channel catfish around the same types of structure and cover where you might fish for black bass and crappie. They often hold in flooded timber, along channel drop-offs, near riprap, on brushy points, near tributary mouths, and on underwater humps. Other top fishing spots include undercut banks, deep timber-filled pools in outside stream bends, big log drifts, and eddy water around fallen trees. Any of your favorite baits will work, from night crawlers and catalpa worms to your own special brew of home-made stinkbait.

There are several Mississippi River access areas in Arkansas, including Sans Souci Landing near Osceola, the Eighth Street Landing in West Memphis, Peters Island in Lee County, the St. Francis Landing (access to Mississippi via St. Francis River) north of Helena, and Panther Forest Landing north of Lake City.

Always be safety conscious on this gargantuan river. Strong current and undertows can get you in a pickle if you aren't careful, and barge traffic is incessant. Keep a safe distance from these big boats, and always wear a life jacket.

No doubt, the "bigness" of this river keeps lots of anglers away. Despite the fact that this is one of the world's premier hotspots for giant catfish, relatively few rod-and-reel anglers ever fish it. If you want to catch the biggest fish of your lifetime, however—a catfish that could run over one hundred pounds—no body of water in Arkansas is better than the Mississippi River.

Fishing Arkansas's Island Retreats

Looking for a fun getaway this season? Why not take that island fishing trip you've always dreamed about? Aaaaahh! Just think of it. Clear, blue waters alive with fish. Verdant shorelines waltzing with a turquoise sky. No phones. No traffic. No chores. Just you and your loved ones. Fishing. Swimming. Camping. Exploring. A world apart.

Sounds like Fantasy Island, huh? Or maybe Hawaii or Tahiti or the Grand Caymans. Well, believe it or not, you can find all this and more on two Arkansas lakes—Ouachita and DeGray.

Surprised? Most people are. Islands are rare here in mid-America. And those you can find usually are hazardous during sudden rises, or they're off-limits altogether.

Lakes Ouachita and DeGray are notable exceptions. These U.S. Army Corps of Engineers impoundments are tucked away in the Ouachita Mountains just a short drive from Hot Springs National Park. Both are dotted with islands that punctuate lake maps like a blizzard of periods, colons, and exclamation points. Together, these scenic lakes embrace over one hundred islands large enough to offer safe, comfortable camping and fishing.

Ouachita and DeGray have big islands, medium islands, and tiny islands, too. Some are chained in miniature archipelagoes like popcorn on a Christmas garland. Some are isolated in mid-lake. Some are little bigger than an urban backyard; on these you have a subconscious conviction that all rules are suspended and anything can happen. Others are more than a mile long and expansive enough that you must constantly remind yourself you're on an island at all.

Best of all, these islands provide a great retreat for a fun fishing getaway. The weed bed lagoons and rocky shores encircling the islands attract extraordinary numbers of popular sport fish—sassy bluegills and redears, tail-walking largemouths and spotted bass, jumbo white bass and pole-bending catfish. DeGray Lake sports world-record-class hybrid stripers, and Lake Ouachita is home to

---

Huge stringers of bluegills and other sunfish often are caught by anglers fishing around the islands in lakes Ouachita and DeGray.

fifty-pound-plus striped bass, hefty walleyes, and even a sizable population of chain pickerels. These are great places to scratch your freshwater fishing itch.

BREAM

For many anglers, a day of fishing on Ouachita or DeGray means only one thing—bream fishing. These lakes bristle with untold numbers of bluegills, redear sunfish, and longear sunfish. Whether you set up camp and stay for the weekend or just visit for an afternoon, the islands are a first-rate place to experience bream-busting at its best.

You'll find most bream in weed beds that encircle the islands like Hawaiian leis. Both lakes have enormous beds of elodea, coontail, and milfoil, and big bluegills and redears usually hold near the edges of these weed patches.

Pinpointing the perimeter of the weeds is important. Cast too far, and you're constantly getting snagged. It's best to present your bait so it falls right at the edge of the weeds.

Scout from a boat first, wearing polarized sunglasses to cut glare and help you see the weed beds. Or better yet, don a swim mask and snorkel and get a fish-eye view. Underwater visibility ranges from three to twenty feet, usually twelve, so this method is also a good way to find big-bream hideouts.

A trip I made to the islands one summer exemplifies the usefulness of underwater scouting. Six of us beached a party barge on a small island and started wade-fishing for bream. During the first two hours, we caught and released over a hundred bluegills and longears, but only a handful were big enough to keep.

One of our party decided to do some snorkeling since the fishing wasn't too great. After swimming the length of the beach, he suggested fishing a different location where he'd seen several big bluegills and redears. That did the trick. Over the next two hours, we caught seventy-five saucer-sized bream, including several weighing over a pound.

Because fluctuating lake levels limit vegetation growth near the banks, weed beds around many islands are too far to reach by casting from shore. Fishing from a boat is a ready remedy, but a cooler, more refreshing tactic is to wade out in a pair of shorts and tennis shoes until you're at the proper distance to make an accurate cast. Be sure to wear shoes. The lake bottoms are covered with thin, sharp rocks, and without footwear, you'll come out looking like you stepped in a nest of wildcats.

Standard island bream fishing gear consists of an ultralight combo spooled with four- to six-pound line, a cage full of crickets, a couple boxes of worms, and a cooler of drinks to stave off thirst. Rig up tight-line fashion (no bobber), with one or two split shot clamped on your line about twelve inches above a small, long-shanked Carlisle hook. Cast to the weed line, keeping one finger on your line so you can feel the tap of a striking fish.

If you prefer fishing with artificials, try using $\frac{1}{64}$- to $\frac{1}{32}$-ounce lead-head jigs. Use a jigging pole or cane pole to work them in weed-bed pockets when boating. Lower the lure to the bottom and jig it with a slow hop to elicit a strike. When casting from shore, use the same basic technique. Let the jig fall to the bottom and hop it in using a slow retrieve. When a bream hits, a snap of the wrist is all you need to set the hook.

Both lakes also harbor sizable populations of jumbo crappie, but they're rarely taken around the islands, except in the few spots where dense stands of timber cover island points.

STRIPERS, WHITES, AND HYBRIDS

Ouachita has striped bass, DeGray has hybrid stripers, and both lakes have healthy populations of white bass.

The best fishing for these species is during spring, late summer, and autumn when all are likely to be slashing through schools of shad on the surface. These feeding frenzies usually occur near dawn and dusk, often in waters around the near-shore islands. Anglers watch for surface disturbances indicating a school of feeding fish, then boat to the fringe of the school, and cast shad-imitation plugs, spoons, and jigs into the melee. Light tackle is appropriate for whites, which run one to four pounds, but when targeting hybrids and stripers, go heavy.

Ouachita stripers frequently top thirty pounds, and on DeGray there's an excellent chance you'll hook a fifteen- to twenty-pound hybrid.

Island fishing isn't as good for these species during summer and winter, but good fish sometimes are taken by trolling spoons, jigs, and deep-diving crankbaits along river and creek channels that meander close to the islands. A good sonar unit and bottom contour map can help pinpoint this structure.

CATFISH

One of the best ways to enjoy an island fishing excursion is sitting around a campfire at night, tending poles baited for catfish. Blues, channels, and flatheads are common in both lakes, and they often feed on shallow ridges and flats connecting the islands. Hooking a cat over fifty pounds is a distinct possibility.

These lakes are usually clear, so confine your fishing to night when possible. For big blue cats, live or cut shad are the bait of choice. Monster flatheads often fall for live sunfish. Channel cats are taken using everything from chicken liver to Ivory soap. Use a large sinker to carry the bait to the bottom, then put your reel in free spool, prop your rig on a forked stick, sit back, and relax while you wait for a bite.

PLANNING A TRIP

The islands on Ouachita and DeGray are super places for fishing adventure. Help keep them open to all by being extra careful and responsible during your visits. Carry out all trash, don't cut standing trees, be careful with fires, and hold down the noise. Keeping human impact to a minimum will encourage the Corps of Engineers to leave the islands open, so future generations can enjoy the experience of island fishing and camping on Ouachita and DeGray.

Be aware of safety considerations, too. Small boats are OK for island hopping in calm weather but can be dangerous in open water when high winds produce big waves. Have each person on board wear a life jacket. It's also wise to carry a battery-powered radio to monitor weather reports. Boating Ouachita and DeGray can get pretty hairy when it's windy.

And when you're headed to the islands, don't forget the most important rule of all—you can't carry too much bait. So far, there aren't any island bait shops. And with fishing this hot, you'll want to keep a hook in the water as much as possible.

Warm Up on Arkansas's Summer Warmouths

"Goggle-eye hole," Curt Moore announced, snatching up a sculling paddle and swinging the johnboat toward a dark, flooded recess in the bottom of a hollow cypress tree.

"How many you reckon are in that I one?" I asked.

"Three, maybe four."

"Really?" I said, incredulously. "What makes you think there'll be so many?"

"Just a feeling," Curt replied. "Watch and see."

Curt maneuvered the boat in close, then, using a long jigging pole, he dropped a cricket smack-dab in the middle of the cavity. The tiny orange cork above the bait hit the water, wobbled momentarily, then shot out of sight. A brief struggle ensued as Curt tried to wrest the cricket-eater from its underwater hideout. But within seconds, he had subdued the ten-ounce fish at the other end of the line.

"That's one," he said, tossing the fish to me to put in the fish basket. "And a nice one, too."

I turned the creature in my hand, examining it more closely. It quivered all over in a manner characteristic of the species. The mouth was large, bass-like. Yet the contours and size of the body closely resembled a bluegill. The fish's colors changed as I held it, from very dark, blackish-green to a lighter brownish-gold. The cheeks were emblazoned with several dark slashes radiating outward from its red eyes. Before I opened the fish basket, Curt was tossing another almost identical fish my way.

"Are you counting, Sutton?" he snapped. "That's two."

Curt's father, W. T., now attempted to join the action. When we first approached the tree, Curt intentionally positioned the boat so W. T. was beyond reach of the goggle-eye hole. Not to be outdone, W. T. paddled his end around and dropped a small jig into the water beside Curt's bobber.

Warmouths don't grow large, but they're abundant in many Arkansas lakes and fun to catch on light tackle.

"Would you look at that?!" said Curt, turning to me. "Can't find his own honeyhole, so he moves in on my spot."

"It ain't nice to be greedy," W. T. replied with a chuckle. "And it would be a good idea if you talked less and paid more attention to what you're doing. That way you might notice when a fish takes your cork under."

Curt's bobber had disappeared, and when he tightened his line, he met firm resistance. During his moment of inattention, the fish had taken the bait, darted away, and snagged the hook in some hidden recess of the tree. A swearword left Curt's lips at the same time W. T. set the hook in a dandy goggle-eye.

"That's three," W. T. said, unhooking the fish. "What happened to the fourth one, son?"

Before Curt could reply, I pulled number four over the transom.

I've been catching goggle-eyes, or warmouths as they're more properly known, since I first started fishing forty years ago. But until I began fishing with Curt and W. T. Moore, they were usually taken accidentally while seeking other species of fish. Mind you, I never had anything against warmouths. Catching them is great fun, and they're delicious to eat. Yet I never gave any thought to targeting warmouths specifically. I didn't know you could.

All that changed on the trip described above. We were bream fishing on an eastern Arkansas oxbow lake that day, and now and then Curt would point to a hollow tree or other such hideout and announce cheerfully, "Goggle-eye hole!" Almost without exception, each of these spots produced several nice warmouths.

I got curious. "How did you know there'd be a goggle-eye in there?" I asked Curt.

"They just like spots like that—dark holes inside these old cypress trees, the real thick branches in the water around beaver lodges. Drop a jig, cricket, or worm in a place like that and you'll catch a goggle-eye almost every time."

"We catch a lot of 'em bass fishing, too," W. T. added. "They'll hit almost anything you throw out there, and you'll often catch 'em on lures almost as big as they are."

That day, I became a true fan of these spunky little panfish. Now, when I'm fishing, I find myself watching for "goggle-eye holes" and rarely pass up the opportunity to see if a warmouth is lurking inside. Using techniques I learned from Curt and W. T., I've caught hundreds while fishing the lowland waters in eastern Arkansas.

Most warmouths are caught and released by anglers seeking bluegills, crappie, bass, or other fish. Some folks shun them because of their small size. The typical fish is eight inches long or shorter and weighs no more than half a pound, if that. They aren't the most handsome member of the sunfish clan; in fact, they're downright homely. They lack the furious spirit and determination of a hooked bluegill, and some fishermen complain they have "soft flesh with a muddy flavor."

Despite these supposed shortcomings, though, warmouths have a devoted group of followers in parts of Arkansas, and for good reasons. Sure, they're small, but they're so plentiful in some waters that you can land fifty or more before you catch your first bass. They may not be as scrappy as bluegills, but what panfish is? Warmouths are pretty darn feisty in their own right, and on ultralight tackle they put up a respectable battle.

Warmouths have a big appetite and a mouth to match. They're anything but shy and will gobble up a wide assortment of lures and baits, including crickets, worms, small crayfish and minnows, insect larvae, jigs, spoons, plastic worms, spinners, flies, streamers, and plugs. Poor table fare? In some poor-quality waters, perhaps, but poor taste is mostly a matter of poor preparation. Throw them on ice as soon as you catch them, and most will provide delectable vittles.

The warmouth is a lover of swamps, bayous, sloughs, oxbow lakes, and other warm, sluggish waters with dense timber, brush, or weeds. It's especially common in the warm lowland waters of the southeastern United States but occurs sporadically as far west as New Mexico and as far north as Lake Erie and southeastern Minnesota. Some populations have been established from stockings in Idaho, Arizona, and a few other areas west of the Rocky Mountains.

Some think the name "warmouth" is probably derived from the "Indian war paint" pattern of facial bars radiating backward from its reddish eyes to the margin of the gill covers. In some areas, it is still

improperly called by an old name—warmouth bass. In other places, it goes by nicknames like mud bass, weed bass, stumpknocker, big-mouth perch, jugmouth, and goggle-eye.

Coloration is extremely variable, making recognition sometimes difficult. Warmouths from swamps may be mottled a dark purplish-brown and at first appear to be entirely different from the golden-brown specimens of upland impoundments.

In Arkansas, warmouths usually are found in oxbow lakes, slug-gish delta streams, and fertile man-made reservoirs where weed beds and woody vegetation are abundant.

One nice things about warmouths is their predictability. As I learned from Curt and W. T. Moore, all you must do to find them is look for a hollow cypress tree or stump in a fertile lake or stream. Chances are, if there are warmouths inhabiting those waters, there will be at least one, and maybe half a dozen, hiding inside. For some reason, warmouths love dimly lit hollows, and if the hole is big enough to drop a jig, cricket, or worm in, you'll soon be yanking warmouths out one after another.

Beaver lodges are another favorite hideout. Sometimes beavers build their stick homes where many branches are submerged, and warmouths hide in these dense tangles. The best way to catch them in this situation is using a jigging pole or cane pole to lower a small lead-head jig into the small openings of the beaver lodge. The hole need be no bigger than a half-dollar to harbor a warmouth, and though you'll lose a few jigs, this is one of the best ways to load a stringer with fat little goggle-eyes.

Mini-crankbaits also are good warmouth catchers. Use $\frac{1}{12}$- to $\frac{1}{8}$-ounce minnow or crayfish imitations fished with two- to four-pound-test line on an ultralight spinning or spin-cast combo. Cast around cypress knees, weed-bed edges, stumps, or other good war-mouth cover and get ready for an exciting battle with one of these spunky, big-mouthed fish. Warmouths exemplify the old saying, "Good things often come in small packages."

Arkansas anglers will have little trouble finding good warmouth waters. According to the book *Fishes of Arkansas,* by Henry Robison

Warm up on warmouths.

Warm Up on Arkansas's Summer Warmouths 131

and Thomas Buchanan, "The warmouth is widely distributed over the state in all major drainages but most abundant in the Coastal Plain lowlands. In the more mountainous regions, it is most common in reservoirs and ponds."

"Fish Arkansas," a brochure distributed free by the Arkansas Game and Fish Commission, lists 116 bodies of water throughout the state where warmouths are found. These include 13 warm-water streams, 18 cold- and cool-water streams, 31 Game and Fish Commission lakes, 21 oxbow lakes, 10 Corps of Engineers lakes, 2 state park lakes, 11 U.S. Forest Service lakes, and 10 city, county, and corporate-owned lakes.

One of my favorite warmouth hotspots is Henry Gray–Hurricane Lake Wildlife Management Area near Bald Knob. Within that area are 8 oxbow lakes easily accessible from management areas roads during dry weather. (Several others are accessible by walking in or by boat during high-water overflows.) Big Hurricane Lake is largest at 60 acres, followed by Whirl Lake (30 acres), Mallard Pond (18 acres), Big Bell Lake (16 acres), Honey Lake (16 acres), and then Bollie Pond, Three Sisters Lake, and Little Green Tom, each between 5 and 10 acres in size. All these waters have huge cypress and tupelo trees towering over the shallows, and finding plenty of goggle-eyes and goggle-eye holes is a breeze. Warmouths also are plentiful in Glaise Creek, a long bayou running through the wilderness management area, that has plenty of warmouth cover in the form of cypress trees and fallen timber.

Another place to try for warmouths is White River National Wildlife Refuge in Arkansas, Monroe, Phillips, and Desha Counties. There are more than 200 natural lakes within this 150,000-acre bottomland refuge, all loaded with plenty of scrappy warmouths.

Among the more easily accessible lakes are Buck Lake, Upper Swan Lake, and Moon Lake off Highway 1 just east of St. Charles; Frazier Lake east of the Highway 17–153 junction south of St. Charles; and a huge complex of lakes (Escronges, Columbus, "H," and Prairie, to name just a few) accessible from gravel roads southeast of Ethel off Highway 17. Essex Bayou, Big Island Chute, and borrow-ditch lakes adjacent the White River Levee also are worth checking out. All these waters have plenty of easily recognizable warmouth habitat, and anglers fishing around cypress trees, buckbrush, and fallen timber should have little problem catching dozens of goggle-eyes during a summer visit. Boat ramps are almost nonexistent, so using a light, easily carried johnboat or canoe is advisable.

Outside oxbow lakes and lowland streams, the best warmouth waters are man-made impoundments owned by the Game and Fish Commission. Good bets include Lake Conway, Lake Bob Kidd, Lake Bois d'Arc, Calion Lake, Mallard Lake, Lake Overcup, and White Oak Lake.

Other good warmouth waters include Horseshoe Lake, Old Town Lake, and Lake Chicot (oxbows), lakes Millwood and Ouachita (Corps of Engineers lakes), lakes Erling and Georgia Pacific (corporate-owned lakes), Mercer Bayou (Game and Fish Commission), and the Black, Cache, St. Francis, and lower White Rivers (warm-water streams).

If you've never fished specifically for warmouths, take my advice and give it a try. Some claim they aren't worth the bother. But if you're out to have fun, to relax and take in the outdoors, simple pleasures like catching warmouths are enough to satisfy.

JULY

Pinocchio of the Rivers

July 19, 1994. Michael Langley of Malvern, Arkansas, has largemouth bass on his mind as he works a topwater plug in the Ouachita River. Suddenly, there's a violent jerk, and his lure changes direction. Langley hangs onto his rod as a 98-pound, 9-ounce paddlefish takes him, fishing buddy Noel Cranford, and their boat up and down the river near Malvern for almost two hours.

When they finally land the gargantuan fish, they contact state fisheries biologist Tom Penniston, who witnesses the official weigh-in. Penniston helps them prepare paperwork for a new Arkansas state record. Langley's monster eclipses the old record of 77 pounds, 4 ounces set in 1989 in Table Rock Lake. His paddlefish also betters the No. 5 fish on the National Fresh Water Fishing Hall of Fame world-record list. Langley's fish is five feet, eleven inches long.

The paddlefish is the fish world's equivalent of Pinocchio. The most noticeable feature of this unusual fish is its weird nose. Protruding like a built-in boat paddle between its beady eyes is a misshapen snoot as a long as a child's arm.

Other curious features enhance the comic-book image. The paddlefish has no bones, only cartilage. The skin is leathery and scaleless. The tail is sickle-shaped like a shark. And while the paddlefish may weigh over 150 pounds, it feeds only on microscopic animals (plankton) siphoned through a toothless mouth big enough to engulf a basketball. Even its nicknames—spoonbill, spoonbill catfish, shovelnose cat, and boneless cat—add to its unusual appeal.

The paddlefish is a living fossil from the Age of Dinosaurs 250 million years ago. Its single living relative, the Chinese paddlefish, plies rivers in the Yangtze Valley half a world away, while North America's paddlefish are found mostly in large river systems in the Mississippi River Valley. Although these two have survived the test of time, today they face a greater challenge—surviving the activities of man.

Sport fishermen did not create problems for paddlefish. Rather

This nice catch of paddlefish fell to snaggers fishing the White River at Batesville.

it was commercial fishermen at the turn of the century and the polluters, dam builders, and poachers of the present who led to the general decline of this once abundant species.

Until the 1890s, paddlefish rarely were harvested, and, when caught, were used as fertilizer or merely dragged up on the river bank to die. Nineteenth-century anglers may have been repelled by the mysterious appearance of this strange fish, assuming ugliness indicated something inedible.

That same prejudice did not apply to caviar lovers. As sturgeon declined in response to a growing demand for caviar, southerners turned to paddlefish for roe that could be sold as a caviar substitute. Paddlefish were slaughtered for their eggs, and fish merchants smoked the meat and sold it as sturgeon. Soon, word spread that there was money to be made in southern rivers, and fishing pressure quickly grew. Around 2,500,000 pounds of paddlefish were harvested in the Mississippi River Valley in 1899.

Now, survivors face the human pressures of pollution and dam projects. Paddlefish are big-river fish requiring certain flows, temperatures, and bottom conditions for growth and reproduction. Man's modification of big river systems had serious consequences for them. Individual fisheries declined by as much as 95 percent. Paddlefish completely disappeared in New York, Pennsylvania, Maryland, North Carolina, the Great Lakes, and all Canadian waters.

Oddly enough, past conflicts between Iraq and Iran escalated problems for paddlefish. Before those nations engaged in their mutual population reduction plan, they exported much of the world's supply of roe for caviar production. When Middle East roe supplies dried up, suppliers again turned to paddlefish to meet the demand for caviar. And with paddlefish caviar bringing up to one thousand dollars a pound on the world market, commercial harvest—legal and illegal—skyrocketed. In Arkansas alone, legal commercial harvest increased 700 percent between 1975 and 1981. From 1975 to 1985, an average of 296,973 pounds of paddlefish were taken commercially each year in Arkansas.

Paddlefish numbers plummeted, leading to their classification as threatened or endangered in Minnesota, North Carolina, Ohio, West Virginia, and Texas.

Anglers in Arkansas, Oklahoma, Missouri, Mississippi, Tennessee, and Kentucky are more fortunate. In these states, healthy populations still exist, and anglers still can pursue paddlefish for sport. Creel limits, seasons, and size are restricted to ensure the paddlefish's protection, but during open seasons, chances of hooking a big spoonbill are excellent for savvy anglers. In Arkansas, paddlefish occur in the Red, Ouachita, Arkansas, White, and Mississippi Rivers and their major tributaries.

To catch a paddlefish, don't follow Michael Langley's example for fishing technique. Because they feed exclusively on plankton, paddlefish rarely take bait or lures.

Snagging is the only reliable method for hooking a spoonbill. This is a method whereby large weighted treble hooks are yanked blindly through the water, in the hope that somehow the hooks and a paddlefish will intersect.

All paddlefish angling is done in dam tailwaters, because state law prohibits snagging except when fishing from the bank within one hundred yards below a dam. Typical snagging equipment consists of a ten- to sixteen-foot, heavy-action saltwater rod and a large-capacity, bait-casting or spinning reel spooled with 50- to 130-pound-test line. Two large, needle-sharp treble hooks are tied tandem on the line, and a heavy weight (up to 20 ounces) is used to sink the hooks in swift tailwaters. Once on bottom, the rig is jerked through the water until it hits a snag or a fish. Lots of terminal tackle is lost to logs and rocks.

Snagging is back-breaking sport. There's a long cast to get the rig upstream and out in the river; a short delay for the weight to sink; then a violent jerk and quick reeling to recover slack lie; another jerk and more rapid reeling; and on until the line is reeled in. Then another cast and more jerking and reeling until a hook hits its mark.

Hundreds of casts can be made before a hook connects with a paddlefish, but once a fish is on, there's plenty of exciting, white-knuckle action for the fortunate angler. Land a paddlefish, and chances are it'll be the biggest fish you ever caught in Arkansas waters.

Paddlefish are excellent table fare. When smoked, the meat is moist and delicious. Fried, it resembles catfish. Paddlefish also can be broiled, baked, grilled, and used in chowder.

To clean a paddlefish, hang it by the paddle, then make a circular cut through the skin just above the tail. Twist sharply on the tail to remove it, and pull out the attached white, hose-like notochord. Use pliers to skin the fish, and remove entrails and head. Cut the meat into fillets or steaks after trimming off the outer layer of dark-red meat which has an unpleasant flavor.

Fishing for these piscine Pinocchios is a sport like no other. Fortunately, here in Arkansas, we're still allowed to do it. Let's protect these monsters of freshwater so future generations also can experience the thrills of hooking a paddlefish.

JULY

Gar Wars

It was the meanest looking animal I've ever seen. Hundreds of thick, sharp, inch-long teeth studded the broad alligator-like jaws. The mouth was twisted into a malevolent smirk. Dark eyes big as half-dollars turned in their sockets, following my movements. "I'll eat you, boy," it seemed to be thinking. "If you'll just step a little bit closer . . ."

It was nearly as long as the wooden johnboat from which it had just been extracted—eight feet, I'd guess, maybe more. Several loops of sisal rope were bound tightly around the creature's snout, but somehow that didn't make me feel any safer. Two bullet holes from a .38-caliber revolver punctuated the top of its massive head, yet still the brute lived.

I had not touched the fish, but I knew the diamond-shaped scales armoring its body were hard as stone. An old man was chopping at the monster's back with a hatchet, and with each blow he struck, sparks flew.

"He'll go two hundred pounds easy," said Garfield Stacy, the commercial fisherman who had captured the giant in east Arkansas's St. Francis River. "Used to be a lot of big ones in the river. But them days are long gone. Gator gar this big are scarce as five-pound crappie."

The alligator gar had been laid atop a board between two saw horses, and Garfield was steadily whacking away, cutting the hard, ivory-like scales from a narrow strip down the fish's back.

"I'm glad they're gone," he said, working the thick shell away from the meat of the huge fish. "Weren't nothing but trouble any-way. They could eat their weight in game fish every other day. And you couldn't hardly keep a net out, 'cause they tore 'em up.

"Don't reckon we'll see another one this size for a long time. And as far as I'm concerned, good riddance."

I never saw another gar that big. I fished the St. Francis River for many years after that day in the mid-1960s—still fish it when I can—but as best I can tell, the big gator gar are gone.

I used to be glad they were gone. Every time I'd swim the river with my teenage buddies, the wicked eyes of Garfield's monster were

This extraordinary battle with a giant alligator gar was captured at the mouth of the Cache River in the 1940s. (Courtesy of the Arkansas Game and Fish Commission.)

following me. Many nights I've dreamed of that beast. I've felt its teeth sinking into my leg and dragging me under to drown. And I've seen that churlish smile as it stared at me with black eyes and pulled me to the bottom to eat me.

It took a while, but the fear faded, and years later, fascination took its place. It started when I found a box of Arkansas tourist guides published in the 1950s. "Gar fishing with deep sea tackle is one of the great thrills of fishing in Arkansas," one guidebook proclaimed above the photo of a successful angler. "Because the savage battlers often weigh more than 100 pounds, strong nerves are essential in the sport."

Trout hadn't made a splash in Arkansas at that time, but huge alligator gar in the St. Francis, White, Arkansas, Cache, Red, and Mississippi Rivers were attracting anglers from throughout the country. Catching several 100- to 150-pounders during a day's fishing was common then, and the gar-fishing industry was serviced by several guides who specialized in catching these prehistoric monsters.

Reading about this astounding fishery, I started wondering what it must have been like to battle those leviathans. And I started wishing that gator gar still swam in the St. Francis.

In the early 1900s, Arkansans began a decades-long campaign to eradicate the species. Dr. E. G. Gudger, an ichthyologist at the American Museum of Natural History, reported in 1933 in "Fishes and Fishing in Louisiana," published by the Louisiana Department of Conservation, "In certain of the small lakes of Arkansas—and by this I mean ox-bow cutoffs of the various rivers—they are seining these, using trammel nets, and knocking the Gar on the head."

Attempts to eradicate gator gar continued through the next two decades. In "Capturing the Marauding Arkansas Gar," an article published in a 1941 issue of *Spot* magazine, we read:

> Among the most loathsome fish in America is the gar-pike, an ugly, mean but withal sluggish fish that at times attains the astonishing weight of 190 pounds and often exceeds seven feet in length. Apparently a throwback to prehistoric ages, it feeds on lesser fish, is so voracious it eats its own weight every 36 hours . . .
>
> Particularly virulent are the gar-pikes of the White River, near the little town of Stuttgart, Arkansas. And because they raise such havoc with the White River game fish, they are the objects of a determined crusade to eliminate them . . .
>
> . . . alligator gar are a menace to modern animal life and will wreak vast destruction unless they themselves are destroyed by game lovers and sportsmen.

The leader of this crusade, according to the article, was Dr. Sherod A. Drennen of Stuttgart, who started fishing for the creatures in 1934. "At first he used ordinary river line and single hooks," the article noted, "but when he found the lines snapped like peach fuzz threads under the weight of the gar he soon switched to deep sea tackle."

Drennen was one of the first to realize the enormous sporting potential of these gigantic fish. He also learned that gator gar were dangerous and hard to kill. The article continued: "For a long time Dr. Drennen used a high-powered .22 rifle to fire hollow-point bullets into the heads of the vicious brutes as they were being hauled toward the boat, but only an excellent shot planted directly between the eyes could kill them. Sometimes, too, an apparently dead fish would suddenly come to life after he had been landed. One, which had been lying on land for ten minutes, rose on its tail and struck a dock man with its snout, cutting a deep, three-inch gash in his forehead."

The problem of how to kill the gar after it was hooked was solved when Drennen teamed up with L. E. Piper, an archer who worked for the Ben Pearson company in Pine Bluff. Piper demonstrated to Drennen that the steel-pointed arrows he used were more lethal than bullets.

"Dad told me that each alligator gar has two diamond-shaped scales on top of its head," Piper's son Lew, a resident of North Little Rock, recalled in an October 1997 interview. "And unless the arrow hit one of those scales, it wouldn't penetrate the gar's thick hide; it would just bounce off. I imagine it was quite a feat, even for a crack archer like my dad, to hit such a small target while standing in a rocking boat. But he did it time and time again while accompanying Dr. Drennen."

To hunt the gar, Drennen designed a flat-bottomed scow topped by a sturdy overhead platform from which he could cast. Attached to his heavy rod was ninety-pound-test line, a four-foot leader of piano wire, and an 8/o treble hook.

"When the fish strikes, it dives and heads down stream," the *Spot* article noted. "From there on it's a fight with man and fish pitched in a battle destined to go on for half an hour and sometimes as long as an hour. Inevitably, however, the fish tires, and the fisherman slowly and watchfully brings it to gaff. The archer takes careful aim, pierces the tough rhombic hide with one or two of his arrows as the gar breaks water. But sometimes, the gar breaks when right at the gaff, slaps out viciously with powerful sweeps of its huge tail, and tries to sink its sharp conical teeth into the arms of its captors."

Stories like the one in *Spot* gave a bigger-than-life reputation to this once-hated fish, and soon Arkansas was flooded with out-of-state anglers hoping to catch one. One man who guided the visitors was John Fox, now a resident of Ocklawaha, Florida.

"I guided on the L'Anguille, St. Francis, White, and Mississippi Rivers from 1954 through 1958," Fox said in a recent interview. "A friend told me about catching these big gar over in the St. Francis.

I went with him one time and was hooked. It was the most exciting thing I'd ever done."

At first, Fox and his clients fished in much the same manner as Drennen. Later, however, Fox devised a better method.

"We took two metal oil cans and brazed them together," he said. "Both ends were sealed. A cotter pin was brazed to the cans, then we took thirty feet of nylon staging, tied it to the cotter pin, wrapped it around the cans, and secured it with a rubber band. A sinker, swivel, piano wire leader, and treble hook were rigged on the line, and a carp or buffalo head was used for bait. We kept several dozen of these can rigs in the boat."

When a gator gar was seen rolling on the surface, Fox paddled one hundred yards upstream and placed ten can rigs across the river. Each can was tossed out, and the rubber band allowed the line to unwind slowly until the bait was on bottom. Ten more rigs were set one hundred yards below the gar.

"Next thing you know, here comes a can moving down the river," said Fox. "The gar would always carry it to the bank to eat the fish head. Then I'd paddle out; we'd grab the can and tie the line on our pole to the line on the can. We'd reel up past the knot, and when the gar started moving back upstream I'd get my angler to put the reel in gear. When the line got tight, you'd stick him and that son-of-a-bitch would jump out of the water eight and ten feet. Using that method, we'd catch six to twelve of these big gar each day, all over 100 pounds. The biggest I caught weighed 220 pounds."

Charles Alter of DeWitt, Arkansas, was another 1950s gar guide. He fished the White, Arkansas, and Mississippi Rivers.

"I didn't consider it a successful trip unless there were two gar caught by the party that weighed over 100 pounds," Alter said in a 1997 interview. "The biggest ever caught by one of my parties weighed 198, but most of them went from 130 to 160 pounds. I was experienced enough that I could go up and down the river and see where they were feeding, or I knew where they'd be feeding on the bottom ends of sandbars. We'd anchor and set out four or five lines. Pretty soon one of them would take a run and I'd let the fisherman catch him. When you set the hook, that's when the activity starts. Usually that gar's gonna come up and make a big jump, like a sailfish or marlin. And he may jump several times trying to throw the hook."

Bow fishermen also found gator gar attractive quarry. John Heuston of Little Rock was a sports writer for the *Arkansas Democrat* in the early 1960s when he accompanied Dr. Rex Hancock of Stuttgart on such a trip.

"You didn't dare catch one on ordinary bow-fishing tackle because it might jerk you right out in the water," Heuston told me. "But Rex devised a way of getting them. He used an open reel that you wound the cord around by hand. He had a small white cork tied to the end of his bow-fishing line, and when a gar was hit, the line peeled off and this cork floated in the water. Attached to the cork was a metal ring. If he hit a really big gar and it took off, he'll pull that line loose, and before it got gone, he'd hook a fifty-five-gallon drum to the ring on the cork and pitch it overboard. Then the gar would drag this big drum around until it wore itself out and we were able to get it."

By the mid-1950s, Arkansas's alligator gar were getting national publicity. Bill Apple of Little Rock wrote in one publication: "Deep-sea fishing 400 miles from the nearest salt water sounds a bit fantastic, but you can get tarpon and tuna thrills on the rivers of southeastern Arkansas . . . Gar weighing up to 200 pounds have been taken from the lower White River. In one 12-mile stretch 600 gar weighing over 100 pounds were taken in one summer season. This was in an area six miles above and six miles below the mouth of Lagrue Bayou . . . Arkansas's Game and Fish Commission encourages this sport, which is now spreading into northern Louisiana. It helps rid the streams of one of the most devastating predators."

An article in the *Arkansas Gazette* on January 21, 1962, was titled "Alligator Gar's Image Has Changed from Predator to Glamorous Object of Exciting Sport Fishing." "If a fish can be said to have a public image then the biggest switch from a bad one to a good one has occurred in the image of the alligator gar," wrote Matilda Tuohey in the article. "In the last 20 years or so the picture of the big and ugly gar has changed from that of a dangerous predator which must be eliminated to the glamorous but still ugly object of exciting sport fishing. Instead of encouraging wholesale slaughter, the parts of the state which promote gar fishing are now becoming concerned about the decreasing population of the gar."

By this time, said John Fox, alligator gar were gone from the

L'Anguille and St. Francis Rivers. "In 1954, '55, '56, and '57, I had people coming in from all over the country," he said. "And we were catching these gar like there was never a tomorrow. When we got one to the boat, we'd shoot it and just let it sink. We thought we were doing a great service. We were told they'd eat their weight in game fish every forty-eight hours. So if it was 150-pounder, you could look at 150 pounds of fish going out of the river every two days. We thought we were getting rid of all these predators, but, in fact, we were victims of our own greed. The fishing started petering out in 1957 or '58, and I just didn't feel right taking people out any more. I was guiding full time, and by 1959, just five years after I started, I had to quit. We had cleaned the rivers out. The gar were gone."

In the White River, other factors contributed to the gator gar's extirpation. "It wasn't our fishing that caused their demise," said Charles Alter. "It was the cold-water releases from the hydroelectric impoundments. One summer, I spent time checking the difference in water temperature in the mouth of the White River and out in the Mississippi. In the hottest time of the year, water in the Mississippi was still warmer by at least ten degrees. That was after the hydroelectric impoundments had been put to use. Gar don't like cold water, so they moved out. The Corps of Engineers folks said they were going to mitigate for that. And in one sense of the word they did; that's what spawned trout fishing in Arkansas. But you tell me. What would you rather catch? A 150-pound alligator gar or a 10-pound rainbow trout?"

Charlie Burton confirmed Alter's suspicions in a spring 1970 article in *Arkansas Game and Fish Magazine:*

> The population of the big alligator gar has declined in recent years, especially in the White River, possibly due to the change in habitat by the release of cold water from the hydro-electric dams upstream. Consequently, the popular fishery in which the gar was sought by anglers using deep-sea tackle has disappeared.
>
> Destroying a gar was once comparable to slaying a dragon that was wreaking havoc on the countryside and devouring women and children. No doubt the gar's physical appearance caused this typecasting. He looks like a torpedo with teeth . . . and his dentures seem designed for biting holes in grain barges. As he lies almost motionless, near the surface of a stream on a

warm summer day, he appears to be waiting on some unsuspecting fisherman to dip a tasty finger into the water.

But the gar does not prefer fingers and toes. He does not even prefer bass or channel catfish. He prefers shad, minnows, and other small, rough fish. Some states are actively stocking gar as a fisheries management tool to help keep rough fish and game fish in proper balance. Yes, this fish, once feared and hated, is proving to be useful and desired in some instances.

With enough patience, you might still catch a gator gar in some of Arkansas's delta rivers. A big one turns up now and then—usually in a commercial fisherman's net in the Arkansas or Mississippi Rivers—but it's just coincidence when it happens. No one fishes for them anymore.

There is a lesson to be learned here. One of the most fantastic sport fisheries in the world was born and died in Arkansas in less than two decades. If only we had known then what we know now.

Yet still we feign ignorance. Alligator gar up to one hundred pounds are still fairly common in some southern waters—Choke Canyon and Sam Rayburn Lakes in Texas, the Blakeley River in Alabama, the Red River in Oklahoma, the Escambia and Choctawhatchee Rivers in Florida, the Atchafalaya River in Louisiana, brackish and saltwater bays and channels along the Gulf coasts of Texas, Louisiana, Mississippi, and Alabama. But we continue our "gar wars," striving for their annihilation. Most states fail to regulate their taking, claiming they are not sport fish.

Doug Stange said it perfectly in an April 1996 editorial in *In-Fisherman*:

> This is the second largest fish in North America. The stuff of Chamber of Commerce billboards. A monster in appearance and proportion. A fish that jumps higher and fights harder than any muskie.
>
> Large alligator gar need immediate protection from further overharvest. The objective, as always, is to harvest selectively, to use but not abuse, so generations yet coming can marvel at this monster.

Let's hope someone listens before it is too late.

Little Rock's In-Close Crappie

If you know the impact summer weather and water conditions have on crappie fishing patterns, and are willing to invest extra time to locate your quarry, July can produce outstanding crappie fishing on Arkansas's many first-class public fishing waters.

Among the finest summer crappie-fishing lakes are several in the heart of the Natural State near the capital city. Three of the largest, and best, of these are Lake Maumelle, Lake Winona, and Lake Conway, all less than an hour's drive from Little Rock. During July, crappie fishing pressure is relatively light on these lakes. On weekdays, especially, you're likely to find a peaceful atmosphere that adds an extra measure of enjoyment to your crappie-fishing excursions. Best of all, these three impoundments can provide blue-ribbon fishing for anglers wise to the ways of post-spawn "specks."

Let's take a closer look at this trio of crappie lakes and some of the fishing tactics that can help make your July outings a success.

LAKE MAUMELLE

Maumelle is the largest of Arkansas's many city-water fishing lakes. Owned by Little Rock Waterworks, the lake covers 8,900 acres eight miles west of Little Rock. Primary access is along State Highway 10 between Little Rock and Thornburg.

Maumelle harbors good numbers of jumbo crappie. They usually hold in deep-water haunts in July, but many anglers are able to entice them by vertically jigging small jigging spoons or jig-minnow combinations around deep points, humps, and creek or river channel dropoffs. Nearly all the timber on the lake bed was cut when the lake was impounded in 1957, so anglers can't rely on visible cover like dead snags and brush when trying to pinpoint fish. A sonar fish-finder unit is invaluable for locating underwater structure that concentrates schools of fish. Watch for signals indicating deep brush piles, humps of rocky rubble, and stump fields on the bottom in fifteen to thirty feet of water. This is where most big crappie will be.

One big handicap for Maumelle crappie anglers is the clear

water. To make the best of this situation, use only four- to six-pound-test monofilament, and remember the best fishing is during low-light periods—at night, early and late in the day, and during periods of cloudiness and rain. Make long casts whenever possible, and keep a low profile on the water. This helps avoid spooking finicky fish.

LAKE WINONA

Just south and west of Lake Maumelle is another central Arkansas crappie hotspot. Lake Winona, a Little Rock water-supply lake like Maumelle, is in the Ouachita National Forest, seven miles west of State Highway 9 at Paron.

Completed in 1938, Winona is among the oldest of the state's man-made public fishing reservoirs. Like Maumelle, it's clear much of the year, and though it's relatively small—1,240 acres—the average depth is thirty-five feet, with some holes dropping down to a hundred feet. These two characteristics—extreme depth and transparency—make light line important, not only to avoid spooking wary clear-water crappie, but also to get lures down to depths where fish are likely to be feeding.

During July, Winona's crappie frequent deep water, often holding along the channel of the Alum Fork of the Saline River, which was dammed to create the lake. Secondary creek channels branching off the main river channel also tend to concentrate crappie, and, as might be expected, a sonar fish-finder is helpful in pinpointing this type of underwater crappie structure. Watch the sonar for blips indicating suspended fish around stump beds, points, cuts, and other prominent features along the channel drops. Some blips will be catfish, bass, bluegills, or redear sunfish, which are also stocked in Winona, but many will be slab crappie waiting for a meal.

Small shad are the primary crappie forage in this impoundment, and artificial lures imitating these animals are good lure choices. A $\frac{1}{10}$-ounce silver jigging spoon allowed to flutter down through the water on slack line provides a convincing imitation of a dying shad and will often be nailed by a hungry crappie. Live minnows and $\frac{1}{16}$-ounce, silver, tinsel-tail jigs also are good producers.

During much of the summer, when the water temperature is warm, many crappie will be close to shore in dead timber near steep ledges. The fish also may be tightly schooled in brush on rocky points, anywhere from fifteen to thirty feet deep, depending on water clarity and sunlight. If it's a fairly dry month, and the water remains clear, the fish will drop down into deeper water, and anglers might catch them working a small jig-minnow combination bounced stair-step fashion down the points. When the water is highly colored after heavy rains, crappie may lie in shallow water, four to five feet deep, right up against steep banks. A good presentation in this case is to slowly work a live shiner below a bobber parallel to the bank face.

LAKE CONWAY

This 6,700-acre Arkansas Game and Fish Commission lake, adjacent to Interstate 40 in Faulkner County, has some of the most consistent action for big crappie anywhere in the state. Unlike many Arkansas waters, Conway's summer crappie fishing is usually equal to, if not better than, fishing during the spring spawning season. In July and August, one-and-one-half- to two-and-one-half-pound crappies are not uncommon.

Most summer crappie anglers use four- to eight-pound line on cane poles, fiberglass poles, or ultralight tackle and fish live minnows, tube jigs, or marabou jigs along inundated creek channels and lakes. The Green's Lake and Adam's Lake areas on the east side are good bets this time of year. The flooded timber adjacent the boat lanes at the Highway 89 bridge (just east of Interstate 40 at the Mayflower exit) is especially good for post-spawn fish, and plenty of big slabs are taken from this spot by anglers fishing from the bank on both sides of the highway bridge.

The lake also is jammed with man-made brush piles that hold plenty of summer crappie. Many anglers sink their own brush piles, and these hotspots can be found around boat docks and other areas throughout the lake at varied depths.

Some anglers use sonar units to locate good brush and treetop areas along lake-bed creek channels and holes. But patient fishermen without this high-tech gear can locate excellent crappie water simply by working visible cover. The key to catching post-spawn crappie is to keep moving from one spot of woody cover to another until a school of feeding fish is located. Most anglers vertically fish with jigs and minnows on a tight line directly above this cover; little tackle is lost this way. Drift-fishing or trolling for crappies is difficult on Conway and seldom practiced because of heavy timber and brush.

Summer crappie fishing can be tough at times, but anglers savvy to the ways of post-spawn slabs can catch plenty of dandies while fishing lakes Maumelle, Winona, and Conway. When the weather is pressure-cooker hot, crappie fishing on this trio of impoundments is hot, too. Get it while it's hot.

JULY

Consider the Carp

Have you ever intentionally caught a carp? That may seem like a ridiculous question to an angler in Arkansas where carp usually are considered trash fish. But not long ago, the lowly carp was a prize catch to the lucky fisherman. The carp was a highly valued, respected, and pampered food fish.

The common carp, a large member of the minnow family, has been cultivated as a food fish throughout Eurasia for at least four thousand years. It originally was found in the Asian watersheds of the Black, Caspian, and Aral Seas and may have been present in portions of western Europe and eastern Asia.

Carp have been a prized commodity for centuries. They were introduced to the ponds of Austrian nobility in 1227, and carp were transferred from the Danube River to Greece and Italy during the Roman Empire a millennium before. Carp were introduced to England in 1496 exclusively for the use of royalty.

As carp escaped royal ponds and populated more European waters, they became readily available to the average citizen. Many who emigrated to the New World left Europe having developed a taste for the rich fish. Yet, when they moved to America, many immigrants were aghast to discover this country had no carp. Jews, accustomed to using carp in the preparation of gefilte fish, were dismayed. So were many Scandinavians, Belgians, Austrians, French, and Germans who served carp at weddings, Christmas, New Year's, and birthdays. All assumed the land of milk and honey would have carp as well.

Thousands of people wrote their new government, asking that carp be made available. In 1876, the government heeded their request, transporting 345 carp from Europe and stocking them in ponds in Baltimore and Washington. In 1877, these carp produced over six thousand fingerlings that were shipped to applicants in twenty-four states. The spread of carp in North America had begun.

An 1874 report by Spencer Baird, head of the U.S. Fish Commission, said of the carp, "No other species . . . promises so great a return in limited waters." Baird also noted further benefits of the

Below Dardanelle Dam on the Arkansas River, an angler wages war with a hefty common carp.

carp, including "(1) its high reproductive rate, (2) its adaptability to artificial propagation, (3) its hardiness, (4) its ability to adapt to environmental conditions unfavorable to other fishes, (5) its rapid growth, (6) its good table qualities, (7) its harmlessness in its relation to other fishes, and (8) its ability to populate waters to their greatest extent."

From 1879 through 1896, the Fish Commission distributed 2.4 million carp. With the aid of special railroad cars with holding tanks, every state in the continental United States, except Montana, received fingerling carp by 1882.

At first, the profusion of carp met with a receptive market. Millions of pounds were purchased at fish markets in St. Louis, New York, Kansas City, Philadelphia, and other cities. But before the first decade of the twentieth century passed, the carp's short reign in America was coming to an end. Too successful in its new home, the carp was displacing more desirable species in public waters. Carp muddied formerly clear fishing waters and uprooted vegetation searching for food. As commercial harvest methods for saltwater fish improved, and beef, chicken, and pork became cheaper because of more efficient production methods, carp as a food fish fell out of favor. By 1896, the U.S. Fish Commission discontinued stockings.

In this country, the carp never recovered its former glory. Yet, in Europe, the carp still is held in high regard and ranks only behind rainbow trout and Atlantic salmon as a sport fish. It's considered one of the most difficult fish to catch, and an English "carpman" considers it good to hook and land a dozen of the wary fish during a thousand hours fishing.

Here in the United States, the carp is widely ignored. And when noticed at all, it's held in disdain.

Why do anglers look down on a fish prized by millions of anglers across the Atlantic? Why do they grimace at the thought of eating a fish still meticulously prepared by chefs in the finest European restaurants? Why do they thumb their noses at a fish esteemed throughout the Orient and the rest of the world?

There are good reasons. Carp muddy the water of lakes and streams. Prolific carp can crowd out game fish. Carp destroy fish and waterfowl habitat by uprooting aquatic vegetation. Carp adapt to the most polluted conditions produced by man and are often seen finning near the surface in stagnant water. Carp are not the type of fish most anglers would have mounted for the den wall.

Nevertheless, carp are here to stay, and they still possess the attributes that make them so popular in other parts of the world. They're challenging to catch, superb fighters, widely distributed, and abundant in many waters. Ten- to twenty-pounders hardly raise an eyebrow. The U.S. record weighed fifty-seven pounds, thirteen ounces, though Romania produced a carp over eighty pounds. The Arkansas record from Lake Hamilton (1985) weighed fifty-three pounds. Contrary to popular opinion in this country, carp also are superb food fish. In fact, the carp is said to be the most popular freshwater food fish in the world.

We're stuck with this bewhiskered alien, so why not make the best of it? If you want to broaden your fishing horizons and catch a different species of fish, one that's overly abundant and possesses all the qualities of a blue-ribbon sport fish, consider the carp. Following are some basic tips for catching the fish Izaak Walton described as "queen of the rivers."

TACKLE

A heavyweight carp moves with the power and speed of a striped bass, can outfight a largemouth, and makes a hefty trout look like a sissy. Carp fight long and hard, and, if hooked in weedy or brushy waters, it's a sure bet they'll entangle themselves and the line.

Knowing these things, the avid carp angler generally selects a medium- to medium-heavy rod with progressive taper, at least six feet long. The longer the rod (up to eleven or twelve feet), the better the angler's chances of handling a large fish.

Choose a medium-weight spinning reel possessing a good drag, one that can hold at least 120 yards of twelve-pound-test line. Spin-casting reels are OK if they have sufficient line capacity and a quality drag, but bait-casting reels provide resistance to the pull of the line when a fish starts a run, and carp are likely to drop the bait at the first hint of resistance.

Single and treble hooks are used for carp fishing, usually in sizes No. 6 through 2. They should have sharpened points and heavy-gauge wire construction, so they won't bend or straighten.

Quill or cigar bobbers often are used, but ball-shaped floats present resistance that often spooks biting carp. Have on hand an assortment of split shot, egg sinkers, and bank sinkers, and some small barrel swivels to use as sinker stops. A large landing net is a definite asset for handling big fish.

FISHING RIGS

Carp are bottom-feeders, and two bottom-fishing rigs will serve the carp angler in most situations. The first holds the offering in slow, steady river currents. To make this rig, tie a double surgeon's end loop on your line's end. Make the loop the diameter of a golf ball. Then use a Palomar knot to tie a No. 6 to 2 baitholding hook to the doubled line. Eighteen inches above the hook, make a dropper loop knot, and onto it tie a ¼- to ½-ounce bank sinker by way of another Palomar knot. Carp are smart and shy, so a rig like this with no swivels or other hardware usually works best.

The other rig, designed for still water, is simple to make. Thread a 1/2-ounce egg sinker on your line, then tie a barrel swivel to the line's end. To the other end of the swivel, tie an eighteen-inch section of ten- to fourteen-pound-test monofilament. To this leader, tie a No. 6 to 2 baitholding hook. Use a Palomar knot or improved clinch knot to tie the hook to the leader and to tie the leader to the swivel.

FISHING FACTS

The Arkansas carp angler typically uses whole-kernel corn, doughballs, or chunks of bread or half-boiled potato for bait. Carp strike other baits, natural and artificial, but these are among the best because carp relish them and other fish rarely mess with them.

One author on carp fishing states that corn is far and away the best of these baits. Another swears by half-boiled potatoes. Yet both agree that doughballs also are extremely productive and fun to prepare. Nearly every carp fan has his own special recipe concocted from ingredients that might include cornmeal, flour, sugar, vanilla, gelatin, anise extract, oatmeal, molasses, corn syrup, wheat germ, wheat flakes breakfast cereal, and/or peanut butter. Cornmeal, flour, and a sweet or pungent scent are the core of most recipes, but it's fun to experiment with your own variations.

To get you started, here's a dough-bait recipe from *Carp in North America,* published by the American Fisheries Society. The ingredients are one cup of sugar, two cups of white flour, and three cups of cornmeal. Mix the ingredients in a bowl. Slowly add water and mix to the desired consistency. If the dough needs stiffening, add more flour and cornmeal. To thin it, add more water. Flatten the ball, wrap it in a cloth bag, and place it in boiling water for twenty minutes. Cool the dough, then put it in a plastic bag and refrigerate. To add other fillers, blend them in before cooking. For scents, knead them in after cooking, once the mixture cools enough to handle.

Once the bait has been selected and prepared, the carp angler casts his rig to a likely looking spot, allows the bait to sink to the bottom, then tightens the line to remove all slack. The rod is held in hand or braced against a forked stick stuck in the ground. The reel is free-spooled so biting fish feel no resistance, and so the angler doesn't lose a rod to the quick run of a large fish.

Line movement indicates a fish has found the bait. Usually, carp pick up the bait and start swimming away. When this happens, set the hook hard and prepare for action. A hooked carp fights like a lassoed steer.

Carp occur in a wide range of Arkansas waters—large reservoirs, shallow ponds, swamps, delta rivers, mountain streams, even some tidal rivers and creeks. They bite year-round, even in winter, and can be caught throughout the day and night. Many experienced carp anglers do best at dawn and dusk, or at night, especially in summer.

Carp seek deep-water areas in winter, but during the rest of the year the best areas to fish are generally shallow, weedy habitats. In lakes and ponds, look for carp near vegetative cover in shallow bays, tributary mouths, and shallow flats adjacent to channel drops. Stream hotspots include shallow backwaters, the upper and lower ends of riffles, shallow pools, and shallow structure in dam tailwaters.

Like mosquitoes, carp are part of the Arkansas ecology whether we like them or not. It's not likely they'll exceed the popularity of fish like largemouth bass and crappie, but they're certainly due a measure of respect that is presently lacking.

The attitude most Natural State anglers have toward carp is perhaps summarized by an exchange of words I had one summer day with a bass angler who trolled past my carp-fishing hole.

"How's fishing?" he asked.

"Pretty good."

"Whatcha catchin'?"

"Carp."

"Really? What for?"

At that time, line started peeling off my reel, and I set the hook on a dandy carp. The fish threw spray into the air, then popped my line and was gone. The fisherman stared at the swirling water.

"That looked like a nice one," he said.

"Yeah. It was."

Then, sheepishly, he asked, "Mind showing me how to catch one?"

JULY

AUGUS

Battling Bowfins

"Try casting your worm by those bushes," I said to Larry Stark one hot August afternoon on an east Arkansas oxbow lake. He did as suggested and began crawling the lure over the muddy bottom. It traveled maybe three feet before it happened—something picked up the plastic worm and started off with it. No *thump-thump* as when a bass hits; something just picked up Larry's worm matter-of-factly and swam away with it. The worm obviously belonged to that something the minute it picked it up.

"Reel up the slack, Larry—fast!" I instructed. The "something" out there was now traveling at a steady clip straight toward the johnboat, creating a wake at the water's surface as it picked up speed. Larry spun the reel handle quickly, but to no avail. The fish was moving too fast. Then suddenly, astoundingly, the creature smashed head-on into the boat—*kerwhang!*—and made an about-face.

"Now you're in for it," I said.

Larry's slack-jawed face suddenly looked pale. He spun the reel handle furiously, and when the line tightened, he set the hook with a powerful backstroke. Something thrashed violently in the tannin-stained water, creating a huge boil that parted the carpet of green duckweed floating on the surface.

"Jumping Jehoshaphat!" Larry shouted, or something to that effect. His rod was doubled over, and his opponent was stripping off line, making the drag on his reel screech like a banshee.

The battle continued for perhaps two minutes, then the leviathan sounded, made a loop-de-loop around a heavy branch, and erupted from the water. It thrashed its scaly reptilian head side to side like a bulldog shaking a rat, then broke Larry's line like it was nothing more than rotten thread.

The battle finished, Larry slumped back in the boat seat and let out a long sigh.

"That, my friend, was a grinnel," I said, smiling.

Larry Stark, a resident of North Branch, Minnesota, called me

The bowfin is common in many of Arkansas's bottomland lakes.

the summer of 1992 to arrange a bowfin-fishing excursion. He was working on a book at the time, "Fishing America," which would describe trips to fish for different species in each of the fifty states. The target for Arkansas was bowfins, and I agreed to be Larry's guide.

We fished for bowfins three days in a variety of eastern Arkansas lakes. And in three days we never put a single bowfin in the boat. Not because we couldn't find them. We did. And we hooked our share. One nice bowfin, a five- or six-pounder, jumped over the corner of the boat before it busted my line. Several more monsters waged battles lasting several minutes. But the bowfins always came out on top. They usually do.

As his trip ended, Larry commented on this extraordinary fighting fish. "I always heard bowfins were nothing fish," he said. "Boy, was that wrong. I never imagined they'd put up such a battle."

The bowfin is a living fossil, the last surviving member of a family that swam the earth with the dinosaurs. It has several nicknames, including mudfish, dogfish, cypress trout, and blackfish. Arkansans know it best as "grinnel," though more vulgar monickers often are used by frazzled fishermen with broken lines, mauled lures, and shattered poles.

Bowfins are the stuff of legends. In Louisiana, for instance, folks say that a cooked "choupique" will uncook itself if left untouched overnight. In other parts of the South, some believe that, given a ritual burial during the proper moon phase, a bowfin will metamorphose into a live snake.

Though these tales obviously have no basis in reality, the truth about bowfins is no less astounding. For example, the bowfin's lung-like air bladder allows it to survive under remarkable conditions. James Gowanloch, in his book, *Fishes and Fishing in Louisiana*, wrote, "They have actually been plowed up alive in lowland fields of Louisiana, weeks after flood waters have fallen and the land has become dry enough for cultivation to begin." A Canadian report describes a bowfin that was dug up from the earth where it lived in a chamber four inches below the surface, one-quarter mile from the nearest river.

The bowfin is a primitive fish seldom sought by anglers, despite its supreme fighting ability.

Bowfins flourish in the rivers, oxbow lakes, bayous, and swamps of eastern and southern Arkansas. Fish are their preferred food, but they will consume almost any animal.

Jim Spencer of Little Rock, Arkansas, is one of few ardent bowfin anglers I've encountered. He's fished for the species throughout the South, and in 1973, he claims to have caught a bowfin on an Arkansas bayou that tipped the scales at an even twenty-two pounds—eight ounces heavier than the current world record from South Carolina. (The Arkansas state record weighed seventeen pounds, five ounces.)

"I wasn't particularly record-conscious in those days," Spencer said, "and after weighing the fish and showing it off, I gave it to a friend who fed it to his hogs."

Spencer went on to relate just how exciting fishing for bowfins can be.

"I once pitched a spinnerbait to the far end of a log and hustled it back to the boat. The lure was within two feet of my lowered rod tip, and I was about to lift it from the water when everything blew up in my face.

"It was possibly the most violent strike I'll ever see in my life, regardless of the species. No white marlin ever slashed a trolled skip-jack any harder than when that grinnel hit my fast-moving spinner.

"The water around the lure erupted like a miniature volcano, and it seemed that most of the displaced water landed on me. I set the hook purely out of fright, and when the fish felt the bite of the steel hook, it swapped ends and pulled off fifteen feet of line against the heavy drag before I could even get the rod tip up. It was all I could do to hang on to my fishing rod.

"I backed off a quarter-turn on the drag in case the fish decided to make another run. It was a good thing I did, because the fish shook its head a time or two and plowed off in a new direction. The fish ran off twenty feet of line this time, and I barely managed to stop it before the fish reached a log pile.

"But that run took the starch out of the fish, and a couple minutes later, I had the ten-pound bowfin beside the boat. It was still making short, powerful lunges in every direction, but I was finally in control."

Spencer leaned over the boat and used pliers to twist the lure free. "The grinnel lazed in the water two feet from my face, eyeing me sardonically," he recalled. "Then it gave a flip of its tail and was gone, leaving me with a well-chewed spinnerbait and another good soaking."

Most bowfins are caught by fishermen angling for other species. Crappie anglers regularly get their cane poles broken while fishing with minnows. Bowfins also test the rods of many bass anglers who fish Arkansas's bottomland waters.

When fishing specifically for bowfins, use the same tactics used when fishing for largemouth bass. Work lures around dead timber, weed beds, cypress trees, buckbrush, and other cover, and get ready for action. Your fishing tackle should be sturdy. I use a seven-foot, medium-heavy rod and a heavy-duty bait-casting reel spooled with fifteen- to twenty-five-pound-test monofilament. The new super-strong braided fishing lines made from Kevlar and other materials will probably work even better. These lines have no stretch, which enables better hook sets on bony-mouthed bowfins, and because they're extremely resistant to abrasion, they shouldn't be as prone to damage from the bowfin's sharp teeth. Heavyweight bowfins can easily bite through twenty-five-pound-test monofilament.

The variety of lures that will entice bowfins is as expansive as the variety of lures used for bass fishing. Black plastic worms have been my best producer, but I've also caught grinnels on spinnerbaits, spoons, crankbaits, jigs, and topwater plugs. Among natural baits, minnows and crawfish seem to be the top producers.

Sight-fishing for bowfins is one of the most exciting forms of the sport. In summer, bowfins often rest at the water's surface, gulping air to compensate for decreased oxygen levels caused by hot weather. The angler sights a bowfin on the surface, then casts a baitfish-imitation plug in front of it, allowing the lure to remain motionless except for an occasional twitch. If actively feeding, the bowfin will soon make a headlong dash for the plug. When it does, hang tight to your rod. The strike of a surface-feeding bowfin is like the strike of a lightning bolt, and the angler who's not prepared may find his favorite rod and reel headed for Davy Jones's locker.

Fishing for bowfins is best during warm months. They'll even hit in midday in summer when other fish slack off. My friends and I often fish for bream or crappie during the morning, then switch to bowfins when the panfishing action tapers off.

It's important to remember that the mouth of a bowfin is studded with dozens of small, razor-sharp teeth. And bowfins are notorious for making quick side swipes and clamping down on a finger or other body part when you least expect it. Handle live bowfins with great care, and carry pliers for removing hooks. If you plan to keep your catch, thump it on the skull with a fishing club before bringing it aboard.

Don't try to rush a bowfin to the boat. If possible, quickly work the fish away from cover and wear it down in open water.

And remember, bowfins aren't school fish, so you're not likely to catch more than one or two in a small area. Keep on the move, looking for new hideouts.

Arkansas has many waters with healthy bowfin populations. Most are in the bottomland areas of eastern and southern Arkansas.

My favorite bowfin-fishing locale is Dagmar Wildlife Management Area, seven miles west of Brinkley in Monroe County. Dagmar encompasses several bodies of water where bowfins grow fat and sassy. My favorite is Gator Pond, a twelve-acre borrow-ditch lake created when Interstate 40 was constructed. Fishing the brushy, log-infested edges of this lake often produces several bowfins in the three- to ten-pound range.

Six-acre Bowfin Overflow, another borrow-ditch lake adjacent to Interstate 40, is, as the name suggests, another superb bowfin honeyhole. This lake lies at Gator Pond's east end and is accessible only by dragging a canoe or other small craft over a levee between the two lakes. Because it's rarely fished, it produces bowfins in the super-heavyweight class.

Other Dagmar waters where bowfins are common include Robe Bayou, Hickson Lake, and Teal Pond.

Another top-notch bowfin area is White River National Wildlife Refuge in southeast Arkansas. White River encompasses over two hundred oxbow lakes, sloughs, bayous, and rivers where bowfins are plentiful. The lakes south of Ethel—Escronges, Bear, "H," Columbus, and others—harbor many big grinnel, and there's plenty of action found on bayous like Indian Bayou in the north end of the refuge, Essex Bayou in the middle reaches, and Scrubgrass Bayou in the south. Buck Lake, Little Moon Lake, Moon Lake, and Upper Swan Lake, all accessible from Highway 1 just east of St. Charles, also are worth checking out.

Bowfin anglers can find good fishing opportunities on many other Arkansas waters as well. Among the best are Felsenthal Reservoir on Felsenthal National Wildlife Refuge near Crossett, Horseshoe Lake in Crittenden County, Old Town Lake in Phillips County, Mercer Bayou in Sulphur River Wildlife Management Area in Miller County, the lakes and streams on Henry Gray–Hurricane Lake Wildlife Management Area near Bald Knob, and bottomland streams like Bayou Bartholomew, the L'Anguille River, the lower Saline and Ouachita Rivers, and Champagnolle Creek.

Although bowfins aren't noted for their table quality, people occasionally keep some to eat. In the 1930s, a state forester wrote, in Gowanloch's *Fishes and Fishing in Louisiana,* "The choupique is considered an essential food in the backwoods and hinterlands. These folks usually catch large amounts of choupique, behead them, clean them and split them up the back to the tail and then sun dry them and pack them away in dry salt, similar to the dry codfish. They are used for various dishes such as fishballs, jambalaya and gumbo."

For the best flavor, always clean the fish quickly, cut away any red meat along the lateral line, and pack the fillets in ice. If you let a bowfin die and clean it later, the meat becomes mushy and cottony. Even when properly cared for and prepared, the flesh is very strong tasting.

To make bowfin croquettes, boil bowfin fillets in a pot of water until the meat flakes easily with a fork. Remove the fish, allow it to cool, then flake the fish and add salt and sage to taste. Blend well, and fashion the mixture into thin patties. Turn each patty in cornmeal and fry in a hot skillet with a little shortening. Serve piping hot.

Bowfins are ignored by most Arkansas anglers. But these prehistoric fish have much to offer the angler in search of fish-fighting fun. Five- to ten-pounders are common in many Arkansas waters, and a hooked bowfin puts up a fight unrivaled by the sportiest of our game fish.

Give these misfits a try. There's always a chance you'll catch the next world record. Jim Spencer proved it's possible right here in the Natural State.

Just be sure you don't feed it to the hogs.

Drummin' Up Summer Fun

August is prime time for catching the freshwater drum, but it's doubtful many Arkansas anglers will give it a try. This unusual misfit is among the most underrated sport fish in Natural State waters, even though it's closely related to redfish, croakers, and other popular saltwater game fish.

The freshwater drum actually has many endearing qualities. It's common in large rivers and lakes throughout the state, strikes fiercely, battles tenaciously, and reaches weights exceeding fifty pounds. The drum also takes a wide variety of natural and artificial baits and is good to eat, a fact confirmed by the millions of pounds caught and sold by commercial fishermen each year.

Why, then, is the freshwater drum ignored as a sport fish, not only in Arkansas, but throughout its range? Perhaps it is scorned because it has large, rough scales and a down-turned mouth like carp, suckers, and other so-called "rough fish." Maybe it's because a hooked drum doesn't leap in spectacular fashion like trout or bass. Whatever the reason, those who've discovered the joys of drum fishing won't be miffed if other anglers continue to ignore this silvery maverick. After all, it's tough nowadays to find an abundant, easy-to-catch, hard-fighting, heavyweight sport fish that doesn't draw a lot of attention.

The freshwater drum is the drum family's only representative that doesn't live in saltwater. A distinctive silvery fish with a blunt nose, humped back, and long dorsal fin, it derives its name from a peculiar ability to make loud booming or "drumming" sounds. At night on some Arkansas waters, these intriguing sounds seem to come from all around, and those unfamiliar with the source may be puzzled by the weird noises emanating from the water.

The sound is believed to originate from muscles and tendons vibrating against the swim bladder. Males start drumming with the approach of the spring spawning season, and the drumming sounds

---

Freshwater drum are abundant, easy to catch, and good to eat. This nice specimen was caught in the Mississippi River.

become longer and more frequent as spawning peaks. The drumming diminishes through summer and ceases by September.

The freshwater drum also is commonly known as the gaspergou, sheepshead, white perch, and jewel-head. The last name developed because the drum has hard, pearl-like ear bones called otoliths. These "lucky bones," as they're called in the South, are believed by some to have supernatural powers and may have been used as charms by American Indians. Otoliths found in archaeological sites suggest that freshwater drum once reached weights up to two hundred pounds, far larger than the current fifty-four-and-one-half-pound all-tackle world record.

Having fished in the heart of Arkansas drum territory most of my life, I've caught many drum while fishing for bass, catfish, crappie, and other species. But like most Arkansas anglers, I always considered drum trash fish, and none were kept. That all changed on an August fishing trip with my son Josh.

Josh and I hoped to waylay some big bluegills on one of the oxbow lakes in Hurricane Lake Wildlife Management Area near Bald Knob. But as darkness fell, our stringers still were bare, a fact I attributed to the oppressive summer heat. Josh requested a last-ditch effort for catfish, so on the way out of the wildlife management area, we pulled off the road to fish where a small creek ran into Whirl Lake.

I wasn't prepared for the action that followed. My first hookful of night crawlers had hardly settled to the stream bottom when I got a ferocious strike. The fish fought deep and pulled hard like a big channel catfish, but, to my admitted dismay, it was instead a very large drum.

Josh, unencumbered by my own prejudices towards drum, cast another gob of night crawlers to the same spot. Again, there was an immediate response, and Josh was soon whooping with excitement as he thrilled to the tug of his own huge drum.

"Get it off quick, Dad," he said as I later tried to disgorge the hook. "I want to catch another one!"

I must admit I was quickly caught up in the excitement. Over the next hour, we caught sixteen drum. The smallest weighed under two pounds; the largest was over ten. Josh made me vow to come back again, and I readily agreed.

Back home, I related the story of our drum fishing excursion to my fishing buddy, Lewis Peeler.

"Sounds like a lot of fun, especially during this heat wave when nothing else is biting much," he responded. "Why don't you take me over there and show me how it's done?"

So it was, two weeks later, I found myself back at Hurricane Wildlife Management Area trying to drum up some more summer fun. This time, however, instead of fishing the small tributary creek on Whirl Lake, we fished the White River from a big white sandbar near the management area's eastern edge. Although we didn't catch any thirty or forty pounders, we caught drum continuously for four hours. We landed over a hundred before we quit counting, including several in the ten- to fifteen-pound range.

Following these trips, I decided to learn more about freshwater drum. Reading the scant literature I could find, I discovered drum are found throughout much of the central and eastern United States, from Canada south to Mexico and from the Missouri River drainages east to the Atlantic seaboard. Although seldom sought by sport fishermen, they are commercially important, and millions of pounds are harvested in trap nets and seines in the Great Lakes and most major river systems within their range.

Freshwater drum occur in bottomland rivers throughout Arkansas, including the Mississippi, Arkansas, lower White, St. Francis, Black, lower Saline, and lower Ouachita. They also are common in oxbow lakes adjacent to lowland streams, and in many man-made reservoirs, including lakes Hamilton, Bull Shoals, and Conway. The current state-record drum—a thirty-three-pound, twelve-ounce behemoth—was caught in Bull Shoals Lake.

Drum inhabit deep pools in Arkansas waters, dwelling near the bottom. Adults root through mud and debris for snails, small clams, crayfish, small fish, and insect larvae. Spawning occurs from April through July after adults move out of reservoirs and rivers into tributary streams. Average weights vary in different waters, but in many lakes and streams, two- to five-pound drum are abundant, and ten- to fifteen-pounders aren't uncommon.

Regardless of where you fish, confine your search for drum to bottom areas in water ten to forty feet deep, preferably where some

Sandbars in east Arkansas's White River provide ideal sites for summer drum-fishing excursions.

current is present. River fishing hotspots include deep pools around river sandbars, dam tailwaters, creek channel or river channel junctions, eddy washouts near outside bends, and fast-sloping gravel bars submerged in deep water. On the White River at Hurricane Wildlife Management Area, we found fish holding on a deep channel drop near midstream. On the Arkansas River, I often catch drum in the roiling tailwaters directly below dams. These fish often are associated with deep scour holes around rock wing-dams.

Good lake-fishing areas include creek and river channel drop-offs, underwater humps and depressions, tributary mouths, long rocky or sandy points, and riprap areas adjacent to deep water. Deep water on the lake side of a dam also can be productive.

Several baits will entice drum. I've found night crawlers to be exceptionally productive when gobbed on a small hook, but many drum anglers prefer a tail-hooked crayfish or minnow drifted along the bottom. Live shad, small jigs and spoons, crayfish- and baitfish-imitation crankbaits, and small spinners also are good producers. You can employ casting, trolling, or still-fishing as conditions or preferences dictate.

A major key to successful drum fishing is presenting your bait or lure on or very near the bottom where drum feed. Fish live bait tight-line style (no bobber), using a slip sinker just heavy enough to carry it to the bottom. Retrieve artificials so that they, too, work along the lake or stream bed.

One of the best traits of drum is the fact that they'll bite around the clock, even during the dog days of summer. If action slows during the day, however, try fishing at night. When temperatures are excessively hot, drum sometimes feed more actively during evening hours.

Drum are school fish and often concentrate in huge numbers within a small area. This means you may fish one area without so much as a nibble, while the action may be almost nonstop in a different location. Keep on the move until you find fish, but once you catch one, work the same area thoroughly for others in the school.

Drum have fairly small mouths, so I generally use No. 1 or 1/0 hooks, even when seeking large fish. Long-shanked hooks enable simple hook removal on most fish. But deep-hooked drum are always a problem, so carry a hook disgorger for releasing fish you don't want to keep.

Using ultralight tackle magnifies the pleasures of catching drum. Nevertheless, I've caught drum using everything from a tiny ultralight spin-cast combo spooled with two-pound-test line to a heavy-duty fourteen-foot spinning outfit rigged with thirty-pound line.

Don't overlook the table qualities of drum, either. One of the most widely mistaken notions about these fish is that they're "full of bones" or simply "not worth eating." Both these contentions are incorrect.

Contrary to popular belief, drum do not have the many small "Y-bones" found in carp and buffalo. Filleting your catch and removing all dark red meat along the lateral line produces boneless strips of meat that can be broiled, baked, fried, smoked, canned, or made into chowder. The cooked meat is firm, not flaky, but quite delectable.

"Poor Man's Lobster" is one simple drum recipe I often use. Cut drum fillets into finger-size pieces and drop into boiling, salted water. Cook the strips for three to four minutes each and remove from the water. Sprinkle each piece with salt and lemon juice and serve with melted butter and cocktail sauce.

Because their flesh is similar to that of their cousin, the redfish, freshwater drum also are a good substitute in blackened redfish recipes.

The freshwater drum won't ever replace such popular species as largemouth bass and crappie in the hearts of Arkansas anglers. But it certainly deserves more respect than it's getting. Though it's more bulldog than acrobat, the drum is a superb fighter. It is widely distributed and very common in many Arkansas lakes and streams.

The drum's finest virtue, though, is its cooperative nature. Summer's heat gives many fish lockjaw, but drum are eager biters, even at midday. Make a trip for drum this August, and you can be catching fish instead of just fishing.

AUGUST

Arkansas's Most Unusual Fish

Eels cause grown men to blench and bolt. I remember, for instance, watching a man land an American eel on the Arkansas River. When he set the hook, the angler was pleased with the reaction. The fish surged away, stripping line against the drag. The man grunted and cranked, smiling all the while.

When the two-and-a-half-foot fish was finally beached, the man's demeanor abruptly changed. I doubt he could have been more horror-stricken had he landed a twenty-foot anaconda. He dropped—no, threw—his rod, ran to his pickup, extracted a .357 revolver, and proceeded to plug the "beast."

When the gun was empty, he smiled again, turned to me, and said matter-of-factly, "I hate @#$+*&* eels."

I decided not to share my penchant for a delicately herbed *anguille au verte*.

"Don't judge folks by appearances alone," my mother used to say. Such is my advice to anyone getting acquainted with the American eel.

Ugly? No doubt about it. The eel is ugly to the bone. The slinky body is long and snakelike. Beady eyes punctuate a small, pointed cranium. Its underlip protrudes in a perpetual pout, and its slug-colored hide is ensconced with thick, snotty mucous. Hold a bass in one hand and an eel in the other and it's hard to believe they're both fish.

Despite their repugnant appearance, however, eels are edible, indeed delectable, and worthy opponents on rod and reel. Catch-and-release (or catch-and-run-away) may have been invented by Arkansans who caught eels by mistake, but among families of Old World origin, no Christmas is complete without eels for the table. This winter specialty keeps thousands of commercial fishermen at work netting tons of live eels to sell in Boston, Chicago, and New York.

I caught my first eel several years ago while catfishing from a houseboat on Arkansas's lower White River. Luck was with us. An eight-pound flathead adorned a stringer full of two- to five-pound channel cats.

A barred owl's eerie call echoed through the river bottom as I

Many fishermen are repulsed by the American eel's serpentine appearance, but these unusual fish are hard fighters and provide superb table fare.

threaded more night crawlers on my hook and cast downstream from the boat. The sinker hit mud. The line swung tight. Then, *tap. Tap, tap. Ziizzzzzzzzzz!*

Line peeled off my reel at a disconcerting rate. I reared back and set the hook. The fish fought much harder than the flathead I'd taken earlier.

"This is a big one," I said to my host, Bill Peace. "A hefty flathead or blue, I'd say."

"Just an eel," he replied.

"An eel, you say? You think a long skinny eel could fight like this? No way. How could it hold the water with a body like that? This is a big cat. You'll see."

"*You'll* see," he said.

The run that ensued was as magnificent as had been the strike. The hook and line held firm, and after a brief but violent struggle, I managed to turn the fish toward the boat. But no, it was off on another run and took several more yards of line. Five minutes passed before I brought it close enough to net. Thirty-six inches of slippery, slimy eel wriggled in the mesh.

"Don't look like no flathead I ever saw," Bill quipped.

"But you'll have to admit it fought like one," said I.

"Oh, indeed," Bill replied. "We catch a lot of them when we fish with night crawlers. And each and every one will make you think you've hooked the biggest catfish in the river.

"Can you believe it? Nobody fishes for these things on purpose. Tell someone you're going eel fishing, and they'll look at you like you have two heads. If they only knew . . ." He chuckled.

For twenty-three centuries, man speculated on the origin of the eel. Aristotle was convinced they rose spontaneously from mud. Roman scholar Pliny the Elder believed young eels came from bits of skin adults rubbed off on rocks. Scandinavians postulated another fish, the Aalmutter, was the "eel mother," while Italian fishermen espoused the idea that eels copulated with water snakes. In early America, it was generally assumed that eels arose spontaneously from horse hairs that fell in the water. These whimsical notions had support until 1924 when scientists discovered facts as astounding as the age-old beliefs were fantastic.

Adult American eels leave our coasts, from the Gulf of St. Lawrence to the Gulf of Mexico, and migrate to the open sea to spawn. Spawning was once thought to occur in the Sargasso Sea between Bermuda and the Bahamas, but more recent evidence suggests breeding grounds are much farther south. European eels, which are very much like American eels, spawn in close proximity to their cousins in a one-way migration spanning three years and five thousand miles. Young of each species disperse in opposite directions.

The spawning is cloaked in mystery; no one has ever witnessed it. Another unsolved mystery is what happens to adults after they leave our rivers. No adult eel has ever been taken in the open ocean. The spawning site was determined solely through collection of just-hatched eels.

Floating eggs hatch into "leptocephalus" larvae so unlike adults that they once were thought to be another species. Tiny and leaf-shaped, they are so transparent that print can be read through their body. They drift with the Gulf Stream, arriving at our coast in a year. At this time their resemblance to adult eels is unmistakable, and they are called "glass eels" or "elvers."

Male eels remain in brackish or fresh water near river mouths. Females ascend the rivers for hundreds of miles and are known to move overland on rainy nights around low falls and dams. Though sporadic in occurrence, they're found in nearly every state east of the Continental Divide. In Arkansas, they occur primarily in larger rivers, but they are no longer as common as they were prior to the construction of large dams. They hide by day in the cover of deep pools and feed at night on fish, crayfish, and invertebrates, live and dead.

Males average twelve to eighteen inches. Females reach fifty-two inches and exceed seven pounds, though the average is much smaller. The all-tackle world-record is an eight-pounder from New York. The Arkansas state record is a three-and-one-half-pound eel caught in Lake Dardanelle in 1993.

Sometime between age five and twenty, females migrate downstream. They and the mature males change from olive-green to silver, cease feeding, and move out to sea. Once offshore, they disappear over the continental shelf. Like Pacific salmon, they die after spawning, and, almost miraculously, the minute larvae find their way back to the shores of their ancestors.

Fishing for eels can be as strange as the fish themselves. Rob Buffler, in his book *Fishing for Buffalo,* reports, "Because eels sometimes actually leave the water and crawl up on land, they are the only fish (except walking catfish) that can be caught by casting *away* from the water . . . Eels feed on worms in low-lying areas, so we key in on these spots, casting to places on land where an eel might hold."

In a July 1996 issue of *Virginia Wildlife,* Jack Randolph described another unusual fishing technique—bobbing for eels—that requires no hook. "One by one, the nightcrawlers are threaded on fine sewing thread by running the needle completely through the worm from one end to the other," he wrote. "When you had about six feet worth of worms you wrap them into a ball and tie the ball with stout line.

The line, about a cane pole length, is tied to the tip of a cane pole and you are ready to fish. In theory the eel would grab the bob and the thread would become entangled in its teeth."

In extremely cold areas, eels lie in mud during winter. In some states, they can be taken by probing repeatedly the mud of river bottoms with a gig.

Most eels are caught using more conventional fishing techniques. Rig as you would when bottom fishing for catfish; bait your hook with a gob of night crawlers, a crayfish, or a minnow, then let your rig swing tight in the current. Even at night, when most eels are caught, you'll have no trouble detecting a strike. Eels hit hard and fight like much larger fish.

To "deslime" a live eel, place it in a container of coarse salt. To remove the skin, nail the head to a board or secure it with a loop of cord, cut a ring around the head with a knife, then use pliers to skin it like a catfish.

Or try the method Greg Gosik of Highland Springs, Virginia, says his grandfather taught him. "Just cut a ring around the head, peel just a small part back (a half inch), take a piece of strong paper like grocery bag paper and wrap it on the eel at the cut. Hold the head in one hand and pull the paper and skin with the other. Comes off easy."

Eels have a delicate texture and full flavor. They're excellent smoked, grilled, fried, baked, and in soups. One simple way to cook them is to fillet the meat, boil for thirty minutes, drain, season with salt and pepper, then dip in beaten eggs and roll in bread crumbs. Fry for five minutes, then serve with hot spaghetti sauce poured on top.

We won't pretend the American eel isn't one of the strangest fish swimming. But like the old saying goes, "You can't judge a book by its cover." Don't overlook the fine sporting and culinary qualities of this, one of Arkansas's most unusual and neglected fish.

Get the Jump
on Summertime Whites

Sunrise that summer day was spectacular. Broad strokes of tangerine orange painted the flowing waters where the White and Mississippi Rivers unite in southeast Arkansas. The sun was a crimson orb on the eastern horizon.

Little eddies of water danced past the drifting johnboat. The air was still and hot. My fishing companion, Bill Peace, shaded his eyes with a hand, as if saluting the dawn.

"There. There they are," he said, pointing to starboard.

A fountain of inch-long shad spritzed from the water, flashing like silver coins skipped across the smooth surface of the river. I glimpsed a fin beneath the fountain, and the swirl of a predator's tail.

Bill flipped on the trolling motor and moved us quickly toward the breaking fish. "Get ready," he said. "The fun is about to begin."

The surface of the water now churned like a boiling cauldron. Perhaps half an acre was so disturbed, as marauding hordes of white bass began a feeding frenzy unlike anything I ever saw. Shad spurted from the water in all directions, struggling to escape the ravenous predators below.

I fired a cast into the melee, and the instant the jig touched down, I felt—and saw—a vicious strike. Bill was ready now, too, and in less time than it takes to tell it, he, too, was battling a hefty white bass. The fish fought furiously, but we brought them quickly to the boat, shook them off the hook, and cast again. The response to each cast was almost instantaneous, and once again we savored the powerful, circling run of a sizable white bass.

The action went on cast after cast for the better part of an hour, then the school dispersed, and the river was once again calm. I would like to tell you exactly how many fish we caught during those sixty minutes, but in all honesty, I cannot. We released every one, and the adrenaline surge I experienced precluded any possibility of accurate mathematics. There were scores, though—of that I have no doubt. And that hour of ultralight fishing encompassed some of the most mind-boggling fishing action I've ever experienced.

Topwater fishing isn't the only way to catch white bass, but it's certainly the most exciting. One writer described this type of fishing as a "sensory overdose." You see strikes. You feel strikes. You hear strikes. And the action continues minute after minute until the fish disperse or you surrender to exhaustion.

If you'd like to experience it yourself, now is one of the best times to try, for summer offers some of the year's most consistent topwater action for white bass. Small, young shad—the principal prey of white bass—are feeding on plankton near the surface, especially early and late in the day. White bass follow in sometimes vast schools, making periodic raids to gorge on the baitfish. Casting to these surface-feeding schools is called "jump-fishing," because the bass, the baitfish, and the anglers are jumping here and there during the course of these feeding frenzies.

"The junction of two big rivers is a great place to catch summer whites," says Peace. "But it's not the only place. Anywhere there's water coming into a river is good—a creek mouth or a river run (chute) that connects an oxbow lake to the river. The whites will be most active where there's some clear water. For instance, when water is dropping out of the oxbow lakes, it runs across the woods and into the river. The river itself may be muddy, but the whites are usually where the clear water from the oxbows is flowing in."

Another location for first-rate white bass action is the tailwater channel just below the lock in a navigation structure. Barges and other boats enter the lock, then the water is raised or lowered so the craft can continue its travel.

"When they're releasing water out of the locks, white bass really go crazy," says Peace. "The water is swift, stirring up baitfish, and the whites come there to work over the schools. In this situation, you're also likely to catch some skipjack herring, and even some striped bass and black bass that are feeding with the whites. Anytime that water starts running, the action heats up."

Peace makes the most of surfacing whites by throwing tandem-rigged lures into their midst and, often as not, catching two fish per cast. He has two basic lure combinations he uses, his favorite being a tandem rig with two ½-ounce tube jigs. Both jigs are tied to the main line, one above the other, and worked through the school.

"In clear waters, lots of fishermen prefer shad-colored lures," he notes. "But this isn't necessary, or even preferable, in a big delta river due to water clarity. Darker colors are better, because fish can see them better in dingy water. Black and blue are two of the best colors in this situation."

Another combination Peace favors is a ½-ounce jig tied above a ⅛-ounce jig with a small safety-pin spinner. The heavier jig stays well beneath the upper lure at a level where larger whites often are holding. Double hookups are common.

"This is a killer rig, especially when you use black-and-chartreuse tube bodies," he says. "Retrieve it through whites breaking on top, and you can catch a boatload."

Many summer white bass anglers use a run-and-gun technique to get within casting range of surfacing fish. When they spot fish surfacing in the distance, they gun their outboard and head for the action, cutting the engine at the last minute, cocking the boat to one side and drifting in on bass before they have a chance to go down. Peace prefers a quieter, more stationary approach.

"Once we've spotted fish breaking on top, I prefer to move in using my trolling motor, being as quiet as possible to avoid spooking the fish and causing them to sound," he reports. "The fish will come up, stay up a while, then go down again. Then, usually, they'll come back up again. Several schools may be working the same general area, and while you're fishing, you may look and see whites working here, there, and yonder.

"Most anglers have a tendency to want to move as soon as a school goes down. But I've found it's better to stay in one place until I know for sure the fish are gone. Often, the action will start up again in a few minutes, sometimes within casting distance of your boat. Patience pays off."

Big bottomland rivers provide thrilling hot-weather action for topside whites, but large man-made reservoirs are the preferred fishing waters of many Arkansas anglers. If substantial populations of gizzard and/or threadfin shad are present, these waters also may be jump-fishing hot spots.

One prime lake for surface-schooling white bass is 28,220-acre Beaver Lake near Fayetteville in the northwest Arkansas Ozarks. Beaver is a U.S. Army Corps of Engineers impoundment that frequently yields "schoolies" as large as three pounds, although the average caught by Beaver Lake regulars like Brad Wiegmann weighs about one to two pounds.

"August and September are the best months for catching whites on top," says Wiegmann, who's been a fishing guide on Beaver Lake for nearly a decade. "In September last year, my wife and I caught ninety-seven in one hour.

"Two of the best places to look for them are around feeder creeks and over long points. These areas may hold whites day after day. Look for feeding white bass by boating up and down the lake, or look for other boats gathered together. Most folks won't mind you joining the action if you're considerate enough to work your way slowly toward the school."

Anglers who fish the jumps often rely on birds to guide them to the action, and Wiegmann is no exception. He watches for gulls hovering over schools of whites and picking off dead or crippled shad left by the gluttonous fish. If there's no gull action, he looks for surface activity—shad or white bass breaking water.

"At times you'll move in close and you'll notice the shad are real skittish," Wiegmann notes. "They'll be zipping and moving real fast, skipping out of the water. The white bass are watching for that action, and that's when they're gonna start breaking. Smart anglers are ready for action."

Wiegmann prepares by rigging some rods with small spinners or topwater lures, and others with small spoons or crankbaits. Worden's Roostertail spinners (¹⁄₁₆ to ¼ ounce) are, he says, "the best bait for breaking white bass, bar none." But he also uses topwaters like the Smithwick Devil's Horse, the Boy Howdy, Cordell's Crazy Shad prop bait, small buzzbaits, Heddon's Zara Pup, Storm's Chug Bug popper, and subsurface lures like Norman's Little N crankbait, Rapala's Shad Rap, Bagley's Killer B, and Luhr-Jensen's Crocodile spoon. Shad patterns and chartreuse work best in Beaver Lake's clear water, he says.

"When you see fish breaking, sit down and motor over close," he says. "Put your trolling motor down so you can follow the school, then stay so you're about a cast away. Just before the fish start breaking, you may want to starting throwing a spoon or other subsurface lure. Then once they're coming up, start throwing topwater baits or small spinners. When they go down again, try a spoon again. A big school of whites will tend to break up into several smaller schools if you stay with them. But stay with one school until you don't catch any more fish in that area."

For Wiegmann, typical white bass tackle consists of a six-foot, medium-action rod and a bait-casting reel spooled with twelve-pound-test line for casting heavier lures, and a six-foot spinning rod and spinning reel spooled with six-pound-test line for smaller lures.

"It's a good idea to have something with heavier line on it close at hand," he says. "Usually whites will be a consistent size within a school. Some schools will hold mostly big ones; some will hold mostly small ones. The average size is about a pound, but there are times when two- to two-and-a-half-pounders are pretty consistent.

"The thing you must remember is black bass, hybrid stripers, and stripers often run in or near the schools of whites, at least here in Beaver Lake. And you never know when you could end up with something really big on the end of your line."

Like most fishermen adept at fishing the jumps, Wiegmann has learned that school fish often adhere to a strict schedule. Barring weather changes, they tear into shad at about the same place and the same time day after day. What the surfacing schedule hinges on, of course, is the daily movement of shad throughout the reservoir, but the feeding binges in which white bass drive shad to the surface may occur so regularly you can set your watch by when the first school shows up.

"Early in the morning and late in the evening are best for this type of fishing," Wiegmann says, "because that's when the whites are ganging up on shad. During the day, it usually slows up. The best times are an hour to an hour and a half before sunset or after sunrise. Sometimes you'll get good schooling action for twenty minutes. Sometimes they'll come up and go right back down. Some days are much better than others. Success is mostly a matter of how much patience you have."

Although their fishing techniques vary somewhat, Bill Peace and Brad Wiegmann are in total agreement when summing up their fascination with jump-fishing.

"I guide for striped bass, black bass, and other kinds of fish, too," says Wiegmann. "But for pure, out-and-out, fish-a-minute fun, nothing beats jump-fishing for summer whites. I love it."

Peace is even more to the point.

"You'd have to be legally dead for this kind of fishing not to excite you."

Amen to that.

AUGUST

SEPTEMBER

Arkansas Striper Bonanza

It's a little-known fact, but Arkansas was the first state to stock striped bass in inland lakes.

Striped bass live in saltwater and spawn in freshwater. But in the 1940s, biologists discovered stripers can live in freshwater impoundments with no ill effects. Dam construction in South Carolina in the early 1940s trapped stripers in freshwater lakes, and by 1950 these fish were growing well and reproducing prolifically.

The presence of stripers in Arkansas is attributable to Riley Donoho of Fort Smith, appointed to the Game and Fish Commission in 1956. Donoho was visited by a fellow who told him about a saltwater fish, the striped bass, landlocked in South Carolina's Santee-Cooper lakes. The stripers were described as terrific fighters weighing up to fifty pounds.

Donoho took the message to the commission and received approval to send men to South Carolina to obtain stripers. In November 1956, four nights of seining produced 1,500 two- to ten-inch striped bass. These were kept in a holding pond before transport, but all died. Seining started again, and, eventually, 350 fingerlings were hauled to Arkansas. Two hundred seven survived the trip. One hundred eighty were placed at the Lake Hamilton Fish Hatchery, and 27 were stocked in Lake Ouachita. This was the first introduction of stripers in Arkansas waters.

Plans were made to collect adult fish prior to spawning season in spring 1957. It was thought that stocking adults would save several years in establishing a reproducing population. In April 1957, eighty-two adult fish from South Carolina survived the trip to Arkansas. Thirty-three went into Lake Greeson, and forty-nine into Lake Ouachita. Efforts in 1958, 1959, and 1960 produced additional stripers for stocking Lake Ouachita.

To the biologists' disappointment, these early stockings were ineffective. The fish didn't spawn in inland lakes. Methods for

This 51-pound striped bass, one of the heaviest on record in Arkansas, was caught in Lake Ouachita, one of the state's premier striper hotspots.

producing large numbers of striper fry had to be developed before a transplant was successful.

Research in South Carolina in the early 1960s produced effective methods for producing fry fish by hormone-induced spawning. Arkansas began obtaining more fish, and during 1965 and 1966, 3.4 million fry were stocked in Lake Dardanelle. Unfortunately, these efforts also failed. The fry died or were eaten by predators. None of the early fry stockings produced an inland fishery for striped bass.

Arkansas began studying methods of rearing stripers to fingerling size in hatchery ponds. By the mid-1960s, this was accomplished. Seventeen percent of the fry survived to fingerling size in 1966, and that fall 63,617 fingerlings were successfully stocked in Lake Dardanelle. Over the next nine years, over 2 million fingerlings were stocked in Arkansas impoundments, and striper fisheries were established in lakes Dardanelle, Norfork, Greeson, Maumelle, Beaver, Bull Shoals, and Ouachita. Since then, striped bass fisheries also were established in lakes Catherine and Hamilton, in the Red River, Little River, lower Ouachita River, Mississippi River, and additional reaches of the Arkansas River.

Today, the striped bass is considered one of state's finest trophy sport fish. Stripers up to thirty pounds are common in several reservoirs and rivers, and fish over fifty pounds always are possible.

Because stripers reproduce only in the Arkansas River, the Game and Fish Commission maintains populations through stocking. Most years, over a million are stocked in Arkansas waters.

Stripers are abundant in some waters and provide great opportunities for those seeking trophy-size fish, but they still rank low among the fish favored by Arkansas anglers. A 1987 fishing preference survey found that striped bass ranked seventh among the sport fish fished for most frequently. Only 3.2 percent of the survey respondents said stripers are the fish they seek most often. Largemouth bass, crappie, catfish, trout, bream, and smallmouth bass all ranked higher.

A 1984 study produced similar results. Striped bass ranked ninth behind largemouth bass, crappie, catfish, trout, bream, smallmouth bass, walleye, white bass, and hybrid striped bass.

Why aren't Arkansans more interested in striper fishing? 1984 survey participants listed seven reasons. Almost 23 percent said they didn't have enough time to fish; 20.4 percent didn't regard stripers as desirable; 19.8 percent said they didn't know how to catch stripers; and 18.7 percent didn't know where to catch them. The remaining reasons given for not seeking stripers were it's too far to travel to catch them (11.4 percent), equipment is too expensive (6 percent), and there are too many people seeking stripers to allow for an enjoyable trip (1.1 percent).

We can't help those without time to fish, but let's address other issues for those wanting to catch these freshwater giants.

First, let's look at the striper's desirability. If you've never hooked one, you've missed one of the greatest thrills in Arkansas fishing. Ten- to forty-pound stripers are often caught in this state, and fish this size are among the most solid fighting adversaries in freshwater. Hook one, and you're in for one of the most exciting battles of your lifetime.

Despite popular misconceptions, stripers are excellent table fare. Many people don't properly care for their catch, with poor quality meat as the result. Ice your fish soon after it's caught, and remove dark red meat along the lateral line. The flesh is white, flaky, and well-flavored. The secret of cooking stripers lies in the freshness and proper care of the fish, not in gourmet recipes.

Not knowing proper fishing techniques also inhibits many would-be striper anglers. Reading these basics should prove helpful.

In spring, stripers school in small areas, and locating and catching them is easier than during other seasons. In spring, stripers migrate from main lakes up major tributaries on spawning runs. These migrations are halted by dams, so tailraces below dams are prime fishing areas.

Most tailrace striper fishermen anchor in fast water and cast baits upstream, letting them bounce along the bottom. Others work topwater plugs or fish live bait below the gates. Tailrace pros prefer bucktail jigs or shad-imitation grubs. Also, shad or other live baits are hooked and tight-lined or worked below a bobber. Lines testing twenty-five to sixty-five pounds aren't out of place, and a long, stiff rod is a necessity.

In summer, stripers move to deep water following shad and searching for suitable temperatures. Locate them using sonar to probe channels, falling points, steep banks, and other deep-water habitat. Most stripers will be in seventy-two degree water, and once fish are located, baits are lowered to them.

Summer striper anglers use jigs, spoons, or live bait to catch fish along river channels, off deep points, or in areas with a constant flow of fresh, cool water. In some lakes, deep-water trolling with down-riggers catches summer stripers. Spoon jigging also is productive.

Autumn finds striped bass schooling and chasing shad on the surface. Action often continues day after day in the same locales. Fishermen watch the water surface for feeding fish, then rush in and cast before the stripers dive. Topwater plugs or light-colored jigs popped across the surface draw strikes when fish are surfacing.

Winter striper fishing varies with water and weather conditions. Surface action may continue, but some fish move deeper. Rock riprap, deep creek mouths, underwater timber, and deep points and break lines where rivers meet lakes are good areas. Vertical jigging with spoons and jigs is good. Trolling deep-running crankbaits with jig trailers also works.

Many anglers say they'd don't know where to go to catch stripers or that good striper lakes are too far from home. Because there are only fourteen Arkansas waters with established striper fisheries, it's true good striper fishing isn't always conveniently located. But for those willing to make the effort, there's plenty of superb fishing to be found.

Bull Shoals Lake shouldn't be overlooked, for there, in May 1987, a state-record 53-pound striper was taken. The Missouri portion of Bull Shoals has produced a 47-pound, 4-ounce striper.

Many consider Lake Ouachita Arkansas's top striper lake. The lake produced a 51-pound striper in March 1988 and three previous record holders—48 pounds, 40 pounds, and 40 pounds, 9 ounces. Twenty-pounders are common, and 30- to 50-pound fish frequently are taken. Ouachita could produce Arkansas's next state record.

Beaver Lake has given up several 40-pound-plus state-record stripers, the largest weighing 45 pounds, 12 ounces. The lake record on Greeson is an impressive 39 pounds, and numerous stripers over 25 pounds are taken there yearly. Fifteen- to 20-pound stripers are common in the Arkansas River, Lake Maumelle, and Lake Norfork.

Granted, catching a big striper isn't easy. It takes knowledge, hard work, hours on the water and lots of luck to be successful. But thanks to the efforts of the Game and Fish Commission, these exciting sport fish are no longer just creatures of the ocean. The striped bass, once found only in saltwater, is now available in Arkansas's freshwater impoundments. And those willing to make the extra effort can experience fishing thrills galore.

SEPTEMBER

Rod-and-Reel Gar

Line peeled off the spool of Lewis Peeler's spinning reel with an ominous *zizzzzz*.

"Not yet," Dean Peace coached. "You've gotta let him run."

The monofilament continued feeding out, and I wondered if Lew would have enough to play the fish once he set the hook.

"This is the hardest thing to learn about gar fishing," Dean said. "You have to let the fish run until you can't stand it anymore, then you let him run some more. When he stops, that means he's turning the bait to swallow it. Once it's down, he'll start moving off again. That's when you set the hook."

"If he doesn't stop soon, he'll have all my line!"

In the lantern light, I could see beads of sweat running down Lew's face. His shirt was soaked with perspiration, and mosquitoes fogged around his head. In the river before him cruised dozens of long gar as thickly laid as fence pickets.

Suddenly, the clicker on Lew's reel fell silent.

"He's stopped," Dean whispered. "Steady now. Don't do anything till he runs again."

All was quiet for a minute or so, then it started again. *Click. Click. Click. Click-click-click. Zizzzzzzzz.*

"Now!" Dean shouted. "Now!"

Lew reared back on the rod, once, twice, and again, and the dark water opened with a roar to let out a fish that seemed as long and thick as a Civil War cannon. The huge thing flipped clear over, turning uppermost its white belly, and fell back into the water with a tremendous crash. The spray from its splashing sparkled in the moonlight.

The run that ensued was as magnificent as had been the strike. The hook and line held firm, and, after a brief but violent struggle, Lew turned the big gar toward the boat. But no, the fish was off on another run, and it took the remaining yards of line. Snap! Lew's rod whipped straight and a remnant of limp line trailed on the water.

Considering their extraordinary fighting ability, it's surprising so few Arkansas anglers pursue gar. Here, a shortnose gar puts up a battle for a White River angler.

"That was a *big* gar," Lew exclaimed.

"Darn right, and the third we've hooked," I replied. "Too bad we didn't bring heavier tackle."

"I might as well have hooked a passing barge," he said. "I couldn't do anything with him."

"Can you believe it?" said Dean, laughing. "Nobody fishes for these things. Tell someone you're going gar fishing, and they'll look at you like you're a Martian. If they only knew . . ."

Despite their stupendous fighting ability, gar have earned little respect among anglers. In fact, that's probably a bit of understatement. Venomous snakes and rabid skunks get as much respect as gar, and when a gar is brought alongside a boat, the typical reaction is to smash its head with a paddle and toss it back for the cannibals. Most fishermen absolutely despise them.

Why such hatred? The creature's menacing appearance provides one reason. The long, snake-like body is covered with a wicked-looking armor of thick, interlocked scales. The gar has an incessant smirk accentuated by rows of sinister, needle-sharp teeth studding its jaws. Look into the eye of this reptilian outcast, and you get the distinct impression that, given the chance, it would chew your legs off, and perhaps a few other appendages as well.

Some folks contend gar aren't fit to eat, while others curse them as gluttonous scourges of sport fish. Still others dislike the gar's uncanny knack for stealing bait and mangling artificial lures.

No one cannot deny, however, that the gar is a noteworthy opponent on rod and reel. These powerful fish race and jump like tail-hooked tarpon, and landing a true heavyweight is one of freshwater fishing's most exciting challenges.

Four species of gar inhabit Arkansas. The most common and widespread is the longnose gar, which is found throughout most of the eastern United States. It's abundant in many of the state's large streams and reservoirs and frequently weighs 10 to 15 pounds. The National Fresh Water Fishing Hall of Fame all-tackle world record from Texas's Trinity River weighed 50 pounds, 5 ounces. This gar's long, slender "needlenose" sets it apart from other species.

The spotted gar has an affinity for the quiet, weedy waters of lowland lakes. Most are small, 2 to 3 pounds average, but the world record from Lake Seminole, Florida, tipped the scales at 28.5 pounds. Unlike most other species, the spotted gar has distinct spots on the head, body, and all fins.

The shortnose gar ranges through most of Arkansas. It tolerates muddy, turbid waters better than most other gar and, as a result, is common in our larger rivers. Oxbows, reservoirs, and other quiet waters also provide a home. This is the smallest gar species, rarely over two feet and 3 to 5 pounds. The broad, stubby snout distinguishes it from the longnose. To separate it from the spotted gar, count the scales along the lateral line—fifty-eight or less on the spotted, sixty or more on the shortnose.

Largest of the gar is the alligator gar, a fish that commonly weighs 100 to 150 pounds and reaches a documented nine feet, nine inches in length and 302 pounds. This fish inhabits large rivers, lakes, bays, and coastal marine waters from central Texas to western Florida and north to southern Illinois, but nowhere is it common. The gator gar is unmistakable, deriving its popular name from the short, broad snout similar in appearance to that of an alligator.

June, July, August, September—these four months serve up Arkansas gar fishing at its finest. In good waters, you'll have little trouble finding fish. They're usually near the surface and rolling noisily, especially near dawn and dusk and at night. A lunglike air bladder allows them to gulp air to aid the gills in breathing.

Gar inhabit all types of waters from small creeks to giant impoundments, but the best fishing is in oxbow lakes, bayous, and sluggish delta rivers. Once you're on the water, look for these predators in the same areas you'd pick for catfishing. River hotspots include lock and dam tailwaters, outside stream bends, sandbar or river channel abuttals, quiet backwater pools, and the mouths of in-flowing tributaries. On lakes, key your efforts in shallow reaches near the edges of woody and weedy cover.

If you want to catch a big gar, 20 pounds or more, it's imperative to use heavy tackle—30- to 80-pound-test line, a stout rod, and a sturdy reel with an excellent drag. For the smaller, more common gar, a durable rod and reel with 15- to 25-pound-test line may be adequate. Most serious gar anglers also use several feet of steel leader as insurance against the gar's sharp teeth and violent thrashing.

The longnose gar sometimes is dubbed "needlenose," a reference to its long, slender, toothy beak.

Fishing topwater plugs is the ultimate form of gar fishing fun, but to be successful, the angler must be endowed with an extraordinary measure of patience. The angler sights a gar on the surface, then casts a baitfish-imitation plug a few feet in front of it, allowing the lure to remain motionless except for an occasional twitch. If actively feeding, the gar will soon propel itself toward the bait with a furtive flick of its fins. There will be no headlong dash for the plug as you might expect. Instead, the gar will move very slowly, thinking itself disguised as a stick or log.

Do not move the lure when you see the gar swimming toward it. If the bait remains still, the gar will swim forward until the lure is alongside and very near its head.

This is where the fun really begins. The gar will remain stock-still so long as the lure remains motionless. But give it just the slightest wiggle and bam! The gar gives a sudden, convulsive, sideways jerk of its head and grabs the intended prey between its jaws. In the next instant, the angler tries to set the hook with several hard upward thrusts of his rod. If he's lucky, one of the trebles will be driven into the bony snout, and the gar will take to the air in a dazzling show of aerobatics. If not, he targets another gar and prepares for another round of fun.

Another successful gar-fishing tactic employs a four- to six-inch length of ⅜-inch nylon rope attached to a wire leader. The fibers on the loose end of the rope are unraveled, bucktail style. This "lure" is then cast near surfacing gar, which seem to find it irresistible. When one strikes, the nylon threads tangle in its teeth, holding it securely while the angler plays it in—if he's lucky. No hooks are required, and it really works.

Another clever technique uses a lasso of sorts. A noose of thin, strong wire is made, and a baitfish is run through with the wire, so it's strung on the loop. The idea is to get the gar to thrust its bill through the loop or to seize the wire while trying to get the fish. A quick yank then snares it by the bill and the excitement begins.

Dean Peace of Jonesboro, Arkansas, uses a slightly more conventional rig when fishing for gar near the juncture of the White and Mississippi Rivers. He prefers live, four- to six-inch-long shiners for bait and rigs them on a 5/0 to 6/0 treble hook tied six inches or so below a bright orange, four-inch-diameter bobber.

"You'll catch a few gar using a single hook," Dean told me the night Lewis Peeler and I fished with him. "But your chances of hooking one are greater if you use a well-sharpened treble hook. I run two of the three hooks through the shiner, then cast the rig upstream and let it float back through schools of gar feeding on the surface. The big bobber is easier to see at night and doesn't seem to bother the fish at all."

On the August night when I fished with Dean, this rig proved extremely productive. The bobber would dive like a submarine when a gar took the shiner, then, following Dean's advice, we'd wait for the fish to stop, swallow the bait, and begin a second run before setting the hook. The response was always instantaneous—several feet of thrashing, splashing gar testing our prowess with a rod and reel. Often as not, the big bruisers were just too much to handle on the bass tackle we were using. But before the night was over, we managed to land a few longnose gar in the ten- to fifteen-pound range.

Sitting on the houseboat that night, my buddy Lewis pretty well summed up the gar-fishing experience.

"This ain't no sport for sissies," he said. "Skeeters eatin' you up, sweat burning your eyes. Every time you throw a bait out, it's like casting into a castle moat full of alligators. You never know what'll hit next, but you know it's likely to be big and mean and have one wicked set of teeth. You don't really feel safe unless you've got a .38 strapped on your leg."

Of course, what Dean Peace said was true, too. When you tell folks you've been gar fishing, they're gonna look at you like you're some kind of alien.

If they do, just smile and act nonchalant. Remember, the folks pointing fingers and laughing won't be crowding your favorite gar holes. And most good gar fishermen would just as soon keep it that way.

They Call Him the Streak

When a friend of mine hooked his first yellow bass, he was in for a surprise. The hook set provoked extraordinary resistance. Line zizzed off his ultralight reel. His rod doubled over. "I've hooked a good 'un," he proclaimed.

The outcome was never certain. The angler gained line. The fish took it back. The angler reeled. The fish resisted. I watched, grinning, as the two-hundred-pound man struggled to land a fish the size of an aspirin bottle.

Persistence and skill paid off. Two minutes into round one, my heavyweight buddy KO'd his flyweight opponent. As he swung his "good 'un" into the boat, a puzzled grimace jumped on his face.

"What the heck is that?" he asked.

"Yellow bass," I replied.

"Do they get any bigger than that?" he queried.

"'Bout twice that size."

"Are there many of them in here?"

"Scads."

"Then the crappie fishing's over."

A hundred yellow bass later, my friend proclaimed, "The most fun day of fishing I've ever had."

If you require hefty fish for your angling jollies, read no farther. Yellow bass won't interest you. Most weigh mere ounces. Record-class fish are barely over two pounds. There are unsubstantiated rumors of five-pounders snatched from Louisiana waters, but a two-pound, four-ounce specimen from Lake Monroe, Indiana, is the largest officially documented.

If you enjoy fish-a-minute fun on ultralight tackle, however, these scrappy little fighters can keep you happy for hours on end. Yellow bass are so abundant in some waters that catching one hundred or more a day is a snap. Their small size belies their militant fighting ability, and when glamour fish get lockjaw, yellow bass can turn a potentially dismal fishing trip into a delightful one.

Yellow bass are true bass, close relatives of white bass, striped bass, and hybrid stripers. Whites and yellows are sometimes confused

Yellow bass seldom exceed one pound, but they're abundant in many Arkansas waters, making them great targets for anglers who enjoy a fight on ultralight tackle.

but easily distinguished by examining the two dorsal fins. On yellow bass, the fins are slightly connected by a thin membrane; the fins are separate on whites. Both species have distinct black stripes on the sides, but on yellow bass the lines are broken and offset above the anal fin.

The common name is appropriate yet understated. The fish have a rich golden hue about their sides, which transforms to glistening topaz on pre-spawn males. Colors are less pronounced on juveniles and fish from turbid water.

Yellow bass nicknames are colorful as well. In the rivers and oxbows of east Arkansas, they're barfish, an appellation said to have originated from the species' tendency to congregate on shallow sand-bars near dawn and dusk. In other parts of their range, anglers use such monickers as brassy bass, yellowjack, stripe, gold bass, yellow perch, striped jack, streak, and streaker.

Yellow bass range through the lowland rivers of eastern and southern Arkansas. They reside principally in the Mississippi, St. Francis, White, Arkansas, Ouachita, and Red River drainages, where they inhabit quiet pools and backwaters, impoundments and natural lakes. They are scattered in occurrence. A lake here and a river there may offer good yellow bass fishing, but many others in the same area may not.

Should you read the scant literature available on yellow bass fishing, you'll gain the impression that yellow bass are always caught in deep water near the bottom. This is hearsay perpetuated by misinformed reporters. It's true that yellow bass rarely exhibit the surface-feeding sprees for which white bass are famous, but studies indicate they often feed on small crustaceans, insects, and fish in mid-depths or near the surface. Deep, open water is a common haunt, especially at midday, but adults feed in shallow water early and late in the day and are often caught around stumps, weed beds, riprap, cypress knees, and brush.

Many lures and natural baits are productive. One of the best is a small lead-head jig—$\frac{1}{100}$ to $\frac{1}{32}$ ounce—dressed with a marabou, tinsel, or tube skirt. Live worms, crickets, and small minnows also are effective, and fly fishing with small streamers or wet flies will produce outstanding catches of yellow bass in prime fishing waters.

Fishing with ultralight tackle heightens the enjoyment of catching these neglected panfish. Yellow bass fight like big bull bluegills, and when you're playing one in on a whippy spinning rod or jigging pole, its scrappy, circle-and-run fighting style may sucker you (like my buddy) into thinking you've hooked a much larger fish. Two-pound-test line would seem appropriate, despite their spunk, but barfish often streak round and round underwater cover like cypress knees and snags. I usually opt for six- to eight-pound monofilament and can account for more of my lures, and more fish, at the end of the day.

There's no off-season for yellow bass. In spring and early

summer, adults spawn over gravel bars, sandbars, or rock reefs in water only a few feet deep. Huge schools may congregate in small areas at this time, and a properly placed bait rarely goes untouched. During summer's heat, the biggest yellows often follow schools of young shad. Watch for tiny baitfish skipping near the surface and cast to them with small lures. Near dawn and dusk, shallow structure produces, especially rocky edges and bars.

Trolling and drift-fishing with small jigs are first-rate methods for pinpointing schools during cool months. Start by using a variety of jigs rigged at different depths. For instance, use four poles, setting two jigs two feet deep and two at six feet. Use various sizes and colors—some $\frac{1}{32}$ ounce, some $\frac{1}{64}$ ounce, some black, some yellow, some silver. This allows you to test different baits and depths until a pattern is established. Once you ascertain that yellow bass favor a certain depth or jig style, then rig all poles to conform to that preference.

Considering their sporty aggressiveness and their abundance in some waters, yellow bass would seem to demand more respect than they usually get. Nevertheless, most anglers pay little attention to these fish, preferring instead to fish for largemouths, crappie, bream, catfish, or other popular species.

Obscurity can't efface the first-class sporting qualities of these spunky game fish, though. Yellow bass offer a wealth of entertainment value. Before you pass them by, remember the old adage, "Good things often come in small packages."

SEPTEMBER

So Many Sunfish

To experience the real meaning of fishing fun, go out on a nice September morning, find a shady spot on the bank of your favorite fishing hole, set up a lawn chair, bait your fishing pole with a cricket or a worm, then sit back, relax, and watch your bobber. Chances are, it won't be long before you'll catch one of the many species of sunfish inhabiting Arkansas waters.

You never know for sure what will take your bait, but it'll probably have an unusual nickname. I thought about this recently while fishing in a little oxbow lake off the lower White River.

Dabbling a cricket in a hollow cypress produced a pretty longear sunfish, a fish also known here as the "sun perch" or "pumpkinseed." The flier or "shining bass" is rare there, but my crickets proved irresistible to one nice specimen taken from a brush pile in shallow water. During the course of the day, I also caught several "stumpknockers," small, brightly colored panfish more properly known as spotted sunfish, and a few "ricefield slicks" or green sunfish.

Despite their unusual names, these members of the sunfish family are fun to catch on ultralight tackle. They don't rate a mention in most panfish popularity polls, but they're delectable table fish and inhabit many waters throughout Arkansas. Fishermen who savor the spice of variety often include one or more of these scrappy little fighters on their menu of targeted species.

LONGEAR SUNFISH: THE RAINBOW WARRIOR

It would be hard to imagine a fish of any sort more beautiful than the longear sunfish. This gorgeous little creature is emblazoned with a rainbow of colors—aquamarine back and sides with gold and emerald speckles, a face of green or tangerine, a lemon-yellow to orange belly, and opalescent veins of turquoise striping the cheeks, nose, and gill covers. Males are even more brilliantly colored than the gaudy females, especially during the spawning season when the breast turns cherry red or fiery orange. Both sexes sport long, black, white-edged ear flaps that protrude from the gill covers like ebony earrings.

Beauty isn't the longear's only gratifying attribute. This little buster is an aggressive, doughty warrior, too, and on the table, it is delectable. Yet most panfish anglers busy with bluegills, crappie, or other fish pay it little mind. When someone catches one, it's usually deplored as too small and tossed back. That's regrettable, for this handsome sunfish is an unsung delight that can render countless hours of angling enjoyment.

The longear sunfish is abundant throughout Arkansas. The scant references you will find describe it as a fish of crystal-clear creeks and small, gravel-bottomed rivers. It is, indeed, a characteristic inhabitant of these types of waters, but this rainbow warrior is not a specialist restricted to a narrow range of habitats. Longears are native to and quite abundant in oxbow lakes, meandering delta rivers, bayous, and other lowland waters, and they have adapted quite well to life in all sorts of man-made impoundments. In fact, it is difficult to find any type of fishing hole in Arkansas where a longear couldn't thrive. Warm or cold, big or small, deep or shallow—if it's not too polluted, longears will call it home.

In 1985, a one-pound, twelve-ounce longear from Elephant Butte Lake, New Mexico, achieved world-record status. In Arkansas, a one-pound, two-ounce fish from Table Rock Lake is the record. But finding a longear that weighs even one pound is about as likely as winning a state lottery. Three to five ounces is the size of an average adult, with anything topping that granted instant trophy status.

Their diminutive stature shouldn't deter you from fishing for longears, though. Some waters are literally swarming with four- to six-inchers, and many folks would readily agree that catching lots of little guys is better than catching few or no bigger fish. Longears are extremely cooperative in this respect, taking worms, crickets, tiny crayfish, wax worms, small minnows, and a variety of other live baits with obvious gusto. Tiny artificials serve well to entice them, too, everything from 1/32-ounce jig-spinner combos to No. 14 dry flies and inch-and-a-half mini-crankbaits. Longears aren't especially shy, and it's common to see several chasing a lure.

Regardless of what type fishing outfit you prefer to use—fly

There are many species of sunfish inhabiting Arkansas waters.

fishing, spinning, spin-casting, poles, or whatever—keep it extra light to get the most from these bantam brawlers. Light line—one- to four-pound-test, tops—also should be a standard, along with small bobbers, hooks, and sinkers.

On small rivers and creeks, look for longears in and about shallow-to medium-depth pools and slow runs with scarcely perceptible current. They seem especially fond of steep, rocky ledges and undercut banks out of stiff flow.

In oxbow lakes and lowland streams, longears usually hang out near cypress knees, half-submerged horizontal logs, and other types of sizable woody cover. Lake and pond fish seem to concentrate around weed-bed edges, steeply sloping rock or gravel banks, and, quite frequently, around fishing piers, docks, and similar structures.

Although methods for catching longears are astoundingly varied and numerous, a cricket or worm fished on a small hook beneath a bobber is about as consistent and simple a tactic as has ever been devised. Regardless of how you fish for them, however, if you want to sample the bounty of longear fishing, you'll probably have to alter your current standard for "keeping size." Most longears you'll land probably won't resemble anything you've ever called a keeper before, but even the four- and five-inchers pack two surprisingly thick fillets on their tiny skeletons. Dress these mini-panfish, salt and pepper to taste, and roll in yellow cornmeal. Then fry them for a minute or so—no longer—in vegetable or peanut oil heated to 350 degrees. Strip out the dorsal fin, pull the two flaky white fillets away from the bones on each side, and settle yourself down to enjoy one of Mother Nature's finest treats.

One further suggestion: be sure to catch a lot!

GREEN SUNFISH: THE PROLIFIC PIONEER

Of all our sunfish species, none is more abundant and adaptable than the green sunfish. This colorful little sprite is a prolific colonizer tolerant of warm, turbid water. It is a pioneering species, readily populating new bodies of water, and is among the first fish to repopulate streams after periods of drought.

No creek is too small for it, no river too large. Turn its stream into a lake or pond, and it will stick around and do just fine, thank you. In fact, if a body of water is even remotely capable of supporting fish life, the green sunfish is likely to be there. "Ubiquitous" is perhaps the best way to describe it.

If you've never seen a green sunfish, you've probably never fished freshwater. It occurs in virtually every body of freshwater in the continental United States and is one of the easiest fish to catch. Bait makes no difference. If a green sunfish can see it, it's likely to take a bite. Worms, crickets, minnows, and small crayfish work as well as anything. But small plugs, jigs, spinners, spoons, popping bugs, and other artificials will do the trick, too. If it has a hook, it will catch a green sunfish.

The green sunfish is like an old acquaintance you run into at the supermarket—you may recognize the face but can't place the name. Few fish have such a variety of colloquial names. Some Arkansans know it as the black perch, shade perch, blue-spotted sunfish, rice-field slick, or rubbertail. In other locales, green perch, goggle-eye, branch perch, blue bass, and buffalo sunfish are commonly used nicknames. You'll seldom ever hear an angler talking about catching a green sunfish, though. "Perch" or "goggle-eye" maybe, but not green sunfish.

Regardless of what you call it, the green sunfish is a gutsy little fighter worthy of your attention. It always seems to be hungry or mad at the world, looking for a fight. It's not exactly an angling challenge. In fact, the saying "shooting fish in a barrel" might have been coined to describe fishing for green sunfish. But on ultralight tackle, this adaptable little devil makes quite a showing of itself. It has a no-fooling strike, and if you've never sampled deep-fried green sunfish fillets, you've missed a real treat.

Green sunfish are long, robust fish with a big mouth like a bass. The back and sides are usually olive to bluish green, the undersides are yellow-orange, the short ear flaps are black with white or yellow-orange margins, and the cheeks have distinctive worm-like blue squiggles. The pectoral fins are short and rounded, and the tips of the pelvic, anal, and tail fins are often a yellow to orange color. The young have dark, closely spaced bars on the sides.

The best places to look for "slicks" are quiet pools of rivers or creeks and along shorelines of lakes and ponds. Small creeks incapable of supporting other sport fish often yield good stringers of hand-size green sunfish.

They almost always are found near cover. It could be a root wad, weed bed, brush pile, or logjam. Maybe boulders or rocks in a stream, or riprap along the face of dam. Even the shade of an overhanging tree will do. If there's cover, green sunfish will be there.

Their only major flaw, in terms of angling quality, is size. Adults can grow eight to ten inches long and reach a pound in weight, but even that size is unusual. Unless they become overpopulated and stunted (a frequent problem in small ponds and lakes), most will run around four to eight ounces. The world record from Stockton Lake in Missouri was a true heavyweight at two pounds, two ounces. The Arkansas record, caught in a farm pond, weighed one pound, eleven ounces.

Judge the green sunfish for what it is, not what it looks like. Sure, it may be a tad on the small side. But it's also widespread, abundant, hard-hitting, fun to catch, and excellent on the table. The green sunfish is an applaudably aggressive citizen of waters throughout the state. So applaud it, catch it, and eat it.

SPOTTED SUNFISH: BUTTERFLY OF THE FISH WORLD

Though it's not very well known, the spotted sunfish is distributed throughout the Southeast, from eastern Texas through the Florida peninsula and north along the Atlantic slope to southeastern North Carolina. It is also found in the Mississippi River basin, from Louisiana north to Illinois. In Arkansas, it occurs primarily in the streams, rivers, and oxbow lakes of eastern and southern lowlands.

Spotted sunfish rarely weigh even half a pound, but their consistent scrappiness, pretty colors, chunky physique, and sweet-tasting meat make them favorite panfish with fishermen in many areas, especially Florida. Few Arkansas anglers fish purposely for them, but as an incidental in a mixed bag, there's no reason to keep them off the stringer.

No butterfly or songbird is more splendidly colored than spawning males of this species. Carmine and tangerine spots on the belly and sides glisten like jewels embedded in dark matrix. The rear margins of the dark dorsal, anal, and caudal fins are aflame with orange. Along the back, against a dark greenish or bluish background, are sparse iridescent ribbons of crimson and blue. The female bears none of this gaudiness, being greenish overall with a yellow belly and spots of dull yellow or orange. Some races in Florida, Georgia, and other Deep South states are marked with brown, blue, or black spots instead of red or yellow and once were considered separate species.

On some oxbow lakes in Arkansas, I have watched spotted sunfish flip from the water and smack against stumps and cypress knees to dislodge dragonfly nymphs and other insects. This habit has earned them the curious and often-used nickname "stumpknocker." Other handles include spotted bream, scarlet sunfish, red perch, and chinquapin.

I've caught spotted sunfish on worms, crickets, small spinners, and popping bugs, usually in calm or moderately flowing water near some type of woody or rocky cover. They often hide around cypress knees and stumps in oxbows and around boulders, fallen trees, and small eddies in streams. From these spots they attack insects, small crayfish, and other frequently taken foods.

Unfortunately, it's a rare occasion when you'll take more than two or three individuals from a single patch of cover. That's one of the reasons this sunfish is so little known. But despite its relative obscurity and small size, the pugnacious spotted sunfish is a real treat for any fun-seeking angler.

FLIER

The flier is another member of the sunfish family sometimes encountered by September anglers, usually in southern portions of the state in oxbows, bayous, creeks, and swampy backwaters of large rivers. Its range encompasses much of the southeastern United States, but it is common nowhere. Catching half a dozen a day, even in prime waters, is quite a challenge. The average size of this sunfish is only a few ounces, and though it's an excellent table fish, few anglers consider it worthy of their attention.

Showy, oversize fins impart a subtle, rounded beauty to these little fish. The sides exhibit an intriguing pattern created by dark spots punctuating each silvery scale. Each eye is slashed by a dusky vertical bar. The soft dorsal fin on juvenile fish bears a distinctive black ocellus or "eye spot" ringed with vivid red-orange. Fliers resemble their close relatives, the black and white crappies, but differ from them in having ten to thirteen dorsal fin spines (versus six to eight).

In *Fishes of the Central United States,* Joe Tomelleri and Mark Eberle note the origin of the fish's name: "In its enthusiasm for floating insects, this sunfish sometimes bursts acrobatically through the surface of the water, a habit having earned it and its winglike fins the title of flier or flying perch." Colloquial names include round flier, round sunfish, shining bass, and long-fin sunfish.

Fliers are slow growers. Six- to seven-inch fish are usually four or five years old. Those less than seven inches feed primarily on small crustaceans, but larger fish are insect eaters.

First-rate baits for large specimens (occasionally a pound or more) include live crickets, dragonfly and damselfly nymphs, and small grasshoppers. Bluegill tactics catch them, but fliers are more inclined to rise to the surface for their food. You'll do better by rigging with no sinker or bobber, allowing the hooked bait to float on the surface and wiggle enticingly. Fly fishers catch them with popping bugs, flies, and nymphs.

Longears, green sunfish, spotted sunfish, and fliers don't get very big, but size isn't everything. If you've ever spent a long day on the water fishing unsuccessfully for some highly touted game fish, you can appreciate how a few quick skirmishes with these bantam brawlers can lift your sagging spirits.

If you're looking for a way to relax this month, to get away from it all, to capture the fun and excitement of no-frills fishing, head for your favorite fishing hole and rediscover the joys of "catch-what-bites" fishing.

SEPTEMBER

Sunfish are excellent targets for anglers wanting to share the joys of fishing with children.

OCTOBER

Bassin's Fall Lineup

Autumn provides superb largemouth bass fishing opportunities for Arkansas anglers. Bass move from deep summer haunts to shallow feeding areas as water cools, and the average angler can more easily fish for them. When this happens in spring, bass are preoccupied with spawning activities, but during fall, food is their foremost concern. Fall bass seem ravenous and willing to travel farther to take a lure.

Let's look at some of the Natural State's premier hotspots for consistent autumn bassing success.

LAKE COLUMBIA

This three-thousand-acre impoundment, owned by Columbia County, was built to supply water to Magnolia, but planners didn't forget the lake's recreational importance. Visiting anglers catch good numbers of one- to five-pound largemouths.

Near dawn and dusk, bass move to shallows to feed on fish fry, and a small minnow-imitation topwater can waylay the big ones. Fish this type of lure with an O-ring or snap rather than tying right to the lure. The ring or snap gives the lure better movement when twitched. Give the rod short twitches and allow it to resurface after each twitch. Cast around standing timber and brush piles near shore and get ready for action.

LAKE ERLING

This seven-thousand-acre Lafayette County lake offers excellent fishing for panfish, but big largemouths steal the limelight. Hundreds of thousands of Florida-strain bass have been stocked here, and local anglers often catch trophy-class fish. One- to four-pounders are common, and Erling anglers have caught lunkers over ten pounds.

A good fall technique is finding a stump-covered hump near the

Stickbaits produce good spotted bass when fishing waters in the Sunken Lands along northeast Arkansas's St. Francis River.

old Bodcau Creek channel and working it with a buzzbait. Big bass move in and out of such places regularly during fall; a buzzbait is perfect for checking them. These lures can be cast long distances, and with their long-range sound attraction, you can fish lots of water in a short time. Buzzbaits also produce when worked around cypress trees, through lily pads, and around logjams and beds of coontail.

LAKE BOB KIDD

Another first-rate autumn hotspot is Lake Bob Kidd in Washington County. This small, often-overlooked impoundment produces lots of big bucketmouths in fall.

This two-hundred-acre Game and Fish Commission lake has lots of dead timber and stumps. You can fish from a boat, but if bank-fishing is preferred, there are plenty of prime bassing areas accessible along the north shore. Big fall bass often hold around lily pads in the lake's shallow upper end and over a large flat that's casting distance from the dam.

Working chugger plugs around stumps and snags is a good autumn bassing tactic here. Chuggers have a deeply concave mouth designed to make loud pops when retrieved on top. Cast one close to a stickup and let it remain motionless a few seconds, then pop it once and prepare for a strike. Retrieve using a series of short jerks punctuated by periods of no movement. Chuggers work great near dawn and dusk and are good choices for small lakes like Bob Kidd. Good ones include the Rebel Pop-R, Storm's Chug-Bug, and the Arbogast Hula Popper.

MILLWOOD LAKE

An October bassing excursion on this 29,200-acre southwest Arkansas lake (seven miles east of Ashdown) likely will produce an outstanding catch of fish, and fishing improves with each passing season.

With the exception of a large, open-water area near the dam, most of Millwood is blanketed with timber. Some of the most popular bassing areas include the timbered channel drops near the east end of Okay Boat Lanes North and South, the Hickory Slough area north of Yarborough Landing, and timbered flats on the lake's west end. Visit with personnel at the state park marina or other boat docks to pick up fishing tips for the time of your visit. These folks will gladly assist you by sharing the wheres and hows of Millwood bassing —hotspots where bass are likely to be hitting, the best time of day for fishing, productive lures, and so forth.

Because Millwood is relatively shallow and is fed by several tributaries, the water level fluctuates constantly. Reading water fluctuations and knowing where to fish at what level are keys to finding bass here.

As a general rule, when the water level rises, bass follow creek channels up onto shallow flats and into flooded woods. As the water level falls, fishing is best in the main body of the lake because bass leave flats and move toward cover along inundated creek and river channels offshore. A sonar unit can be helpful for finding the secondary pockets or fingers on creek channels where bass often hold.

Lure choices run the gamut from jigs to deep-diving crankbaits. In October, prop baits worked over beds of hydrilla and lily pads and along the edges of stumps are very productive, especially near dawn and dusk when the water usually is calm. Lures of this type include old favorites such as the Smithwick Devil's Horse, Cotton Cordell's Boy Howdy, Luhr-Jensen's Nip-I-Diddee, and the Heddon Torpedo.

The least twitch of one of these lures makes a fuss on the surface, but, usually, the faster and more noisily you retrieve them, the better action you can expect. Experiment with everything from short hopping twitches that barely move the lure to smashing jerks that sputter the water furiously.

ST. FRANCIS SUNKEN LANDS

The Sunken Lands along northeast Arkansas's St. Francis River were formed by the 1811–12 New Madrid earthquake. Few people know about the region's superb spotted bass fishing, but at times, fishing here produces numerous two- to three-pounders in a single hour.

The best bassing is in borrow-pit lakes created during river levee construction. These lakes occur from the Missouri border south to

Marked Tree on both sides of the river inside the levees, and most are open to the public. Access is usually by gravel ramps off county roads.

Spotted bass lurk near woody borrow-pit cover, the perfect setting for fishing stickbaits. These long, slender lures, such as the Heddon Zara Spook, have no propellers, lips, or other built-in action-makers, but they're extremely effective when the angler knows how to walk, wobble, and weave them across the surface with a combination of rod movement and reel retrieve.

What makes stickbaits so exciting to use is the possibility of catching a real lunker. Most such lures are large, and when retrieved slowly and correctly, they attract jumbo bass.

Try fishing stickbaits around windy points or isolated shoreline stickups in Sunken Land waters. Toss the lure to a good-looking spot and let it sit until all the ripples subside. Then barely twitch the rod, making the lure dance and twist from side to side without moving it from the spot. Let the lure rest again, twitch it a little more, then make your retrieve. The slower you fish these lures, with long pauses between motions, the better the results.

To experience some of the superb bass fishing for which Arkansas is world renowned, try some of these blue-ribbon waters this October.

Hotspots for Flathead Catfish

Flathead catfish are giants among Arkansas fish. Only alligator gar grow larger. A 139-pound, 14-ounce flathead caught in the Arkansas River below Terry Lock and Dam is the largest ever documented. It was caught on a snagline. Another Arkansas River specimen—an 80-pounder—is the state-record rod-and-reel catch.

Arkansas encompasses scores of lakes and rivers offering excellent fishing for flatheads. Action peaks in October and November. Coming up with a list of the best is like trying to pick the state's best restaurants. It's darn near impossible, and lots of excellent establishments are bound to be left out.

Nevertheless, following are short reviews of seven bodies of water renowned for great flathead fishing. Some are best known for their trophy potential. Others have well-deserved reputations for fast action—lots of cats caught in a day's fishing, with an occasional lunker in the harvest to keep you on your toes. All offer excellent October fishing for the savvy catter.

ARKANSAS RIVER

The Arkansas River is the undisputed queen of Arkansas flathead waters. No other water body in the Natural State has produced as many record-book flatheads. Fishing is excellent throughout the warm months on the entire length of river from Ft. Smith to the river's mouth near Yancopin.

Top hotspots along the river's length include the tailwater of Ozark–Jeta Taylor Lock and Dam south of Ozark, where an eighty-pound flathead, the current state record, was caught in 1989; the tailwater below Dardanelle Lock and Dam near Russellville, an area which has given up two state records and numerous fifty-pound-plus flatheads; and the tailwater below Dam 2 on the Arkansas River's lower end below Tichnor, an area which produces astounding numbers of big flatheads every year. A sleeper honeyhole is the stretch immediately below Terry Lock and Dam where Bruce and Mackey Sayre caught the biggest flathead ever recorded in May 1982.

Heavy tackle is must. Rods should be eight- to fifteen-foot, heavy-action models, and reels—whether level-winding or spinning —should have drags in good working order. Hooks should be no smaller than 7/0 to 9/0 when fishing exclusively for large flats, and you'll need plenty of egg sinkers heavy enough to hold your bait on the bottom. Use top-quality, 50- to 150-pound-test line.

Small bluegills, live shad, and live skipjack herring are the baits of choice. Most anglers catch their own using hand-thrown cast nets.

A good, simple rig is the egg-sinker rig. Run an appropriately sized egg sinker up on your main line and tie a sturdy barrel swivel below it. To the other eye of the swivel, tie a twenty-four-inch leader to which you've tied a hook. Impale a baitfish on the hook, leaving the hook point exposed.

LAKE CONWAY

Few bodies of water in the United States churn out the number of monster flatheads produced by central Arkansas's Lake Conway. This sixty-seven-hundred-acre Arkansas Game and Fish Commission lake (off Interstate 40 just west of Little Rock) is the largest ever constructed by a state wildlife agency. Its waters are shallow, heavily timbered throughout, rich in shad and sunfish, and full of logjams and deep holes—in other words, prime habitat for giant flatheads.

Scores of thirty- to sixty-pound Conway flatheads are taken every year, some by anglers fishing for other species, some on trotlines, a few by rod-and-reel anglers who enjoy the challenge of battling big cats in heavy timber. Serious local cat men believe that hundred-pounders swim here, but the dense timber makes it almost impossible to land one. Small live sunfish are the leading bait choice.

Because most Conway flathead aficionados won't reveal their favored honeyholes, it can be hard for a first-timer to locate an area harboring big flatheads. The best way is to obtain a map showing old lakes inundated when the Conway was filled. Flatheads prefer the sanctuary these deep areas offer. Adams Lake, Greens Lake, Cub Pond, Round Pond, Gold Lake, Goose Pond, and Holt's Lake are

The lower White River, where this 25-pound-plus flathead was caught, is one of the Natural State's blue-ribbon fishing spots for these gigantic catfish.

all excellent locations for placing a trotline or bait-fishing with a rod and reel.

ST. FRANCIS RIVER

This broad bottomland river forms the border between Arkansas and Missouri's boot heel. Continuing south through east Arkansas's Delta, the St. Francis passes Lake City, Trumann, Marked Tree, Parkin, Forrest City, and Marianna before spilling into the Mississippi River just north of Helena. Two public recreation areas on the river—St. Francis Sunken Lands and St. Francis National Forest Wildlife Management Areas—offer access for a first-rate flathead fishing junket.

The Sunken Lands are scattered along thirty miles of river from Monette to Marked Tree. A flat-bottom boat with a small outboard is the primary mode of travel for catfishermen here. Boats can be launched at three concrete ramps—one at Stevens Landing east of Trumann, one at Oak Donnick south of Tulot, and one at Siphons north of Marked Tree.

St. Francis National Forest Wildlife Management Area lies eighty miles south of the Sunken Lands. The area's eastern edge is in the low, flat land along the St. Francis, L'Anguille, and Mississippi Rivers. Catfish on this end of the river tend to run a bit larger, and it's not unusual to catch thirty- to forty-pounders. There's likely to be more action, too, since the Mississippi River, a mother lode of giant flatheads, is a short distance downstream. The two river junctions—St. Francis–Mississippi and St. Francis–L'Anguille—serve up exceptionally good flathead fishing.

Look for St. Francis River flatheads near break lines in river bottom structure. Deep holes, outside channel bends, and areas above and below sandbars are good places to fish. The portion of the river traversing the Sunken Lands also has numerous logjams where flatheads hide. Live bream are the preferred bait.

WHITE RIVER

The White is another of Arkansas's premier flathead rivers. It has its narrow beginnings in northwest Arkansas and flows 690 miles to its junction with the Mississippi. However, due to the cold-water discharges of lakes Bull Shoals and Norfork, the really superb White River catfishing doesn't begin until you reach Clarendon in Monroe County. Boat access is available in White River National Wildlife Refuge, at St. Charles, and other locations along the river.

Outside bends of the river are among the most productive hotspots, especially where trees have toppled into the water and the river has gouged deeply into the bank forming undercuts. Potholes or slight depressions in the river bottom also tend to concentrate flatheads, as do the upstream sides of underwater humps, and shallow flats and drops near tributary mouths. Live fish are the best baits, with live green sunfish, goldfish, shiners, and small carp topping the list.

Rod-and-reelers find the superb catfishing along the lower ten miles from the Corps of Engineers barge canal to the Mississippi River. There's good access for bank and boat fishermen alike at Norrell Lock and Dam, eight miles south of Tichnor. This section of the White contains drop-offs, holes, brush, bends, and other structures attractive to flatheads, and a limit of outsized cats is common for many anglers.

LAKE HINKLE

Lake Hinkle, twelve miles west of Waldron, typifies a superb flathead catfish lake. About 70 percent of this 960-acre lake is flooded timber. Dead snags, stumps, and submerged treetops provide abundant protective cover that flatheads prefer.

Creek channels, several small ponds, inundated roadways, and flooded fencerows are among the bottom features of this west Arkansas lake. All these features are used by structure-oriented flatheads. Hinkle also provides a dense population of prime flathead forage—shad, small minnows, crawdads, and small sunfish—allowing the cats to reach extraordinary sizes. Thirty- to forty-pound flatheads are fairly common, but the possibility of hooking a much larger fish is excellent.

Many catters concentrate their efforts in deeper water near the dam. This area is preferred for two primary reasons: (1) it has more open, snag-free water, thus providing a better chance of landing a heavyweight fish; and (2) a caged fish-rearing operation adjacent to the dam creates a zone of fertile, forage-filled water that attracts many giant flatheads. Preferred baits include live crawdads for smaller flatheads and live bluegills, longears, or green sunfish for trophy-class fish.

L'ANGUILLE RIVER

The L'Anguille River, a tributary of the St. Francis, is a relatively unknown hotspot for flathead catfish, but this small farm-country stream gives up some real monsters. Seventy- to eighty-pounders are caught here every year. Unfortunately, thick hard-to-fish cover makes it darn near impossible to land the river's giants on rod and reel.

Fishing is best downstream from the U.S. Highway 70 bridge near Forrest City, but the entire river from the Cross-Poinsett county line to Marianna is alive with five- to twenty-pound flatheads. It's difficult to travel more than a few hundred yards at any point on the river due to extensive logjams, but these barriers are favorite hideouts for big flats. Trotlines baited with goldfish or bream account for most of the catch.

Almost all land bordering the L'Anguille is privately owned, so beware of trespass problems.

LAKE GRAMPUS

The name "Grampus" comes from French explorers and is derived from a French word meaning "fat fish." It might well refer to the jumbo flatheads native to this 350-acre lake. Five- to fifteen-pounders are common, and lucky anglers occasionally land specimens topping forty. Despite being a first-rate flathead lake, Grampus is largely overlooked by anglers who usually fish man-made reservoirs.

Fifteen miles east of Hamburg in south Arkansas, Grampus is an oxbow of Bayou Bartholomew. Flatheads cruise waters throughout the lake, but usually are caught around cypress trees, buckbrush, brush piles, and underwater stump fields. Shad and small sunfish entice most, but smaller flatheads frequently hit earthworms and crawfish as well.

Arkansas River Stripers

In terms of the number of fish it produces, the Arkansas River is one of the best striper waters in Arkansas, and perhaps in the nation. This is the only body of water in Arkansas where striped bass spawn naturally. All other waters in the state are maintained with hatchery-spawned fish, and because this is expensive, striper populations in some lakes are limited. If budgets or the availability of fish don't allow stockings in some years, there may be missing year classes of stripers.

During normal years, striper reproduction in the Arkansas River yields millions upon millions of young fish. Compare that to the one million or so young fish per year that are stocked in all other Arkansas striper waters combined, and you can understand why the Arkansas River is full of stripers.

Considering all this, it seems ironic that so few people seem to know about this astounding fishery. We hear often about the extraordinary striped bass fishing on Lake Ouachita, Beaver Lake, Lake Maumelle, and other waters, but somehow the Arkansas River has managed to escape notice. Few people fish the river for stripers, and fewer still have learned how to locate and catch these challenging sport fish.

There are at least two reasons why the Arkansas River striper fishery has drawn little attention. First is the fact that running water poses more of a challenge than lakes, and most anglers are oriented to still-water situations. Lake conditions remain pretty stable, but on rivers, everything changes with the water flow, and many physical features of the stream can be different from day to day. Most anglers won't take time to learn the special tactics required to catch these river brawlers.

The second reason why the Arkansas doesn't get more striper fishing pressure is the fact that striped bass here seldom exceed twenty pounds. In most river pools, five- to ten-pound stripers are incredibly abundant, and ten- to fifteen-pounders are not uncommon. Occasionally, you're find a newspaper sporting the photo of a lucky angler who's boated an Arkansas River striper topping twenty, sometimes even thirty, pounds. But stripers that size are unusual here.

The absence of large stripers in the Arkansas River isn't really important to most anglers. There are few days when a dedicated angler with a little striper knowledge can't hook several nice fish, and abundant five- to fifteen-pound stripers provide all the action most fishermen desire.

Stripers are taken year-round along the entire 320-mile length of the Arkansas River in Arkansas, from the river's mouth in the remote Mississippi River bottoms of Desha County to Ft. Smith on the Arkansas-Oklahoma border. In spring, they accompany schools of white bass upriver into the tailwaters below the river dams. Slack water periods, when few or no gates are open, are great times for fishing these tailraces with a medium-action rod, ten- to twelve-pound line, and live minnows. Thread a ¼- to 1-ounce egg sinker on your line before tying on a 1/0 to 2/0 hook, then squeeze a split shot on the line two feet above the hook to keep the sinker from slipping down on the bait. Hook one or several minnows through both lips, from the bottom up, then cast the rig toward the dam and retrieve it with a lift-and-drop action of the rod tip. Sometimes a larger striper will strip or break your line, but using light tackle compounds the thrill you experience when you battle one in.

When water is being discharged from the dam and heavy current is present, drift-fishing, or drift-trolling, is a popular spring striper tactic. Anglers motor to the closest safe, legal distance below the dam, then, using heavy tackle (ten- to fourteen-foot rods, heavy-duty reels, and twenty-five- to sixty-five-pound-test line), they troll a bait or lure behind the boat while the current carries their craft downstream past likely striper hideouts. Bank-fishing also is popular and productive for tailwater stripers, and bank-fishing access is excellent below most Arkansas River dams.

The most popular natural baits for big tailwater stripers are live shad or bluegills hooked through the lips or back using a 2/0 to 6/0 hook. Sometimes the baitfish is carried to the bottom using a sinker appropriate for the amount of current. Other times, the angler uses a brightly colored, baseball-sized float to keep the bait from getting hung as it moves down the tailrace.

Popular artificials include one- to three-ounce bucktail jigs, heavy four- to seven-inch deep-running plugs, and one- to three-ounce silver spoons. Almost any lure resembling a shad will elicit strikes if properly presented.

Stripers migrate to deeper waters in summer, following baitfish and searching for comfortable temperatures. In June, before temperatures soar, look for them around rock wing dikes and jetties. They live up to their common nickname "rockfish," frequenting these jagged outcroppings until warmer weather and diminishing water flows force them upriver. When hot weather sets in, you can find striper concentrations in the upper reaches of each river pool around the main river channel and near the junctures of tributary stream channels.

Summer striper anglers use jigs, spoons, and live bait to catch fish along river channels, off deep points, and in areas with a constant flow of fresh, cool water. Big shad–imitation crankbaits and topwaters are the ticket when fishing rock structures such as wing dikes. Work the lures along the upstream edge of the structure where actively feeding fish usually hold.

Autumn finds striped bass schooling and chasing shad on the surface. The fish roam large areas as they follow bait, but some action continues day after day in the same locales, usually around dawn and dusk. Fishermen watch the water for feeding fish, and, once disturbances are seen, they rush to get in a cast before the stripers dive. Practically any topwater plug or light-colored jig popped across the surface will draw strikes when fish are in a feeding frenzy.

Winter striper fishing varies with water and weather conditions. Surface action may continue, but some fish move to deeper structures. Riprap and rock dikes, deep creek mouths, deep points, and river channel edges are good areas on which to focus a search for fish. During this season, stripers stay near baitfish, so if you have a sonar fish-finder unit, watch closely for big fish suspended beneath schools of shad. A slow, vertical presentation of live shad, a bucktail jig, or a jigging spoon often prompts these fish to bite.

Stripers are caught on every mile of the Arkansas River flowing through Arkansas. There are, however, several perennial hotspots that merit extra attention.

The best striper pool, perhaps, is Lake Dardanelle near Russellville. Dardanelle covers 34,300 acres at conservation pool level, is 50 miles

OCTOBER

long, and has 315 miles of shoreline. Stripers were first stocked here in 1965 and '66 when 3.4 million fry were trucked in from eastern states. These fish grew amazingly fast in the fertile lake. In 1967, Dardanelle produced a six-pound, twelve-ounce state-record striper, then a nine-pound, four-ounce record in 1968, and a twelve-pound record in 1969. Area fishing reports indicate twenty-pound-plus stripers are a possibility today, and two- to six-pounders are common.

In April, larger tributaries such as Illinois Bayou and Piney Creek draw stripers to the shoals for spawning. One place reported to attract hundreds of ten-pound-plus stripers annually is the waterworks dam across Illinois Bayou a short distance before it enters Lake Dardanelle. Before and after the spawn, look for stripers in lower reaches of Dardanelle around the main river channel and the mouths of tributary streams.

Spring and summer fishermen also congregate below Ozark–Jeta Taylor Lock and Dam on the lake's upstream end and below Dardanelle Lock and Dam, which impounds the lake. Hydroelectric power is generated at both sites, and stripers are attracted to well-oxygenated currents and dense shad populations in the tailraces.

One winter hotspot is the discharge bay of the Nuclear One Power Plant on the lake's north side. Cooling water taken from the lake is discharged into a mile-long bay south of London. The temperature of the discharge water is five to fifteen degrees warmer than surrounding lake water. Shad are attracted to the warmer water, and they in turn attract stripers. Many two- to eight-pound stripers are taken by trolling deep-running lures through the bay.

Ozark Lake, the next pool upstream from Lake Dardanelle, offers yet another excellent striper fishery. This pool covers 10,600 acres with 173 miles of shoreline and stretches 36 miles from Ozark west to Ft. Smith.

On this lake, the best area for stripers is below Lock and Dam 13 at Ft. Smith. Local anglers use big slab spoons, heavy twister-tail jigs, and live shad to catch stripers in the spillway area year-round. In early spring, submerged rock jetties on the main river are hard to beat. Jetties at the mouths of coves often harbor stripers.

Another locale often targeted by Ozark striper anglers is the Mulberry River arm. In spring, stripers are taken here as they run to the first shoal on the Mulberry to spawn. In late fall, anglers may find stripers almost anywhere up and down the Arkansas River channel, but fish seem especially numerous around the deep ends of rock jetties and wing dikes.

On the other end of the Arkansas River, in the region where the Arkansas and Mississippi Rivers converge in southeast Arkansas, there are several popular striped bass fishing areas. When water is being discharged, good numbers of small stripers can be caught from the bank below Norrell Lock and Dam south of Tichnor at the mouth of the Arkansas Post Barge Canal, the beginning of the lock and dam system on the Arkansas River. At Morgan Point and Dam 2 (Wilbur Mills Dam) south of Gillett, numerous two- to twelve-pound stripers draw the attention of increasing numbers of spring anglers. Live shad, which can be caught below the dams using a cast net, are the preferred bait.

Every river pool has one or more launching ramps, and most have public-use areas with campgrounds, drinking water, picnic tables, rest rooms, and other facilities.

OCTOBER

Four Great Smallmouth Floats

Mention smallmouth bass to an angler and thoughts of the world-famous fishing available in Canada, the Great Lakes region, and New England immediately come to mind. You don't have to travel north to enjoy superb smallmouth fishing, though. Arkansas is laced with hundreds of miles of cool, upland streams where anglers can indulge in blue-ribbon smallmouth action, especially during the cool months of autumn.

The biggest problem Arkansas smallmouth fans face is deciding which section of which stream to fish. To help in that respect, here's a compilation of detailed information on four great Arkansas smallmouth streams. Each offers easy access, superb scenery, and quality smallmouth fishing. The waters included are among the best in the state.

LITTLE MISSOURI RIVER
(ALBERT PIKE CAMPGROUND TO LAKE GREESON)

The Little Missouri River courses through scenic country in the Ouachita Mountains, and along most of this stream, from the headwaters south of the Big Fork community to the backwaters of Lake Greeson, you'll find fast-paced action for smallmouth bass up to three or four pounds.

The float section of the Little Missouri begins at the U.S. Forest Service's Albert Pike Recreation Area in Montgomery County near Langley. The stretch of river from this campground down to the crossing at Arkansas Highway 84 covers 8.5 miles of good smallmouth territory, but avoid it during high water unless you're experienced at white-water boating. The best section for slower-paced fishing starts at the Highway 84 put-in and carries the angler through beautiful mountain country to Lake Greeson, 10 miles downstream. This stretch is a rough-and-tumble ride, too, after heavy rainfall, but it doesn't require the technical paddling skills of the section above it.

The upper Ouachita River gave up this trophy smallmouth, which was caught on a jig-and-pig worked near a shale ledge.

Smallmouths in the Little Missouri are suckers for live crawfish, and if you take time to turn over a few rocks in feeder creeks you pass, you can quickly gather a dozen or more. Store them in a container of dampened moss or leaves, and rig tight-line style with a small split shot a foot above the hook. Most smallmouths hold on the downstream side of boulders, treetops, and other current breaks, so cast upstream and allow the bait to drift by this cover.

Businesses and government facilities near the river provide angling amenities. There are public campsites at the Albert Pike area, along with a private campground in the same vicinity. Rental cabins, grocery stores, bait shops, lodging, and other services are available in Daisy, Kirby, Langley, and other communities near the river. Several Corps of Engineers and state park campgrounds are also available on Lake Greeson, including one—Star of the West—at the take-out point for the lower float.

CROOKED CREEK (PYATT TO YELLVILLE)

Arkansas's stream inventory includes at least ten Crooked Creeks, but only one has been described as the "blue-ribbon smallmouth stream of the state." That particular Crooked Creek originates near Dogpatch in Newton County and flows eighty miles past the communities of Harrison, Pyatt, and Yellville before emptying into the White River.

While Crooked Creek offers decent spotted and largemouth bass action as well, its real claim to fame is the smallmouth. Ideal habitat and abundant hellgrammites, crayfish, and other smallmouth foods combine to produce large numbers of quality "brownies." Two- to three-pounders are fairly common, and four- to five-pound smallmouths always are a possibility for savvy anglers. Popping bugs and streamers on fly rods offer great sport for smallmouths, and many anglers also use crankbaits, spinnerbaits, and live hellgrammites or crayfish to take Crooked Creek lunkers.

The stream's upper reaches offer opportunities for wade-fishing and occasional float trips, but most recreational use occurs in the lower fifty miles below Pyatt. Float trips are possible past Yellville, but the ruggedness of the float—rocky shoals, tight chutes, and willow thickets—discourages most visits. Also, in late spring, Crooked Creek below Yellville literally disappears, sinking beneath the surface and flowing underground.

The stretch of Crooked Creek between Pyatt and Yellville is among the most popular with smallmouth anglers and can be divided into three segments. The half-day float from Pyatt to Turkey features good fishing, plus lots of riffles, gravel bars, and overhanging limbs. To reach the takeout, go east of Snow for about two miles, then turn south off U.S. 62 onto a country road providing access to the stream. The one-day trip from Turkey to Kelly's Slab also offers good scenery, fast chutes, and good smallmouth fishing. The takeout point is one mile due west of Yellville at a low-water bridge known locally as Kelly's Slab. The half-day float from Kelly's Slab to Yellville is similar to the upper trips but shorter. The trip concludes on the east side of Arkansas Highway 14 at the city park in Yellville.

There are no public campsites on the creek itself, but campgrounds are available nearby at Bull Shoals Lake and Buffalo National River. Supplies and motels are available in Yellville, Cotter, Harrison, Flippin, and other area communities.

KINGS RIVER (MARBLE TO SUMMERS FORD)

The Kings River offers rewards that go far beyond the fine smallmouths with which you're likely to tangle. This is a dream stream—beautiful and pristine. It transports float-fishermen back in time to a simpler, less complicated era. The 56 miles of river between Marble and Summers Ford provide enough blue-ribbon smallmouth fishing to keep an angler occupied for years.

Long, deep pools make the segment from Marble to Marshall Ford (10.7 miles) a good fisherman's float. Overhanging trees and logs sometimes hamper travel, but there are no dangerous hazards, and the scenery is excellent. The put-in is northwest of Marble at a county road crossing. Take out at the low-water bridge at Marshall Ford, an access point northeast of Alabam.

The long run from Marshall Ford to Trigger Gap (21.7 miles) is best as a two- or three-day float, but there are intermediate access points at Piney and Rockhouse Creeks. This is the loneliest stretch of the Kings, and the floater sees few signs of civilization. The take-out is at the low-water bridge at Trigger Gap, 9 miles southwest of Berryville off Arkansas 221.

From Trigger Gap to the U.S. Highway 62 bridge (12.1 miles), the water moves right along, and the stream is normally clear of obstacles. This is the most-floated portion of the Kings, enjoyed by anglers and sightseers alike. About 20 miles of Osage Creek, the mouth of which is just below the bridge, are floatable early in the year and offer good smallmouth fishing.

A 12-mile float from the Highway 62 crossing to Summers Ford (off Arkansas 143) is another memorable run and a popular choice for fishermen. Some fine gravel bars are found in this stretch of the river.

If you want to catch the real Kings River lunkers, take along heavy tackle. Some people expect bass from this smallish river to be smallish, too, and that can cost some trophy fish. A bait-casting reel, medium-action rod, and ten- to twenty-pound-test line are appropriate.

Big smallmouths hit large crankbaits and large tandem spinners with trailing pork rind. Six or seven-inch topwater minnow lures are deadly, and the jig-and-pig is a good producer. Concentrate your casts in still pockets, side sloughs, and pools and skip the fast water.

Berryville and Eureka Springs are located near the Kings River and can meet the needs of most visitors.

BIG PINEY CREEK
(ARKANSAS 123 TO LAKE DARDANELLE)

Big Piney Creek flows largely within Ozark National Forest. The region is rugged and remote, and nearby towns have appropriate names like Fallsville, Limestone, and Deer. Some consider it the classic Ozark float stream.

A veteran fisherman will look at the cool, clear water with its rocky cover and have one thought—smallmouth bass. Brownies are abundant here, and fishing is a year-round possibility for those willing to wade-fish or drag their boats over shoals during drier months.

In fall, however, anglers usually find enough water for a leisurely float-fishing trip.

The section from Arkansas 123 to Treat (Forest Road 1805) covers about eight miles. The water upstream is fast and sometimes difficult to navigate. But on this stretch, the valley is not so tight, and the stream's pace slackens a bit to allow casual fishing. The rapids are rated easy to medium.

The float from Treat to Long Pool continues to offer great smallmouth fishing, but the hills start crowding the creek along this ten-mile run, and the result is rapids with names like Roller Coaster, Surfing Hole, and Cascades of Extinction. Gravel bars are conveniently located just below those rapids, providing ideal spots for a breather, a shore lunch, or, in some cases, a salvage operation. The takeout at Long Pool is a Forest Service campground complete with rest rooms, changing rooms, loading-unloading areas, and a parking lot.

The Piney's next section—Long Pool to Arkansas 164 (or Twin Bridges)—slows down considerably in its five-mile journey. The creek leaves the Ozarks, creating longer pools and mild rapids, then flows a few miles below Highway 164 into the backwaters of Lake Dardanelle.

Supplies can be obtained in Dover and Russellville, and the latter city also offers numerous motels.

The four floats mentioned here are among the best in Arkansas, but you can also find excellent bronzeback fishing on several other mountain streams: the Saline, Ouachita, and Caddo Rivers in the Ouachita Mountains and the Cossatot River, Eleven Point River, Illinois Bayou, Buffalo National River, and Strawberry River in the north Arkansas Ozarks.

When visiting, remember your responsibilities as an ethical angler. Obey fishing laws. Carry out all trash. Avoid trespassing on private land. Leave no signs of your visits.

Our smallmouth streams are special. They always have been and always will be—we hope. Do your part to keep them that way.

OCTOBER

NOVEMBER

Bassin' the Arkansas

If you're looking for a good body of water to ply for November largemouths, consider a trip to the Arkansas River, the state's best-known bassin' stream. The site of several national bass-fishing tournaments, including two BASS Masters Classics and at least three Red Man All-Americans, this broad river serves up superb action for autumn largemouths.

The Arkansas hasn't always been held in high esteem as a bass-fishing hotspot. Prior to 1970, the river was wild and muddy, frequently flooding surrounding countryside. It was fished by the brave and few, usually commercial fishermen or recreational anglers seeking catfish, buffalo, or drum. Bass fishing was excellent, even then, but relatively few anglers challenged the treacherous currents that characterized the river much of the year.

Today, the Arkansas resembles a series of lakes more than a river. In 1971, the Corps of Engineers completed the McClellan-Kerr Arkansas River Navigation Project, the largest inland waterway project in the corps' history. The project included construction of twelve dams in Arkansas, turning the once untamed river into a series of comparatively tranquil reservoirs. The project not only improved navigation on the river, it also improved fishing as well. Tales about huge stringers of giant Arkansas River bass began making the rounds through the nation's bassing fraternity.

By the mid-1970s, local, state, and regional bass tournaments were being held on the river nearly every weekend, year-round. And as more anglers experienced its sensational bass fishing, the Arkansas River gained a well-deserved and highly publicized reputation for producing jumbo largemouths and lots of them. The prestigious BASS Masters Classic was held on the river in 1984 and again in 1985, followed by the 1987 Red Man All-American. Proof-positive of the river's blue-ribbon status came during the 1984 BASS Masters when Rick Clunn amassed a three-day catch of bass weighing 75 pounds,

Fishing the Coal Pile in Pool Two of the Arkansas River produced this dandy largemouth.

9 ounces, smashing his own Classic record by over 15 pounds. All told, 930 pounds, 4 ounces of fish were taken to the scales, over 200 pounds more than the previous record.

DISSECTING THE RIVER

Largemouths and spotted bass inhabit all pools of the Arkansas River, but some of the best November fishing is in the four pools formed by Lock and Dam 5, below Redfield; Lock and Dam 4, below Pine Bluff; Lock and Dam 3, near Grady; and Lock and Dam 2, near Dumas.

Pool two, above Dam 2, contains 96 miles of shoreline at normal navigational pool and has 10,600 surface acres. This pool extends upstream 35.9 miles following the river channel.

This river section has a reputation for producing ten-pound-plus bass. The Pendleton area contains a variety of good bass-fishing areas, including two huge off-river oxbows, Moore Bayou and the Coal Pile, as well as Merrisach Lake.

Coal Pile is on the right bank of the river (heading downstream) at about mile 23. This area offers ideal bass habitat, with logjams, flooded cypress, rocks, channels, and flats to fish. Moore Bayou is three more miles downriver on the opposite side. Flooded timber and shallow water are abundant here. Merrisach Lake, just above Lock 2, is on the Arkansas Post Canal, which leads out from Moore Bayou. Like Coal Pile and Moore Bayou, it is essentially shallow with heavy cover. And like its sister waters, it often produces giant bass.

Continuing upstream, anglers can explore Big Bayou Meto, Mud Lake Bend (a major backwater), and Little Bayou Meto. Nooks and bays off the main river lake also contain good cover and excellent shallow-water fishing.

Pool three is the smallest of these four Arkansas River lakes. This pool has thirty-six miles of shoreline and 3,670 surface acres at normal levels. It's mainly just straight river channel, but there are a couple of backwaters between Richland Bend and Trulock.

This section contains a large number of bank-stabilization structures, which consist mainly of large wooden pilings driven into the sandy bottom. At times, these attract dense bass concentrations.

Pool four begins just below Pine Bluff and contains 5,680 surface acres and fifty-eight miles of shoreline in its twenty-mile length. This is the pool made famous by Rick Clunn. His fabulous three-day stringer of bass came from the Slack Water Harbor area near Lake Langhofer. Clunn found a shallow ledge holding an immense population of black bass and used crankbaits to establish the record catch. In its eight-mile length, the harbor contains a variety of cover and structures, including flooded timber, shallow vegetation, riprap, and two- to eighty-foot holes.

Lake Langhofer and the Slack Water Harbor area contain some of the best backwater areas on this section, but there's also a small often-productive backwater near the Hensley Bar Cutoff. The remainder of the pool is mostly river channel with several miles of channel-stabilization structures.

Pool five extends upstream from White Bluff twenty-one miles, with 6,680 surface acres and a fifty-mile shoreline. This pool contains several backwater areas. Brodie Bend, an old oxbow with acres of timber, is one of the most heavily fished areas, but locales around Case Bar Cutoff and Warings Bend also provide excellent backwater bassing. Several small creeks also enter this pool, and they often hold bass, especially where they enter the main river pool.

TACTICAL TIPS

If autumn rain and runoffs are heavy and the river is high, anglers probably will be forced into backwater sloughs and off-river lakes where topwater plugs, buzzbaits, minnow-imitation divers, and crankbaits can be retrieved around timber, rocks, pilings, and vegetation. Jig-and-pigs take bass around logs and treetops.

With more stable water conditions, backwaters are good early and late with topwaters, buzzbaits, and plastic worms. Midday patterns revolve around the main river channel and include riprap with crankbaits, worms, or spinnerbaits and flipping shoreline cover with worms.

Should weather be unseasonably warm, wing dikes could figure prominently in your angling game plan. These walls of rocks reduce shoreline erosion by directing water downstream. They often stretch

NOVEMBER

hundreds of yards on both sides of the river, especially near dams and along bends. Water around them ranges from five to fifteen feet deep, and if the water is still relatively warm, schools of fall bass will hold near these dikes.

Sometimes bass hold right off the ends of the rocks. Other times, they're at a specific spot along the rocks. And still other times, they're scattered along them. Crayfish and shad are attracted to these boulder-strewn hideouts, so artificials imitating these forage animals are among the best bass-catchers.

In November, the Arkansas could be clear and stable, high and muddy, or anywhere in between. The anglers most likely to catch fish are adaptable and multifaceted, prepared to deal with whatever conditions the capricious river throws their way.

NOVEMBER

Ouachita River Smallmouths

I saw a cartoon that pictured Thoreau at Walden Pond writing a postcard to Emerson. "Dear Ralph," it said. "Talk about boring! Nothing to do but take stupid walks in the dreary woods. You'd hate it! Best regards, Henry."

If Thoreau had written that way, the caption explained, Walden Pond would still be unspoiled.

It pains me to say anything about the extraordinary smallmouth bass fishing on Arkansas's upper Ouachita River. For those of us who treasure the experience of a peaceful float on a beautiful, blue-ribbon smallmouth stream, there's always a conflict between wanting to share a good thing and wanting to protect it. The upper Ouachita seems especially vulnerable because it is a ribbon of unspoiled water in a sea of recreational users. Millions of people visit the surrounding Ouachita National Forest each year, yet few take time to float this emerald treasure.

I have decided, nevertheless, to share what I know of the Ouachita. In my experience, smallmouth anglers are people who stress quality versus quantity, folks who place little or no emphasis on "limiting out." One may therefore mention the secret lairs of the smallmouth without fear of ruining them.

The Ouachita River begins life as a trickle of water just north of Mena, but it is hardly wadable until it nears Cherry Hill. Once it clears Cherry Hill, then Pine Ridge, the stream continues thirty miles eastward, skirting the west Arkansas towns of Oden and Pencil Bluff, to below Sims, north of Mount Ida. The upper river completes its destiny to become lakes Ouachita, Hamilton, and Catherine.

This scenic river is custom-made for smallmouth bass. Its waters are clear, cool, and fast-flowing, and there's a good mix of long deep pools and rapids. There are lots of big rocks, deep runs under steep banks, and downed timber which offer shade, food, and protection from the current. That's where you find smallmouths.

Most local anglers prefer live baits, particularly live crayfish and minnows. However, any artificial designed to imitate the smallmouth's natural prey usually proves productive. Plastic worms and salamanders, crayfish- and minnow-imitation crankbaits, and the pork-frog–jig combination all are worth trying.

Bronzebacks feed primarily by sight, so the manner in which bait is presented is a key element in taking fish. Ouachita River brownies usually rest behind rocks or other current breaks and wait for something carried in the current. You'll catch more bass if you present your bait in the same way, in as natural a manner as possible.

Cast slightly upstream and let the bait drift with the current on a slack line. Guide the lure past and behind as many large rocks as you can pick out, hopping it along with short flips of your rod tip. Make the retrieve slow, too, nice and slow. Use too rapid a retrieve and the smallmouths won't hit it in this cool water.

When is the best time to fish for Ouachita River brownies? If you're most interested in catching a big bass, pick a late fall or winter day. Canoe traffic is light then, sometimes nonexistent, so boat-wary smallmouths aren't as likely to have lockjaw. You may have the river all to yourself, another big plus. November is an especially fruitful fishing month, with colorful hardwoods blanketing the surrounding hillsides.

No matter when you fish, try to be on the river before sunrise. Peak smallmouth activity usually comes during the first couple hours of the day.

In contrast, the worst periods for river smallmouths usually come on the heels of hard cold fronts, regardless of the season. For a day or two after a front comes through, bass fishing takes a nosedive.

The uppermost Ouachita float starts at the McGuire access on the south side of Arkansas Highway 88, halfway between Ink and Cherry Hill, and ends seven miles downstream at the Cherry Hill Access area. The second float covers thirteen miles from Cherry Hill to Pine Ridge. The takeout is a country bridge a mile east of Pine Ridge, just southeast of Highway 88. The third trip is a ten-mile float from Pine Ridge to the Arkansas Highway 379 bridge south of Oden.

From Oden, it's ten miles downstream to the Rocky Shoals Campground at the U.S. Highway 270 crossing. Anglers putting in at Rocky Shoals can take out at Sims Campground, four miles downstream, or at Fulton Branch Campground another three miles downriver. Both these camping-access areas are good starting points for trips to the last two public takeouts—Dragover and River Bluff. It's two miles from Fulton Branch to Dragover, and three miles from Dragover to River Bluff. Several other takeout areas are on the back-waters of Lake Ouachita around the Arkansas Highway 27 crossing.

Excellent fishing isn't the only hallmark of the upper Ouachita. There's also the scenery. The Ouachita features intriguing rock for-mations, forested hillsides, and occasional glimpses of wild turkeys, deer, and other wildlife. With only sparse population along its banks, the river also offers a sense of solitude. The stream's long, lazy pools and sparkling shoals make it especially inviting for families wishing to pause for a swim or picnic along the way.

The upper Ouachita is great for beginning floaters, since rapids rarely exceed medium on the difficulty scale. A canoe provides the best means of river travel, but if you don't have one, canoe rentals and shuttle service are available through several local outfitters.

The upper Ouachita River provides a beautiful, peaceful setting for a smallmouth junket. Visit it when you can, and match wits with ol' bronzeback, the cagiest, smartest, and most classic fighter in southern waters.

NOVEMBER

Playground of the Ozarks

The White is a river with two faces. Born in the homespun Ozark hill country of northwest Arkansas, it flows on an erratic course for 690 miles to join with the Mississippi far to the south and east.

In the northwest, it is a spirited colt of a stream, kicking its cold, white-water heels through wooded Ozark valleys and gaps as rugged and worn as a blacksmith's apron. The eastern section is a sluggish, brutal river that cuts S curves and near figure eights like a giant plow tearing an erratic furrow in an equally gigantic area of delta flatland. There is as much difference between the two portions of the stream as there is between the fast-falling Niagara River in New York and the peaceful Suwannee of Florida.

The section of the White River most popular as a vacation mecca is undisputably its upper portion—that stretch of river that has its headwaters on top of a Madison County mountain and then flows 390 miles down into north-central Arkansas to Batesville. After World War II, four U.S. Army Corps of Engineers dams were built in the upper river basin to control flooding and create power sources. The four resulting lakes—Beaver, Table Rock, Bull Shoals, and Norfork—brought an economic revolution to the entire Ozark region. The tourism industry was born.

The "Great Lakes of the White River" have become a fisherman's paradise and are noted for lunker-size largemouth and smallmouth bass, stripers, white bass, bream, crappie, and catfish. However, no story about White River fishing would be complete without discussing its biggest claim to fame—float-fishin' for trout.

The White didn't become a trout stream until Bull Shoals Dam was built. After the dam was completed in 1951, water in the lake was stored at great depths, making it ice cold when released. This created ideal trout habitat and enabled successful stocking of rainbow and brown trout. Today, for almost seventy-five miles, from Bull Shoals

---

Rainbow trout are the bread-and-butter fish of the White River in north Arkansas.

Dam downstream to Guion, trout thrive in the cold fifty-six-degree water released from the dam.

They grow large. In 1972, Gordon Lackey landed a monster brown weighing 31 pounds, 8 ounces. This stood as the North American record until Leon Waggoner landed a 33 pound, 8 ounce leviathan in the North Fork of the White River in 1977.

Further evidence of the White River system's exceptional trout fishing came on August 7, 1988, when Mike Manley of North Little Rock, Arkansas, landed another mega-trout in the White's North Fork, this one weighing 38 pounds, 9 ounces. That fish stood as the National Fresh Water Fishing Hall of Fame all-tackle world record until Howard Collins of Heber Springs caught a 40-pound, 4-ounce brown in Arkansas's Little Red River in 1992. A week after Manley made his catch, David Wooten of Jordan, Arkansas, landed a 34-pound brown just downstream from Manley's hotspot.

Very few browns grow to such enormous proportions, but 5- to 10-pound brown trout are common, and you have an excellent chance of landing a 10- to 20-pounder. Each year a few 20-pound-plus trophies are boated by ecstatic fishermen.

While bull browns tug at the heartstrings of trophy fishermen, acrobatic rainbows provide the bulk of fast action. Probably more rainbow trout are caught each year in the White than in any other trout stream in America; the Arkansas Game and Fish Commission and U.S. Fish and Wildlife Service stock millions of rainbows in the White River annually, and more than 90 percent of them are caught each year by anglers who come here from throughout the country.

The action is spectacular. Smashing strikes are followed by bull-dogging runs. And it's always amazing how a rainbow trout can hit a lure ten feet underwater and the next instant perform aerial acrobatics that would put a world-class gymnast to shame.

Although White River rainbows don't reach world-record weights, in 1981, the river produced the current 19-pound, 1-ounce Arkansas state record. Ten-pound fish are occasionally taken, and 2- to 6-pound rainbows are common and almost always eager to bite. The pure joy of a White River fishing trip is that everybody can—and usually does—catch rainbow trout here year-round.

Trout-fishing enthusiasts also will be pleased to find nice cut-throat and brook trout in the White River. These species were first stocked by the Game and Fish Commission in the 1980s. The Arkansas record cutthroat, a mammoth 9-pound, 9-ounce beauty, was caught on the White in October 1985, and a 3-pound, 10-ounce record brook trout was taken on the North Fork of the White River below Norfork Dam in October 1984.

Many fly-fishing enthusiasts consider White River the best year-round trout-fishing stream in North America. Low summer water levels expose shoals, riffles, and moss beds concealing hungry lunker trout.

Five- and six-weight fly-fishing outfits are ideal when fished with size 6, 8, 10, or 14 weighted nymphs. Favored lure patterns include the Gold-ribbed Hare's Ear, the Montana Nymph, Whitlock's Squirrel-tail Nymph, and the Woolly Worm.

During winter, switch to size 18 or 22 midge patterns to match these tiny insects hatching in long pools. The sculpin, a small bottom-dwelling fish, is common in the river, and big brown trout like large sculpin patterns, big streamers, maribou leeches, and brown or black Woolly Boogers. Long casting produces outstanding results, and floating lines work fine. Use a strike indicator on the tippet.

While fly-fishing attracts many trout fans, float-fishin' put White River on the map. The art of float-fishin' wasn't born on the White, but it probably was refined to its truest form here by guides floating trout anglers through emerald-green pools walled by limestone bluffs that curve to the sky. Any real trout fisherman who's ever made a float trip will tell you it's properly called "float-fishin'," and you never put a "g" on this pleasurable sport.

The standard White River rig is a long, lean vessel called a john-boat, for some forgotten hill-country reason. It comes fully equipped with captain's chairs for fishing comfort, a drink cooler amidships, a ten- to twenty-horsepower motor to take you back upriver to your resort at day's end, and a guide who knows every riffle and pool. Leisurely transported in a twenty-foot long johnboat past picturesque bluffs, camera bugs can snap away while waiting for the next strike.

The float-fishin' guide is a jack of all trades. He is a historian in regards to the river's past and points of interest along your down-stream journey. He is a self-appointed naturalist familiar with all the area's wildlife and is intimately acquainted with all the monster trout—which are easily seen in the gin-clear water as they lie in their own private pools—calling this one and that by name as he would an old friend. He is a chef par excellence, and the mouth-watering aroma of trout cooking over a gravel bar campfire will have you licking your lips as you soak in the White's spectrum of rustic beauty.

At times it's possible to float and not see another human all day. But during peak fishing season, from early spring to late fall, the river is alive with activity and other float-fishermen. Yet on the White, where guided float trips are a specialty, there is more than ample elbow room, so anglers aren't crowded.

It's worth remembering that fishing season never closes in Arkansas, and even the coldest months have mild, sunny days made just for the outdoorsman. The larger fish usually are taken during the cooler fall and winter months, and cruising the river from October to February is a little like arriving early at your senior prom. The decorations are in place, the punch bowl is filled, and the band is playing. But the crowd hasn't appeared yet, and somehow the whole affair seems to have been laid just for you.

Marshmallows and worms may not seem like a gourmet's delight, but White River trout love them. Your guide may joke that the reason the combination goes over so well with the fish is because most that you catch are females, and everyone knows how the girls love sweets. Actually, though, the reason is a little more logical.

With the dams upriver, the water level on the White fluctuates, sometimes overnight, and at times as much as two to six feet. When the water rises, larger trout move in close to the bank; and even when it goes down again, they often stay there feeding in mossy plants near shore. If you plunk a plain worm down, it gets lost in the vegetation. By squeezing a miniature marshmallow on the line above the hooked worm, you can float the bait above the moss, preventing hang-ups and keeping it visible to trout.

Other popular fishing methods include using canned corn, salmon eggs, crappie jigs, wax worms, and a wide variety of crankbaits, spoons, and other artificial lures. Don't worry if you've never fished for trout on a big river. Your guide can show you how to fish, what bait to use, and, of course, he'll take you to a honeyhole where you're sure to catch fish. He'll also provide fishing tackle and baits if you like.

If you want to hire a guide there are plenty working out of well-equipped marinas up and down the river. When you call to reserve a spot, be sure to specify the kind of trip you want and what you expect the guide to show you.

Specify, for instance, that you're interested in big fish or lots of fish. Specify, also, if you want to make a long float trip or fish a smaller river section within motoring distance of your overnight accommodations.

If you prefer to do without a guide, great. There are only a few tricky shoals, but normally there is enough boat traffic that you can follow other anglers through safe passages. You can bring your own boat and gear, or boats, motors, and other equipment can be rented for a reasonable fee.

When you're not fishing, take time to enjoy the resplendent scenery in this timeless landscape. Each season has its special fascinations—spring's dogwood blossoms and colorful migrant birds, summer's slow-moving serenity and isolated swimming holes, autumn's gold and crimson foliage, winter's icicle draperies on riverside bluffs. The White is truly a river for all seasons—and for everybody.

Take beautiful Arkansas Razorback country, add southern mystique and hospitality, a big dose of fast trout action and the chance of landing a trophy, and you have a perfect trip. Of course, the White River is hardly a secret. On the contrary, it is one of the most famous float-fishin' rivers in the world. And for millions of visitors annually, the White River in Arkansas has become synonymous with the word "playground."

And if you're a trout fisherman, only one word adequately describes this beautiful country: paradise.

NOVEMBER

Winter Floats for Arkansas Spots

November is superb for float-fishing the scenic spotted bass streams in Arkansas's Ozark and Ouachita Mountains. Water levels are just right for canoeing, big "Kentuckies" are actively feeding, and with few people on the water, you can enjoy an extra measure of relaxation.

Spotted bass are aggressive, high-spirited scrappers that guarantee hard strikes, powerful runs, and rod-bending fights. Yet, throughout Arkansas and the rest of their range, these sporty game fish are largely misunderstood, overlooked, and under-utilized. Most are taken unintentionally by anglers fishing for other species.

This seeming lack of popularity is not because the fish are scarce. They're not. Spotted bass comprise a significant portion of the catch on numerous lakes and streams throughout Arkansas and the southern United States.

It's not because spotted bass aren't sporty opponents, either. Inch for inch and pound for pound, they are among the gamest of southern sport fish.

Perhaps the main reason spotted bass are ignored is confusion. Many fishermen think the spots they catch are small largemouth or smallmouth bass. Spots don't grow as big as these closely related species, and while two- to three-pounders aren't unusual, fish of four pounds and more are exceptional in most waters.

Adding to the muddle is the fact that the spotted bass is sort of an "in-between" fish. It has the general shape and coloration of a largemouth, but its compact jaws resemble a smallmouth's. It can't survive in water with low dissolved-oxygen content, water in which largemouths thrive, but is successful in waters that are somewhat warmer and siltier than those supporting smallmouths. Its range overlaps that of both its cousins; and in some waters, including the streams in Arkansas's mountain country, you may catch spotted bass and largemouths; spotted bass and smallmouths; or spotted bass, largemouths, and smallmouths, all on a single trip.

Winter is prime time for catching fat spotted bass in Arkansas's mountain streams.

Fortunately, fishermen who learn specialized spotted bass tactics can catch lots of them by design rather than a few by accident. If you gear your tactics and equipment to the spotted bass's habits and habitat, this handsome sport fish can add an enjoyable new dimension to your bass fishing.

FLOATING AND FISHING TIPS

A light canoe will put you within reach of many prime spotted bass pools on the cool-water streams of the Ozarks and Ouachitas. Winter anglers can launch at a roadside access and enjoy a leisurely float that lasts a few hours or a few days. Water levels usually are ideal this time of year, so you'll seldom have to wade or drag over shoals.

Allow time to take in the sights and have a gravel-bar lunch. The beauty of these mountain streams is mesmerizing, and you'll want to savor every aspect of these majestic uplands.

Though heavier tackle is OK, many anglers fish these streams with an ultralight spinning or spin-casting outfit. Most "Kentuckies" in these waters run a few ounces up to two or three pounds, and light tackle compounds the fun of catching these feisty little stream fish.

Crayfish and small baitfish are the main course at a spotted bass luau, so when using artificials, it makes sense to use those that imitate these animals. Jig-and-pigs are good for this reason, as are plastic grubs and small jigging spoons. Plastic worms and tube jigs also are favorites. Shallow-running crankbaits and spinnerbaits produce during the spring spawning season.

The favorite bait of savvy Arkansas anglers is live crayfish. These are gathered from beneath leaves and rocks in shoreline shallows and stored in a container filled with wet leaves.

The best crayfish size is two to three inches. Rig them on a 1/0 to 3/0, light-wire hook with one or two split shot crimped on your line twelve inches above the bait. Run the hook upward through the last third of the crayfish's tail, so it can be retrieved in a natural, backward manner.

Let the crayfish fall to the bottom, regardless of the depth of water you're fishing. Then keep your rod tip high and apply light pressure to the line so your bait doesn't crawl under a rock. Work the bait by pulling it up off the bottom then letting it fall back down. Don't move it more than six inches at a time, and don't jerk it suddenly. Move the bait slowly.

Working your bait or lure across the bottom near rock ledges is the best way to pinpoint spotted bass, but don't bypass midstream boulders, underwater shale ridges, shoal edges, and other structures.

GOOD STREAMS TO FISH

In the Ozarks of northern Arkansas, you'll find nearly a dozen good spotted bass streams from which to choose—Crooked Creek, Buffalo National River, Lee Creek, Big Piney Creek, Illinois Bayou, Cadron Creek, the upper forks of the Little Red River, the Strawberry River, Spring River, Eleven Point River, and the Current River. The Ouachita Mountains in west-central Arkansas also encompass outstanding spotted bass streams, including the Cossatot River, Little Missouri River, Caddo River, the upper forks of the Saline River, and the upper Ouachita River.

Caddo River (Caddo Gap to Glenwood)

This popular six-mile float offers excellent spotted bass fishing. Kentuckies are fat, averaging a pound, and you may catch and release dozens, including, perhaps, some two- to three-pounders.

Launch at the low-water bridge west of Arkansas Highway 8 in Caddo Gap. Take out beneath the U.S. Highway 70 bridge at Glenwood. In between, you'll encounter small rapids, long gravel bars, and plenty of good bass fishing around boulders and fallen treetops. Try using a bobber to drift night crawlers and small tube jigs past these hideouts.

Upper Ouachita River
(Oden to Rocky Shoals Campground)

Plan to put in early and take out late to get the most from this scenic ten-mile float. The fishing is exhilarating, with fast-paced action for spotted bass up to two and three pounds. Don't dilly dally if you want to thoroughly fish the many rocks and ledges in this stretch of clear mountain water.

The put-in is at the Arkansas Highway 379 bridge south of Oden. The takeout is at Rocky Shoals Campground (Ouachita National Forest) at the U.S. Highway 270 crossing. Fishing tip: work brown jig–pork frog combos along crevices in stream-bottom shale.

Little Missouri River
(Arkansas Highway 84 bridge to Lake Greeson)

Set aside as part of Arkansas's Natural and Scenic Rivers System, the Little Missouri is a strikingly beautiful smallmouth stream. This ten- to eleven-mile stretch—starting west of Langley, with a takeout at Lake Greeson's Star-of-the-West Campground—harbors plenty of feisty spotted bass within its rock gardens and deep pools. Entice them with live crayfish.

Fishing supplies, lodging, and other amenities are available in Daisy, Kirby, and Langley.

Saline River
(Lyle Park to Game and Fish Access near Interstate 30)

The upper portion of the Saline, above Benton, is a clear, cold-water section harboring lots of fat spotted bass. This float begins at Benton's Lyle Park, just off Highway 5 about a mile north of town. Take out at the Game and Fish Commission's concrete boat ramp on the left bank just before you pass under the Interstate 30 bridge. Under normal conditions, this is a three- to four-hour float, but if you fish the deep pools thoroughly, as you should, plan on five to six hours.

Fishing tip: about two-thirds of the way through this float, you'll notice a tall water-pumping facility on the left bank. Just downstream is a low-water dam. Use extreme caution here, stopping to portage around the dam and to fish the deep pool above it. Work lures around the fallen treetops along the bank just above the dam. This is a real hotspot for jumbo spotted bass.

Kings River (Marble to Marshall Ford)

You'll have to look long and hard to find a better winter bass hotspot than this Ozark stream, where all three kinds of black bass—spots, largemouths, and smallmouths—await your pleasure. Long, deep, still pools make this particular section a good fisherman's float. Overhanging trees and logs sometimes hamper travel, but there are no dangerous hazards, and the scenery is excellent. Put in at the low-water bridge one-half mile off Highway 68 at Marble and take out at the low-water bridge at Marshall Ford, an access point 10.7 miles downstream, just northeast of Alabam.

Concentrate your casts in still pockets, side sloughs, and pools, and skip the fast water. Most good spotted bass will be holed up in such areas. The jig-and-pig and small bottom-bumping crankbaits are good producers, but don't use your ultralight tackle here. The Kings harbors lots of gigantic smallmouths, and you don't want to miss a chance at one of those.

This primer on catching Arkansas spotted bass is by no means complete. Yet, hopefully, it has enlightened you about one of this region's most neglected sport fish.

If, after reading this, you decide to give the spotted bass a try, beware. Spotted (bass) fever can be treated by grasping one end of a fishing rod while a spot tugs on the other. But, as anyone who has it will tell you, there's no cure.

NOVEMBER

DECEMBER

Capital City Saugers

A cold, rainy day in early December isn't my usual idea of a good time to fish. But when I heard saugers were biting below the North Little Rock hydroelectric plant on such a day, I grabbed an ultralight rod and a tackle box and headed to Cook's Landing on the Arkansas River.

Drizzle fell from a lead-gray sky. A frigid wind rushed up the river corridor. As I headed down the steps to waterside, I saw a dozen stubborn anglers fishing from walkways by the channel.

Polar bears, I thought. You must be half polar bear to fish in this weather.

"Are they biting?" I asked a man coming up the steps.

"They're biting alright," he replied, wiping his cherry-red nose. "I caught seven, but I can't handle any more of this cold. I'm darn near froze."

As I made my way down, a teenager outfitted in heavy coveralls let out a holler and began reeling in a nice fish. The big sauger had no intention of being hauled ashore, however, and it was three minutes before the youngster landed it. It was a dandy fish, close to three pounds, and it was hooked on a big pink twistertail jig. The boy held the fish high for his friends to see, then fastened it on a stringer that held four smaller saugers.

I dug through my tackle box and found a fluorescent pink, $\frac{1}{16}$-ounce, curly-tail jig and tied it on my ultralight spinning outfit. Then, reaching my hand into the cold water in my minnow bucket, I corralled a two-inch shiner and ran the jig hook through its lips.

"Ain't seen that trick," a fellow next to me noted. "Oughta work though. These buggers are mighty fond of minnows. Fellows down there have caught fifteen or twenty on shiners since I started watching an hour ago. I can't buy my first nibble."

The man was fishing a black Road Runner, a good bait at times, but apparently not this day.

Winter anglers line the shores below Murray Lock and Dam at Little Rock, hoping to catch tasty saugers as they make their upstream spawning runs.

"Here, try this," I said, tossing him a pink twistertail. "Some guys up thataway are doing good with them. I've got plenty in my box."

I cast the jig-minnow combo upstream. My line swung tight, and when I reeled up slack, I felt the rig bumping across the bottom.

On my third cast, one bump was followed by a pickup. It wasn't a jarring strike, just a slight "tap tap" followed by the upstream movement of my line. After a short battle, I landed a one-pound sauger.

As I unhooked my fish, the fellow next to me shouted, "Hot dog!" and began fighting his first fish of the day, another sauger as we soon found out.

The action wasn't fast, but over the next two hours, my new-found friend and I landed seven more saugers, and a trio of white bass to boot.

"Ain't many folks that know about the sauger fishing here," the man said as he watched the tip of his long spinning rod. "Even if they did, I don't reckon many would be out here on a day like this. Beat's sitting in front of the TV, though, and me and the little lady'll eat good tonight. Ain't no better eating in the river than these little guys here."

That's the way it is with saugers. These unusual panfish, cousins of the walleye, don't have many fans in Arkansas. They don't fight much, and the best fishing is on cold days when even a penguin would welcome an electric blanket. But when it comes to table quality, there's not a fish swimming in Arkansas waters that can top them. And on those cold, dark days in winter when other fish have lockjaw, saugers are good ointment for a man with the fishing itch.

The sauger looks prehistoric. Take away the fins and add legs and a long tail, and you'd have a respectable looking lizard. The streamlined sauger has glassy, marble-like eyes, sharp teeth, and blotchy brown and gold skin. Local names include sand pike, gray pike, and jack salmon. Arkansas's state record weighed six pounds, twelve ounces.

Finding saugers isn't difficult if you're willing to brave the cold. The best fishing is in winter below dams on the Arkansas River where the fish are halted during runs upriver. The last three state records came from this large river, and though other streams—the Black, White, Current, Eleven Point, and Spring—sometimes are productive, none comes close to the Arkansas River for quality sauger fishing.

This wasn't always the case. In the 1960s, saugers were a rare catch in the Arkansas. They were abundant in earlier years, but as surrounding lands were cleared and developed, the river became muddier and more polluted. As a consequence, the sauger thumbed its nose at the Arkansas River.

Fortunately, the sauger's disappearance wasn't permanent. Following construction of the McClellan-Kerr Navigation System in the 1960s, water quality improved, and by the early 1970s saugers once again were being caught.

In the fall 1977 issue of *Arkansas Game and Fish Magazine,* fisheries biologist Bob Limbird wrote about the sauger's return to the Arkansas River. He noted that a surge in the sauger population occurred during 1973 and 1974, a period when heavy spring rains produced a constant volume of water flow during the sauger spawning season. Good spawns two years in a row caused the population to increase markedly.

Reading Limbird's story helps us understand why saugers may be abundant in the river some years and seemingly nonexistent during others. He says, "Frequent water level fluctuations below lock-and-dams are detrimental to sauger spawning success. As the water level falls, eggs adhering to the rocks are often left out of the water, causing a high mortality rate. It is during the spring periods when large volumes of water, usually caused by heavy rains, keep the river flow constant that the sauger spawns are most successful." During the years immediately following these good spawns, anglers are most likely to catch good numbers of saugers in the Arkansas River.

Saugers live throughout the river in Arkansas, from Ft. Smith to the river's confluence with the Mississippi. Concentrations occur below every dam at times.

One superb fishery is below Murray Lock and Dam and the North Little Rock hydroelectric plant in Pulaski County. Fair to good concentrations of saugers occur here, and there are excellent bank-fishing facilities on both sides of the river—at Cook's Landing on the north bank and at Murray Park to the south.

Look for saugers here in pools or pockets where current is

DECEMBER

present but greatly diminished. Start fishing near the dam and slowly move downstream. The greatest numbers of fish usually are caught within two hundred yards of the dam and power plant gates, but sometimes you must move farther downstream to be successful. A boat seldom is necessary, but if saugers seem uncooperative, you can launch at the Murray Park boat ramp and motor from one area to another, casting around riprap, wing dikes, or other revetments between the dams and downtown Little Rock.

Normally, there's good water flow below the dams in winter, and saugers are up against the rocks along the banks. If the water is moderately, yet not excessively, high, cast around riprap, wing dikes, and other rock structures to find fish. On the rare occasions when winter water releases are low, look for fish in the deeper water of the spillway.

Water flow also helps determine where to fish—below Murray Dam or in the hydroelectric plant channel. My preference is to fish the area where water flow is constant but at a minimum. These conditions may exist in both channels at the same time, in which case you can take your pick. But as a general rule, flows from the dam and power plant differ. Sauger anglers differ in their preferences, so you might want to try both areas under different conditions to determine which area you like best.

Saugers feed primarily on small baitfish like shad and minnows. They usually are caught using live baitfish or an artificial lure imitating that prey. Of course, that takes in an astounding variety of baits—small live shad (which can be caught with a cast net in dam tailwaters), live shiners, jigs, small spoons, small spinners, small crankbaits, and other popular enticements like Gay Blades and the Little George tailspinner.

In my experience, you'll rarely go wrong using live minnows, lead-head jigs, or a combination of the two. For minnows, tie a heavy sinker to the line's end, so it sinks to the bottom where saugers usually stay. The minnow is lip-hooked on a small, single hook attached to a dropper line tied a few inches above the weight.

Lead-head jigs also must weigh enough so that they fall to or near the bottom. For shallow water, lighter jigs—$\frac{1}{16}$ to $\frac{1}{8}$ ounce—

work well; in deeper or more turbulent water, some anglers go as heavy as an ounce.

When using a jig-minnow combo, consider adding a No. 8 treble hook as a trailer. Tie a short length of line to the bend in the jig's hook, and tie the treble hook on the other end. Hook a live minnow through the lip with the jig hook, then hook one barb of the treble in the minnow's tail. This simple rig nails saugers on the slightest nibble.

Allow your lure or bait to bounce along the bottom with the current. When bank fishing, an upstream cast lets you keep your rig in the water longer. Keep a tight line so you can feel striking fish.

Most Arkansas River anglers use light to medium tackle for saugers. A medium-action rod, spinning reel, and six- to twelve-pound-test line are strong enough to handle them and easy to use in cold weather. Bait-casting reels are difficult to control with gloved hands.

Weather and water conditions are important considerations when planning a sauger trip. Most sauger fishermen insist that the lousier the weather, the better the fishing. The ideal sauger fishing day is when it's cold, dark, windy, and rainy. I've never done much good when the river was high and muddy, as occurs following a heavy rain. The water needs to be fairly clear, and low-water conditions always seem best.

Another variable to consider is time of day. You can do OK during midday, especially on rainy or overcast days. But for big fish in quantity, fish in the dark. The peak time seems to be in the hour or two before dawn, though other nighttime hours can be equally productive.

Fishing on cold, wet days isn't for everybody. For most of us, a warm fireplace is much more attractive than a frigid outing on a big river. If the fishing itch gets too intense to bear, though, don't let the weather keep you housebound. Head for the dam tailwaters on the Arkansas River at Little Rock. Catching fat river saugers is a sure remedy for what ails you.

DECEMBER

Christmas Tree Crappie

When winter rolls around, crappie fishing is the last thing on most Arkansas anglers' minds. Nevertheless, winter is a great season for crappie fishing here. Cold-water crappie feed actively, and anglers who give winter fishing a try may be pleasantly surprised at the number and size of fish they catch.

Winter crappie usually hold near deep cover and structure, making them somewhat difficult to locate. In recent years, though, Arkansas fisheries managers have brought crappie and anglers together by placing man-made fish attractors in many first-rate crappie lakes.

These artificial crappie "condos" usually are made from trees bundled together with wire and sunk with concrete weights. They're especially helpful to anglers unfamiliar with a lake's bottom topography and to those who don't have electronic equipment for locating crappie concentrations on underwater structures. Because fish attractors placed by government agencies usually are marked with specially colored buoys, the angler can find crappie by simply moving from one fish-attractor buoy to another, working jigs and minnows through the woody tangles below.

HOW MAN-MADE FISH ATTRACTORS WORK

Fishermen have been sinking brush and trees to attract and concentrate fish for hundreds of years. Sink a tree in a lake where natural cover has disappeared, and crappie flock to it like a new restaurant in town. These sites provide resting and feeding cover, and spawning habitat.

Old Christmas trees most often are used for making crappie attractors. These are gathered at advertised collection sites, tied in bundles, and anchored with concrete blocks to supplement existing cover. A few days after the trees are sunk, small aquatic organisms

Crappie fans who learn the proper technique for fishing around fish shelters constructed from discarded Christmas trees take home lots of dandy crappie in winter.

gather around the maze of branches. When baitfish discover these minute food animals, they school around the brush piles to feed on them. Game fish such as crappie and bass soon follow, feeding on the schools of baitfish. Fishermen zero in on the concentrations of game fish.

Christmas trees aren't the only material used for building crappie attractors. One variation uses several small hardwood trees bundled together with wire. Wooden stake beds also work well. Long, thin slats of lumber are driven into the lake bed or nailed to shipping pallets for sinking in deeper water. Many state agencies use bundles of old tires with holes punched in them to facilitate sinking. Concrete blocks attached with wire hold the attractors on the bottom.

THE BULL SHOALS–NORFORK FISH COVER PROJECT

One large-scale fish attractor project was implemented in lakes Bull Shoals and Norfork, two large U.S. Army Corps of Engineers impoundments near the Arkansas-Missouri state line.

The corps completed construction of Norfork in 1944 and Bull Shoals in 1952. During construction, virtually all trees were removed from the lake bottoms. Trees not removed have mostly rotted away.

Because the lake levels fluctuate dramatically, aquatic vegetation never has been well established in Norfork and Bull Shoals. Lack of fish cover always has limited fish production. Nevertheless, crappie and other fish grow fast in the clear, high-quality water, and fishing is excellent for those who know where to find their quarry. Unfortunately, lack of cover made it difficult for many anglers to locate concentrations of sport fish.

In 1986, the Twin Lakes Chapter of the Bass Research Foundation approached the Arkansas Game and Fish Commission with a special request. They wanted assistance introducing aquatic vegetation into Norfork and Bull Shoals to improve fish habitat and fishing. At the time, the Corps of Engineers and Arkansas Game and Fish Commission were concerned that establishing aquatic vegetation might conflict with other reservoir uses. The Game and Fish

DECEMBER

Winter crappie fishing is good around fish shelters.

Commission suggested that a large-scale artificial habitat improvement project might accomplish some of the same goals.

A plan involving use of trees from the lakes' shorelines to create fish attractors was presented to the Corps of Engineers and the U.S. Fish and Wildlife Service for federal funding approval through the Sport Fish Restoration Act. Both federal agencies and the Twin Lakes Chapter approved the plan. The project began in 1987.

Since then, six hundred fish attractors have been installed in Bull Shoals and Norfork. Over seventy thousand trees comprise the attractors, which cover over 160 acres of lake bottom totaling thirty-three miles in length.

Each attractor has thirty or more bundles of trees (six or less trees per bundle) and covers an area approximately 40 feet wide and 300 feet long. The bundles were sunk along a contour line corresponding to the depth at which the thermocline usually forms (25 feet deep). On Bull Shoals, the target elevation is 630 feet above mean sea level; on Norfork, it's 525 feet. Fishermen can determine how deep the attractors are by determining the current lake levels and subtracting the above elevations.

In recent years, fish attractors have been placed in many other Arkansas lakes as well. These include outstanding crappie fishing waters like Bob Kidd, Elmdale, Chicot, Dierks, DeQueen, Sugarloaf, Hinkle, and several lakes on Dagmar Wildlife Management Area. All these lakes offer excellent late-winter crappie angling for those who know how to fish sunken brush piles.

FISHING BRUSH PILES

Bill Fletcher of Mountain Home, Arkansas, has guided fishermen on Lake Norfork for more than twenty years. He's done an extensive fish attractor program on his own for his guide service and was instrumental in completing the Lake Norfork project.

"Lake Norfork was over 90 percent cleared when it was built," Fletcher says. "Now the brush piles placed in the lake are magnets for sport fish.

"These brush piles make a big difference for crappie fishermen, especially someone fishing a big, deep lake like Norfork for the first time. One of the biggest helps for me as a guide is I can take some-one out who's never fished here before, and, on a half-a-day trip, I can show them how to locate brush piles with a graph and how to fish them. Then they can come back to the lake and have a success-ful fishing trip on their own."

After choosing a fish-attractor site marked with a buoy, Fletcher runs his boat over the site, using a graph recorder to determine the position of the brush.

"On Norfork and Bull Shoals, the brush piles extend about 100 to 150 feet on each side of the buoy, and about 90 percent are cen-tered on the 20-, 25-foot depth," Fletcher notes. "Begin by using your graph to find the shallowest brush pile, and mark it with a buoy. Crappie in an aggressive or 'biting' posture often line up horizon-tally above the shallowest brush piles, so fish these piles first."

Fletcher recommends a "count-down" technique for pinpoint-ing feeding fish.

"Take your boat 20 to 30 feet away from your marker buoy, and using four-pound-test line and a $\frac{1}{16}$-ounce jig head, cast to the buoy," Fletcher says. "Now count the jig down until you get a hit or hit brush. If you get a hit, use the same count next cast. If you hit brush, use a shorter count.

"The key to catching crappie on fish attractors is positive depth control. Crappie don't feed down, they bite up. So don't fish under them. Sometimes crappie form horizontal schools on the sides of the brush piles, but the same tactics will work if you can locate them.

"You can catch crappie without the brush piles, but they cer-tainly make it easier. You establish that the fish are there and at a certain depth, then boom, boom, boom, you're putting them in the boat."

Now, the old excuse, "Winter crappie are too hard to find," just doesn't hold water. With a map and depth sounder, any crappie fan can find fish attractors holding plenty of slabs. Where fish shelters are marked with buoys, it's easier still.

Don't wait for the spring spawn to enjoy the thrill of crappie fishing. Bundle up and indulge in some first-rate fishing fun. Christmas-tree crappie provide a sure cure for winter's cabin blues.

Cool Cats

Do catfish contain antifreeze? That question crossed my mind as I caught my tenth big channel catfish. It was a polar afternoon in December. The high temperature soared to near forty degrees. Alex Hinson and I were catfishing in a small Arkansas farm pond.

I'd done it once before—fishing for pond catfish in the dead of winter. Thirty years have passed, but I remember vividly the enormous stringer of channel cats I caught that wintry day. I was twelve. Rabbit hunting hadn't been good, but I had a hankering to stay outdoors. So I grabbed a rod and reel and a box of chicken livers from my grandmother's freezer. Soon, I was standing in snow beside my uncle's fish pond, casting to the big cats that lurked therein, but never really expecting to catch one.

To say the fish were cooperative is an understatement. I'd cast a bait into deep water by the dam, and before it hit bottom, a channel cat would take it. One after another, I hauled in the fish. I'd caught plenty of catfish before, but not as many as that afternoon. In just over an hour, I had twenty fat cats croaking atop the snow. My uncle checked them later on the meat scale at his store. Together they weighed in excess of 120 pounds. The three biggest were 10 pounds apiece.

I shared the story with Alex, who suggested we plan a winter junket immediately. Within the week we were sitting in a johnboat over a deep hole in the pond, dropping liver-baited hooks into the murky depths. Before each bait touched down, a sassy channel cat had it. Alex caught a five-pounder, then its twin. I caught several over three pounds. Twenty-three fell prey to our tactics.

What surprised me most was how icy cold the fish were. Each fought like the dickens, and we took great care not to get soaked with freezing water when one splashed alongside the boat. Yet when you touched one fresh from the water, it felt like a Popsicle. How, I wondered, can a cold-blooded creature put up such a fight when its body temperature is barely above freezing? Antifreeze, perhaps?

Big blue cats often fall to savvy winter catfishermen.

Many Arkansas catfishermen still labor under the false impression that catfish don't bite in winter. That's simply not true. Take channel cats, for instance. The experiences outlined above show the exciting potential for catching these fighters during cold months. Even more amazing is the fact that channel cats are now common targets for ice fishermen in northern states. Despite popular misconceptions, they don't lay in the mud and sulk when it's cold. They actively hunt for food and bite readily even when lakes and rivers freeze.

Blue catfish also feed actively throughout winter. Like striped bass, they feed largely on shad, herring, and other schooling baitfish. Consequently, they're more migratory than other cats and are more frequently found in open-water habitat. That makes them tough to find at times, especially for catters who refuse to abandon near-shore fishing tactics. But when you do, the blue cat's tendency to gather in large winter schools can lead to wintertime fun.

Flatheads seldom fall to winter anglers. These big brutes become lethargic in cold water. Food habit studies indicate very little winter feeding. When one is caught, it's usually because the angler has seen the fish on sonar, and he's anchored right over it. With luck, the bait drifts in front of the fish, which takes it. But flatheads won't move far to feed in cold water. You must place the bait in front of their nose.

FEEDING PATTERNS

To target cats successfully in cold water, it helps to understand some primary winter feeding patterns. What are they likely to be eating? When? Where?

One pattern involves winter-killed shad. Gizzard and threadfin shad, two primary forage items for catfish, are intolerant of severe cold. When the water temperature dips below forty-five degrees, both species become cold-stressed. If the cold persists and the water temperature continues dropping, thousands of shad die. This phenomenon, a yearly event on many Arkansas catfish waters, is known as "winter kill."

When winter kill starts, catfish flock around shad schools like buzzards around roadkill. Dying baitfish fluttering down through the water column are inhaled by waiting cats. The pattern may last a day or a month, depending on the weather. But while it lasts, fishing for big cats is at its best.

To capitalize on this cold-weather pattern, use sonar to pinpoint schooling baitfish, then throw a cast net over the school to collect bait. Large shad can be sliced for cutbait, but small whole shad (an inch or two long) work best. Impale two or three on a hook, running the hook through the eyes and leaving the barb exposed. Lower your rig through the school of baitfish to the bottom, reel it up about a foot, and hang on. If the winter-kill feeding frenzy is in full swing, a catfish will soon strike.

One first-rate place for this type of fishing is in the tailwater of a big-river dam, such as at the twelve dams along the Arkansas River. As the baitfish die, they're drawn through the turbines or open gates of dams where they're chopped up and spit out. Catfish gather in the roiling waters below to feed on this seasonal bounty.

No matter where you fish this pattern, always keep plenty of shad ready for rigging. Where one cat is caught, there usually are dozens. Don't be caught without bait when the bite is on.

Freshwater mussels or clams are another favorite food of catfish, especially in winter. It's not unusual in some waters to catch a catfish that rattles from all the mussel shells stuffed in its gut.

The inch-long exotic Asian clam and tiny zebra mussel, now common in many lakes and rivers, are special favorites, but small varieties of native mussels also are relished. Shell and all is eaten. Digestive juices kill the mussel, the shell opens, the flesh inside is digested, then the shell is passed by the fish.

Mussels are favored by winter cats for two reasons. First, they live in dense colonies, called "beds," containing thousands of individuals. Second, mussels are slow. Their rate of speed is comparable to a slug swimming in molasses. Cats don't have to expend any energy chasing them. They can stay in one small area day after day and gorge on the bounty nature provides.

Look for mussel beds near shore in three to six feet of water. They can be pinpointed during low-water periods or found by moving parallel to shore and probing the bottom with a cane pole. (The shells make a crunching sound when the pole strikes them.) Catfish return to the same beds season after season, so when a bed is found, memorize its location or mark it on a map.

An egg sinker rig is ideal for fishing mussel beds. Use mussel flesh for bait, or small chunks of cut shad or herring. Although catfish may be feeding on mussels primarily, they won't pass up a piece of properly presented cutbait.

Cast to the shell beds, allowing your bait to sit on the bottom undisturbed up to fifteen minutes. If no bite is forthcoming, move to another spot and try again. If you catch a cat, fish the water for several yards in either direction. It's likely others are feeding in the area as well.

If the feeding patterns outlined above aren't evident on the waters you fish, the following information may help you capitalize on the superb winter catfishing available in many waters.

WINTER STRUCTURE

Catfish, like bass and crappie, usually stay near distinct bottom structures. Knowing this, you may want to "channel your efforts"— look for catfish holding around deep-water creek and river channels meandering across the lake or stream bottom. Although some channels can be found using bottom contour maps and a good dose of luck, most are located using sonar, an important tool for the cold-water catter.

Use the sonar unit to pinpoint easily definable channels, as well as subtle drops and ledges. Both are catfish magnets, and in winter you're likely to chart dozens of fish concentrated near each structural feature. Most catfish will be on or very near the bottom in relatively deep, well-oxygenated, slow-moving water.

Catfish may be scattered all along a bottom channel, but most gather near channel features such as brush piles, points jutting into the drop-off, adjacent humps, stump fields, dead snags, or pockets cutting into the bank. Big cats prefer deeper water at the base of channel ledges and also like the outside turns of channel bends, locations near the junction of two or more channels, and deep channel edges in or near dam tailwaters.

DECEMBER

Humps on stream and lake bottoms also are hotspots for winter catfish. The tops of humps attract schools of shad and other baitfish, which in turn attract hungry cats. Catfish hold in deeper areas around the hump during bright sunny days, but at night and on cloudy or rainy days, they move into shallower reaches to feed. When a bite is on, fishing a hump in winter can produce catfishing action far better than anything you ever imagined.

If you fish on Lake Dardanelle, Lake Catherine, or other Arkansas waters where a power-generating facility is located, be sure to look for catfish nearby. Catfish prefer areas with noticeable current, and water flowing in and out of these plants creates a subsurface current covering a big area. If plant discharges are warmer than surrounding waters, and they usually are, large numbers of catfish are attracted to structures and cover near outlet areas and stay there throughout winter.

Inundated lakes and ponds offer catfish deep winter sanctuary, and if scattered trees or stumps still exist around the perimeter, the potential for fast-paced action is great. Deep channels beneath bridges, deep-water chutes around river islands, long, timbered points jutting into deep water, potholes adjacent to the deep end of river wing-dikes, lock-wall edges, and tributary mouths—these, too, are among the many areas where winter catfish wait.

POND FISHING

If it's eating-size cats you're after, head straight for the nearest farm pond. Most are stocked with channel cats, and winter is the best season to catch them.

Start by asking the pond owner to point out the deepest hole in the pond. During cold weather, that's where most cats will be. Fish from a boat if you can, lowering a bait straight down into the hole. When it reaches bottom, turn your reel handle a few cranks so the bait is a foot or so above the substrate where cats can better detect it. When bank fishing, adding a small bobber on the line between your hook and sinker accomplishes the same thing.

Chicken liver is a top bait in this situation. Cats quickly zero in

DECEMBER

on the scent and taste of poultry blood dissolving from the tissue. Some catters prefer frozen livers, because they stay on the hook better, but fresh liver has more cat-attracting qualities.

Don't sit in one spot too long. If a cat is nearby, you'll have a bite before fifteen minutes passes. If you don't, move a short distance and try again. If catfish are biting, the action may end abruptly after you've caught a few fish. Once again, it's time to move and try another location.

When you're fishing for winter cats, it pays to keep moving anyway, just so you can keep warm. This is not a sport for anglers who detest the cold. You'll get chilly out there, even when you're wearing proper clothing. Your teeth will chatter, and your hands and feet will feel like Popsicles.

Nice thing is, when the cats start biting, that frigid feeling disappears. Nothing in the world warms you quicker than battling a rod-bending cat.

Nine Winter Fishing Trips

Winter fishing isn't for everyone. For many anglers, the cold months of December, January, and February are a time for fireside reflections or viewing photos of last May's fishing trip on Lake Hookahawg. Hunting when it's cold is bad enough, they say, but if you go out on the water in the cold, on purpose, to fish, you have reached the outer edge of sanity.

That kind of skepticism was on my mind when I began my first extended winter fishing trip with a couple of experienced cold-weather anglers. The trip on the upper Ouachita River started amidst December snow flurries. Stepping into frigid wind, I was convinced that anyone with the good sense to stay indoors would find the weekend much more enjoyable than I.

Yet when we reached the river, and the sights and sounds of the city receded, startling new perspectives invaded my clearing senses. Asphalt highways and high-rise office buildings gave way to vast stretches of untracked backcountry. We canoed through mountain passes cuffed with snow-covered hardwoods. Curtains of icicles sparkled along riverside bluffs. Wood ducks flushed before us. As we paddled farther from civilization, I found myself enveloped in the stark, elemental beauty only winter can create.

Casting jigs in deep pools, we caught smallmouths, spotted bass, and fat green sunfish. They were small fish mostly, but the action was steady and enjoyable. By dusk the first day, we had enough for a gravel-bar supper.

Later, watching fish sizzling over the campfire, I found myself inexplicably content to be sitting comfortably on a remote river bank watching it snow. I knew then I was hooked on winter fishing.

Many people cringe at the thought of fishing in cold weather, just as I once did. Lots of these folks are ardent warm-weather anglers, but they stop fishing when there's frost or snow on the ground.

Actually, the winter months bring superb fishing opportunities in Arkansas, and if you outfit yourself with proper clothing and other outdoor gear, you can be quite comfortable and safe on a winter fishing trip. Largemouths, crappie, walleyes, trout, bluegills, small-mouths, stripers, white bass—all these are caught by savvy winter fishermen. Wintry conditions send fair-weather anglers scurrying home, so this is the season when you're most likely to find your favorite waters pleasantly uncrowded.

Even professional anglers sometimes have trouble catching winter fish. But anglers armed with knowledge of cold-weather behavior patterns usually find their quarry. The main question is where to go and what to fish for. To help in that respect, here's a mixed bag of Arkansas fishing opportunities to be considered by anglers this season.

NORFORK TAILWATER TROUT

It may seem small and insignificant, but the five-mile stretch of river from Norfork Lake Dam to the White River is one of the world's best trout fisheries. This tailwater has produced hundreds of five-pound-plus brown trout, including a thirty-eight-pound, nine-ounce former world record that's still the second-largest brown trout ever recorded. Rainbows comprise a significant part of the catch, with many ten to sixteen inches long. Brookies and cutthroats are here, too. Anglers fishing the Norfork have an excellent chance to catch a grand slam, at least one trout of each species sixteen inches or larger.

Many trout are taken on flies, spinners, and other artificials, but bait fishing with night crawlers, sculpins, wax worms, and other natural baits also produces.

LAKE CATHERINE CRAPPIE

Lake Catherine near Hot Springs is a honeyhole for oversized winter crappie. Fish under a pound are seldom caught; there are many one- to two-pound slabs.

One excellent big crappie hotspot is the Tigger Bay area across from the state park marina. The river channel runs through this area, with many fallen trees extending over the channel banks in ten to fifteen feet of water. Many jumbo crappie suspend in those trees.

Local anglers catch them by anchoring a boat over this structure and fishing jigs, small spoons, and horsehead spinners.

LITTLE RED RIVER CUTTHROATS

Cutthroat trout add a special dimension to the Little Red River trout fishery below Greers Ferry Dam at Heber Springs. Cutthroats were first stocked in 1989. They grew fast, and anglers harvested a high percentage of those released.

Three- to four-pound cutthroats are fairly common now. Many are taken on flies, spinners, and other artificials, but bait fishing with night crawlers, wax worms, and other natural baits is also productive.

LAKE CONWAY CRAPPIE

Unlike many Arkansas waters, Lake Conway offers winter crappie fishing that's usually equal to, if not better than, fishing during the spring spawn. In December, one-and-one-half- to two-and-one-half-pound crappie are not uncommon.

Fish live minnows, tube jigs, or marabou jigs along inundated creek channels and lakes. The Green's Lake and Adam's Lake areas on the east side are good bets this time of year, and the flooded timber adjacent to the boat lanes at the Highway 89 bridge (just east of Interstate 40 at the Mayflower exit) is especially good for winter slabs.

ARKANSAS RIVER SAUGERS AND WHITE BASS

Saugers and whites to three pounds are a common catch in the Arkansas River this month. Fishing tailwaters is the way to load a stringer, with those below the Ozark, Dardanelle, and Murray dams among the best. Be on the water just before dawn and dusk for best success. Use $\frac{1}{16}$- to $\frac{1}{8}$-ounce jigs or jig-minnow combinations; focus on pools, pockets, and eddies where current is present yet diminished. Other good lures are spoons, tailspinners, and small, deep-diving, shad-imitation crankbaits.

DECEMBER

WHITE OAK LARGEMOUTHS

White Oak Lake in southwest Arkansas has been a superb bass fishery since its creation in 1961. Eight-pound-plus largemouths have always been common, and this huge Arkansas Game and Fish Commission impoundment has given up dozens of ten-pound-plus bass, including several fish exceeding fourteen pounds.

White Oak is eighteen miles northwest of Camden. An angler acquainted with the lake can catch good numbers of big bass year-round, but winter months are considered best by most local anglers. Big largemouths are usually around stickups, fallen timber, and cypress trees on five- to eight-foot-deep flats with deep water nearby. A sonar fish-finder helps pinpoint these areas along the inundated White Oak Creek channel. Popular lures include plastic worms, the jig-and-pig, and the jig-and-eel.

LITTLE ROCK CATFISH

Pool Six of the Arkansas River at Little Rock has for years been one of the hottest pools for consistency and numbers. Trophy blues, channels, and flatheads always are possible, too.

Winter months provide plenty of action within the first mile below Murray Lock and Dam and the North Little Rock hydro-electric plant. Bottom-bounce one- to two-ounce jigs tipped with cut shad or herring along the channels for numbers. Cast whole bait-fish into grooves of slow-moving water below the dam for a shot at bigger catfish. Live bluegills fished on float-paternoster rigs or three-way rigs account for many trophy-class blues and flatheads taken this season.

Heavy winter rains may muddy the river, raise the water level, and accelerate current. When flows through Murray Dam exceed fifty thousand cubic feet per second, smaller catfish gather in scour holes and along downstream edges of wing dams and bridge piers. Cast cutbait, chicken liver, or night crawlers for action in these areas. Bigger cats roam the pool day and night, often feeding in shallower five- to ten-foot backwaters. Try drift-fishing with chunks of skip-jack herring or shad. Hotspots include riprapped banks in the tailwater and beneath the Little Rock–North Little Rock bridges, and the first mile of the Fourche Creek tributary just above Interstate 440.

RICHLAND CREEK SMALLMOUTHS

Richland Creek, a tributary of Buffalo River, winds thirty miles through a remote portion of the Ozark Mountains downstream from Pelsor in Newton and Searcy Counties. It's been described as "the most beautiful stream in the state," and anyone familiar with the creeks and rivers of Arkansas will quickly realize the significance of that statement.

Richland Creek is seldom floatable because of its steep drops, big rocks, and narrow chutes, but if you're willing to hike to some of its backcountry stretches, you can enjoy some of the best wade-fishing for smallmouth bass available in the Natural State. The deep pools followed by noisy rapids are a brownie fisherman's delight. Try working the rocky streambed in pools with a jig-and-pig or small crawfish-imitation crankbaits. Locals also use live crayfish, minnows, and other natural baits. Smallmouths rarely exceed a pound and a half in this smallish stream, but there are plenty to keep a winter angler happy for hours on end.

LAKE CHARLES MIXED BAG

Lake Charles, a 650-acre Game and Fish Commission impoundment in Lawrence County, offers a mixed bag of fishing opportunities. Angling for jumbo largemouth bass, crappie, bluegills, and channel catfish is excellent in winter for savvy anglers, and unlike most Game and Fish lakes, Charles harbors a good population of hybrid stripers (up to six or seven pounds) and white bass, too. Open water is prevalent, a condition conducive to good hybrid and white bass fishing, but one that makes it difficult to find concentrations of largemouths, crappies, bream, and catfish. The Flat Creek channel winding through the heart of the lake is a good area for your winter efforts. Anglers also do well fishing points, coves, and the area around the dam. State park personnel have placed brush piles and fish attractors inside the park cove for bank fishermen.

Scores of other lakes and streams offer superb winter fishing for Arkansas's fishing fans. Wrap up your angling year by visiting some of these blue-ribbon waters.

And while you're there, remember this: Natural State fishermen are among the most fortunate in the world, because some of the finest freshwater fishing anywhere—winter, spring, summer, and fall —is found right here at home. We can count our lucky stars.

DECEMBER

Appendix: Arkansas Fishing Information Sources

The following agencies provide information invaluable to all anglers fishing in Arkansas waters.

Arkansas Department of Parks and Tourism
One Capital Mall
Little Rock, AR 72201
501–682–7777
www.arkansas.com

> Information available: free brochures and booklets with information on Arkansas state parks, including maps of state park lakes; free float-fishing information packet ("The Arkansas Floater's Kit") with maps of major mountain float streams.

Arkansas Game and Fish Commission
2 Natural Resources Drive
Little Rock, AR 72205
800–364-GAME
www.agfc.com

> Information available: fishing regulations guides; maps and information on AG&FC lakes and state-owned oxbow lakes; state fishing records, applications, and information; free brochures and booklets on Arkansas fish and fishing; for-sale publications of interest to anglers, including "The Angler's Guide to Arkansas Game and Fish Commission Lakes," "An Angler's Guide to Arkansas Fish," and "The Arkansas Outdoor Atlas" (with 75 county maps showing the locations of public fishing waters [rivers and lakes], boat ramps and access areas statewide); boating law and boating safety information.

Big Lake National Wildlife Refuge
P.O. Box 67
Manila, AR 72442
870–564–2429

Information available: fishing regulations guide; free brochure with map showing area lakes and streams.

Buffalo National River Office
P.O. Box 1173
Harrison, AR 72601
870–741–5443

Information available: maps and information for Buffalo National River.

Cache River–Bald Knob National Wildlife Refuges
Route 2, Box 126-T
Augusta, AR 72006
501–347–2614

Information available: fishing regulations guide; free brochure with map showing area lakes and streams.

Entergy
P.O. Box 1330
Hot Springs, AR 71902
501–321–8500

Information available: free brochure, "A Guide to Lakes Hamilton and Catherine."

Felsenthal–Overflow National Wildlife Refuges
P.O. Box 1157
Crossett, AR 71635
870–364–3167

Information available: fishing regulations guide; free brochure with map showing area lakes and streams.

Holla Bend National Wildlife Refuge
Route 1, Box 59
Dardanelle, AR 72834
501–229–4302

> Information available: fishing regulations guide; free brochure with map showing area lakes and streams.

Little Rock Municipal Water Works
P.O. Box 1789
Little Rock, AR 72203
501–377–1200

> Information available: free map and boating regulations guide for Lake Maumelle; information on Lake Winona.

Ouachita National Forest
P.O. Box 1270
Hot Springs, AR 71902
501–321–5202

> Information available: maps of national forest lands showing lakes, streams, campsites, and more.

Ozark National Forest
P.O. Box 1008
Russellville, AR 72801
501–968–2354

> Information available: maps of national forest lands showing lakes, streams, campsites, and more.

St. Francis National Forest
2675 Highway 44
Marianna, AR 72360
870–295–5278

> Information available: free brochures with information and maps for Lake Storm Creek and Bear Creek.

U.S. Army Corps of Engineers
Little Rock District
P.O. Box 867
Little Rock, AR 72203
501–324–5551

> Information available: maps and information for all agency lakes and state's large navigable waterways.

Wapanocca National Wildlife Refuge
P.O. Box 279
Turrell, AR 72384

> Information available: fishing regulations guide; free brochure with map showing area lakes and streams.

White River National Wildlife Refuge
P.O. Box 308
DeWitt, AR 72042
870–946–1468

> Information available: fishing regulations guide; free brochure with map showing area lakes and streams.

Index